Latin American Political Economy

Series Editors

Eduardo Moncada, Barnard College, New York, NY, USA
Aldo Madariaga, Santiago, Chile
Sara Niedzwiecki, Santa Cruz, USA

Latin American Political Economy publishes new, relevant, and empirically-grounded scholarship that deepens our understanding of contemporary Latin American political economy and contributes to the formulation and evaluation of new theories that are both context-sensitive and subject to broader comparisons. Inspired by the need to provide new analytical perspectives for understanding the massive social, political, and economic transformations underway in Latin America, the series is directed at researchers and practitioners interested in resurrecting political economy as a primary research area in the developing world. In thematic terms, the series seeks to promote vital debate on the interactions between economic, political, and social processes; it is especially concerned with how findings may further our understanding of development models, the socio-political institutions that sustain them, and the practical problems they confront. In methodological terms, the series showcases cross-disciplinary research that is empirically rich and sensitive to context and that leads to new forms of description, concept formation, causal inference, and theoretical innovation. The series editors welcome submissions that address patterns of democratic politics, dependency and development, state formation and the rule of law, inequality and identity, and global linkages.

Juan O'Farrell

Business Power in Agriculture Value Chains

Argentina During the Commodity Boom

palgrave
macmillan

Juan O'Farrell
Caba, Argentina

ISSN 2945-7076 ISSN 2945-7084 (electronic)
Latin American Political Economy
ISBN 978-3-032-06588-9 ISBN 978-3-032-06589-6 (eBook)
https://doi.org/10.1007/978-3-032-06589-6

This Palgrave Macmillan imprint is published by the registered company Springer Nature Switzerland AG
The registered company address is: Gewerbestrasse 11, 6330 Cham, Switzerland

Acknowledgements

I want to thank Sebastián Etchemendy for his invaluable support and inspiration for this project since its beginning many years ago. I also extend a special thank you to Carlos Freytes, Tasha Fairfield, Ken Shadlen, Anabel Marín, Tomás Bril Mascarenhas, Ruth Berins Collier, Victoria Murillo, and Alison Post for their contributions in earlier stages of this project. I am also grateful to the Latin American Political Economy series editors, Juan Bogliacini, Aldo Madariaga, Sara Niedzwecki, and Eduardo Moncada, for their support, and to two anonymous reviewers for their insightful comments.

The research for this book would not have been possible without the financial support of CONICET and Fulbright. The book was translated by Verónica Santos.

Contents

List of Figures

List of Tables

CHAPTER 1

Introduction

In March 2005, Monsanto halted shipments of soybean meal from Argentina at the port of Rotterdam. The agricultural input company demanded royalty payments for the use of its Roundup ready (RR) technology, specifically the RR gene, which makes transgenic soybean plants resistant to the widely used herbicide glyphosate. While Monsanto held patents for this gene in several European countries, it did not have one in Argentina. After detecting traces of the gene in the shipments, the company demanded the seizure of the goods and brought lawsuits against importing companies. Over the following year, it employed the same strategy in ports in Denmark, Spain, and England. Faced with the high logistical costs and financial risks associated with litigation against Monsanto, European importers began to replace Argentine soybean meal with supplies from other countries. The resulting loss of markets led Argentine exporters to pressure the government to negotiate an agreement with the American company.

This conflict struck a critical nerve in an already fragile economy. Soy and its derivatives constitute Argentina's primary export product and a crucial source of fiscal revenue. The country was barely recovering from the 2002 financial crisis, one of the biggest in its history. With exports at a standstill, the government found itself at a crossroads: yield to corporate pressure and impose higher technology costs on Argentine farmers or contest the case in Europe, risking a prolonged dispute and further

J. O'Farrell, *Business Power in Agriculture Value Chains*, Latin American Political Economy, https://doi.org/10.1007/978-3-032-06589-6_1

market losses. It chose to resist and intervened as an interested party in the lawsuits.

Eventually, in a ruling that set a major precedent in the debate over seed intellectual property disputes globally, the EU Court of Justice ruled against Monsanto. The decision argued that the company's patent did not cover the gene itself but rather the function it performed—glyphosate resistance—, which was present in soybean seeds but not in their derivatives, such as soybean meal. While the government celebrated the decision, this episode would not be the last time a multinational corporation attempted to leverage its power to obstruct Argentine exports.

Far from stabilizing, distributive conflicts surrounding export agriculture intensified in the following years. The high profitability driven by the soybean price boom in the mid-2000s, during the so-called "commodity boom," exacerbated tensions within the value chain and between the agribusiness sector and the then incumbent Peronist administration. The most visible confrontation occurred in 2008, when, in response to increased export taxes on soybeans and other agricultural commodities, rural associations organized a trade halt that paralyzed the country for four months. The protests, which spread from the countryside to urban centers, weakened the government's standing, ultimately leading to a congressional vote in which the measure was rejected. Despite this significant victory on the part of farmers, agricultural export taxes during that period remained among the highest in the world. The commodity boom also exacerbated socio-environmental conflicts. The adoption of new technologies, such as genetically modified organisms (GMOs), alongside the rapid expansion of soybean crops, introduced significant health and environmental risks—most heavily affecting rural populations—and led to mobilizations and protests advocating for more stringent regulatory frameworks.

This intensity of conflict around agriculture was not entirely new for Argentina, one of the world's largest agricultural exporters. Agriculture has been a remarkably contentious sector in the country for over a century. Historically, the main source of tension stemmed from the fact that Argentina exported the same goods it consumed—primarily wheat and beef—creating constant friction between producers and consumers. These distributive tensions have long represented one of the primary sources of political conflict in the country.

Throughout much of the twentieth century, agricultural producers—particularly large landowners—represented the country's agricultural economic elite. However, over the past three decades, the structure of the sector has undergone a dramatic transformation. A combination of rapid technological development, economic liberalization, and privatization has increased the economic weight of multinational corporations (MNCs), both as key input suppliers and as intermediaries on whom producers depend for exports. Trading firms like Cargill and Dreyfus control access to foreign currency through export origination, while input suppliers like Monsanto (now Bayer) hold patents on genetically modified seeds—the critical driver of the sector's significant productivity gains since the 1990s. These new actors have transformed what was once a bilateral distributive conflict between agricultural producers and consumers into a more complex dispute involving not only these traditional groups, but also input suppliers and trading companies.

This book investigates the political power of these new actors—i.e., agribusiness MNCs—and their influence on policymaking and distributive conflicts. What are the sources of power for input suppliers and traders? How are these sources of power connected to existing policies and distributive outcomes?

The broader context for this study is the commodity boom that Latin America experienced during the 2000s—an economic expansion fueled by rising international prices for the region's key primary exports. This period also coincided with the rise of governments intent on capturing and redistributing the rents generated by the boom. In this sense, the book seeks to contribute to the broader literature on the political economy of natural resource industries in booming times and to contribute to a deeper understanding of the power dynamics between left-wing or populist governments and the economic elites controlling strategic sectors.

More than a decade after these events, academic literature remains divided as to the power of agrarian elites. From a comparative politics perspective, scholars have highlighted the apparent paradox of a sector with undeniable economic relevance—given its role in exports—but limited political capacity, especially in terms of partisan and sectoral representation. The consensus among political scientists is that the government has been able to sustain high agricultural export taxes due to the political weakness of agrarian elites.[1] In contrast, an opposing view, mainly from

[1] Fairfield (2011), Richardson (2012), Freytes (2015); Fernández Milmanda (2024)

sociology and economic sociology, portrays these elites as a dominant force in national politics.[2] This approach emphasizes their control over the productive model, highlights the negative environmental impacts—aligning with critiques of neo-extractivism[3]—and argues that, in 2008, they managed to prevent the consolidation of the national and popular project promoted by the *Frente para la Victoria* (FPV).

As I will argue in this book, this apparent contradiction in assessing the power of agrarian elites arises from differences in conceptualizing: (i) agricultural business actors, (ii) their sources of power, and (iii) the policy areas in which they intervene. The polarization in responses is also disciplinary in nature: institutionalist analyses in political science tend to underestimate the power of the agricultural sector, often overestimated by structuralist approaches in sociology.

I intend to propose an alternative perspective on the power of agrarian elites in Argentina from a comparative politics approach. Rather than adopting the predominant institutional perspective, I address the issue through value chain analysis and focus on structural power. In my view, this approach allows to capture distributive conflicts often underestimated in the literature and accounts for the influence of agrarian elites in various policy areas beyond the debate over export taxes.

1.1 Business Power and Distributive Conflicts in Agriculture Value Chains

The core argument of this book is that the distribution of sectoral revenues among the various components of the agricultural value chain is shaped by the structural power each segment can wield to resist state regulatory initiatives. In contrast to much of the existing literature—which tends to focus on the overall fiscal burden imposed on the sector—this work examines how the government intervenes in distributive conflicts among key actors: consumers, farmers, input providers, and traders.

Although it is acknowledged—consistent with existing literature—that governments have been able to impose significant costs on the sector as a whole through export taxes, this outcome does not appear to be solely

[2] Basualdo and Arceo (2009), Giarracca (2009), Newell (2009), Lapegna (2017)

[3] Svampa (2013)

the result of institutional weakness on the part of agricultural producers. It seems to stem, instead, from conflicting interests within the value chain itself. These intra-sectoral conflicts have eroded the sector's ability to coordinate politically and created room for the government to disrupt collective action.

The government was only able to impose high export taxes because the most powerful segment of the value chain—i.e., traders—were not negatively affected by them and therefore had no incentive to mobilize against them. In contrast, the segment bearing the cost—i.e., farmers—lacks the structural power to effectively oppose them. As a result, traders managed to appropriate a disproportionately large share of the revenues generated during the commodity boom.

The other major winners were input suppliers, particularly biotechnology and agrochemical firms, which are essential to productivity growth. While they failed to strengthen intellectual property protections for seeds through legislation, they increased profits through private contracts and blocked government efforts to regulate or restrict agrochemical use or promote local biotechnology.

The losers in terms of rent appropriation were agricultural producers and local seed companies. The book explains how producers were harmed by the implementation of export duties and export permits, which significantly reduced their profitability. However, they were partially compensated by a reduction in input costs due to the failure to amend the Seed Law. Other losers include populations negatively affected by agrochemical contamination, the uncontrolled expansion of the agricultural frontier, and deforestation—consequences of weak environmental regulations.

Who are the actors that wield the most power in decision-making and in resolving these distributional conflicts? What factors explain the variability of business power across different policy areas and over time?

The argument of this book is that agribusiness MNCs win over distributive conflicts against local actors because they have greater structural power. Distributive conflicts are resolved through the power that MNCs exert over the government and over other private actors within the chain.

The structural power of agribusiness MNCs stems from their ability to influence access to technology and international markets and technology—elements that agricultural producers rely on to enhance productivity and that governments need to strengthen the economy. This privileged position, in turn, increases their instrumental power, as governments grant them greater access to both formal and informal decision-making spaces due to concerns over the potential economic impact of their business decisions. In contrast, because of their fragmentation and territorial dispersion, farmers may only inflict economic damage through an extraordinary degree of coordination and articulation.

In the case of traders, structural power derives from their dominant position in international grain trade, through which they can influence Argentina's exports at destination ports. This dynamic is a constant in the sector's relationship with any government and is the primary reason why no initiative aimed at increasing direct state control over commercialization could succeed. This power grew as a result of the deregulation and privatization of grain trade since the 1980s, as most trade shifted from state-to-state transactions to business-to-business exchanges.

At the local level, traders can restrict the inflow of foreign currency by delaying settlement of exports, or even temporarily suspending them. The structural power derived from foreign currency control varies over time, as it is conditional on the macroeconomic context. It diminishes when the economy has a trade surplus, high reserves, or borrowing capacity. A stronger economy with greater foreign currency generation capacity places the government in a better negotiating position *vis-à-vis* currency providers. In such circumstances, the government's ability to impose costs on this segment increases through regulatory threats and selective incentives, while the credibility of corporate threats diminishes. These tools raise the cost for companies when they enter into conflict with the government, thereby reducing their structural power.

For agricultural biotechnology companies, structural power derives from their ownership of technology. However, to be effective, it must be complemented by legal and political capabilities to restrict access to that technology. Specifically, biotech companies use licenses and patents as power resources to discipline other actors in the chain and secure their support in conflicts with the government. At its peak, and thanks to their weight in the global seed market, this form of private authority allows them to block local actors from accessing export markets. In this sense, this resource is more significant than conventional disinvestment threats: the threat of exit is not as relevant as the role of these companies as gatekeepers of markets and technology. Conversely, the significance of the local economy's market share for a company's overall business strategy strengthens the negotiating position of government officials and increases the costs for companies seeking to punish the government.

However, the power of agricultural biotechnology companies is insufficient to achieve their ultimate objectives (or offensive power) in Congress when these objectives conflict with those of the ruling party's electorate, mobilized actors, or highly salient issues drawing public opinion. In such conflicts, social legitimacy and electoral incentives prevail over the structural or instrumental power of multinational corporations.

Finally, the laxity of environmental regulations during this period can be explained by the central role of the technological package (glyphosate-resistant transgenic soy) in the agro-export model, which means that regulations follow a commercial logic—prioritizing access to international markets over sustainability considerations. Unlike other regulatory areas, in environmental policy, the interests of the value chain are aligned: input suppliers, producers, and exporters all benefit from weak regulations. The greater the economy's dependence on agricultural exports (as a share of total exports), the more sensitive the trade balance and fiscal outcome are to environmental regulations that limit cultivable land or increase production costs.[4]

1.2 Discussion with the Literature

With this book, I seek to contribute to the comparative politics literature on agriculture in Argentina. In this section, I position my argument within that literature, specifically in relation with two of the works that have more directly addressed the role of business power in agriculture during the period, namely, Freytes (2015) and Fernández Milmanda (2024). Both authors underscore the paradox of the economic strength and the political weakness of the sector. These studies largely focus on characterizing and measuring this weakness and explaining its origins. I agree with the central idea of these works: the instrumental (partisan and electoral) and structural weakness of Argentine agricultural producers

[4] Middle-income countries such as Argentina also contend with a population characterized by widespread unmet needs and strong demands for social policies. In these contexts, implementing strict environmental regulations or rejecting a technology on precautionary grounds entails a high economic cost and, at times, uncertain environmental benefits. Moreover, while the costs are often clearly borne by a specific sector, the benefits tend to be more diffuse.

explains their difficulties in blocking high taxation. However, I diverge from these studies in three key analytical dimensions: actors, power, and policies.

First, I depart from the authors in how they define the agricultural elite. Both identify agricultural producers or landowners as the primary elite actors, while overlooking the segments at either end of the value chain—input provision and foreign trade—both of which are dominated by multinational companies (MNCs) such as Monsanto, Bayer, Cargill, and Bunge, among others. This omission is problematic, as these segments concentrate much of the sector's economic power—the very factor the authors invoke to explain the apparent paradox of economic strength paired with political weakness. It is exporters who possess the capacity to generate foreign exchange, and it is within the input segment that the greatest share of value added is located.

Secondly, both authors adopt a distinctly institutionalist perspective: they focus almost exclusively on instrumental power—limited to the electoral and legislative arenas—while underestimating the role of structural power within the agricultural sector. The latter is not subject to systematic analysis, nor is empirical evidence reconstructed to assess its influence—or lack thereof—on the processes under study. The structural dimension is relegated to a secondary position and is addressed only through general references to the sector's "economic weight," as a catch-all category covering a wide range of productive factors, from land and technology ownership to the sector's economic contributions, such as foreign exchange generation, value added, and tax revenue. As a result of this analytical limitation—linked to the absence of a precise inquiry into the actors involved—the authors also fail to distinguish which actors possess the actual capacity to control and politically mobilize each of these resources. At times, this shortcoming even leads them to equate the institutional weakness of agricultural actors with the political weakness of the sector or the productive chain as a whole. This approach does not seem to explain the government's failed attempts to implement certain policies. As argued throughout this study, during the period in question the government faced significant resistance that compelled it to set aside several of its programmatic objectives—from commercial and environmental regulation to the promotion of local technological capabilities.

Fernández Milmanda (2019, 2024) assigns greater relevance to structural power when addressing alternative explanations to her own, although she does so by engaging with the classical theories of Block and Lindblom from the late 1970s, rather than turning to more recent approaches. According to those classical views, an increase in a sector's economic weight should automatically translate into influence, without requiring political organization. The author argues that, although the agricultural sectors in Latin America were structurally strengthened by rising prices and international demand, this did not always result in strengthened political influence. Consequently, policy variation would be explained by instrumental or organizational factors rather than by structural ones. I agree that the classical versions fall short of accounting for such variation, but, as I analyzed in Chapter 1, more recent studies have developed conceptual and methodological strategies to overcome this limitation—such as incorporating policymakers' perceptions into the analysis.

Third, both authors draw their conclusions based almost exclusively on a single policy area—export duties—while neglecting other key arenas in the relationship between the state and the sector, such as the regulation of inputs such as seeds and agrochemicals and the contest over the management of foreign exchange inflows. Although during the period under analysis the government managed to sustain high export tax rates, in other policy areas the balance of power shifted in favor of private actors. This narrow focus therefore leads to an overestimation of the state's autonomy in shaping and implementing policies related to export-oriented agriculture.

Finally, this book contributes to current theoretical debates on business power, and particularly on structural power (Hacker and Pierson 2002; Fairfield 2010; Culpepper and Reinke 2014; Bril Mascarenhas and Madariaga 2019). First, these authors have historically focused on the role of power in the relationship between firms and governments. The approach proposed here is new in that it combines structural power theory with value chain analysis to examine how firms exercise power not only in their interactions with the state but also in their relationships with other private actors across the chain. Second, structural power literature has largely focused on the capacity for disinvestment or *exit* as the primary mechanism of influence. By contrast, the findings of this research suggest that, in the case of agribusiness MNCs, structural power does not lie in disinvestment—a highly costly and unfeasible option in a country like Argentina, one of the world's leading agricultural commodity producers—but rather in their ability to block local actors' access to markets and technologies. Regarding technology-linked structural power, it is shown to be contingent on specific legal frameworks, including patent regimes, licensing systems, and intellectual property legislation. Third, this book argues that the structural power of firms is shaped by the national context in which they operate. In this regard, I propose a context-sensitive analysis, i.e., a conceptualization of structural power attuned to the Argentine context. A distinctive feature of Argentina's political economy is the recurrent balance-of-payments crises. In this setting, corporate actions capable of disrupting the flow of foreign currency carry significantly more weight than in countries with less exposure to such vulnerabilities.

1.2.1 Methodological Comments

To address these questions, in this book I present a case study of export agriculture policy in Argentina during the administrations of Néstor Kirchner (2003–2007) and Cristina Fernández de Kirchner (2007–2015). I compare three policy areas both across each other and over time: (i) intellectual property rights, (ii) foreign trade administration, and (iii) environmental regulations. The government's capacity to achieve its programmatic goals varies across these areas and through different periods. I have sought to explain these differences by drawing on recent variants of the classic distinction between structural power and instrumental power (Hacker and Pierson, 2002; Fairfield 2010, 2015; Culpepper and Reinke, 2014; Bril-Mascarenhas and Madariaga, 2019). The three selected areas are those with the greatest impact on distributive conflicts related to agricultural exports, each subject to policies and regulations that vary both among themselves and over time.

I draw causal inferences using two complementary strategies: on one hand, I compare policy outcomes on the basis of winners and losers; on the other, I assess the effectiveness of actors' power across three regulatory areas (cross-case) and over time within a single area (within-case) (Gerring, 2001). The aim is to explain the scope of agrarian elite power in regulatory outcomes and distributive conflicts.

This strategy differs from existing studies on comparative politics of structural power. While some works conduct cross-national comparisons (Culpepper and Reinke, 2014), this book presents comparisons within a single country. Likewise, unlike studies that compare economic sectors (such as finance and agriculture in Fairfield, 2015), here I compare regulatory areas within the same value chain. I also attempt to explain power variation by firm type based on their activities (e.g., input suppliers versus producers versus traders), decision-making arenas (e.g., Executive Branch versus Legislative Branch), and economic contexts (e.g., foreign exchange abundance versus scarcity).

A common challenge in such studies is distinguishing whether a government favors a firm due to its power or because the firm's interests align with government preferences or public opinion. Structural power can operate even when interests are aligned, but empirically isolating its specific effect is difficult. To address this challenge, it may prove useful to analyze cases involving conflicts between corporate interests and government programmatic goals (Culpepper, 2015). The period analyzed encompasses the three administrations of the *Frente para la Victoria* or FPV (2003–2007, 2007–2011, 2011–2015), which constitute a relevant case for this study: they enable exploration of the capacity of governments with redistributive and/or statist programmatic objectives to regulate sectors based on natural resources controlled by concentrated multinational corporations.

Although this period was characterized by the "commodity boom," the upward cycle of international prices reversed in 2011, prior to the end of the period under study. This circumstance provides a useful opportunity to examine government-business relations in different economic contexts and explain the variation in power and distributive conflict outcomes across economic cycles.

Specifically, I conduct a multiple-observation analysis within a single case to establish the sequence of events through which firms succeeded or failed in influencing policy decisions, and to identify the most relevant sources of power. For each regulatory area, I analyze key episodes when agendas were set or critical policies decided. I conducted 55 interviews to obtain information on decision-making processes, reform options considered and discarded, and negotiations between business actors and officials that led to these outcomes (Fairfield, 2015). These in-depth interviews were carried out at various points between 2014 and 2020 (see Annex for a detailed list) and included actors from both the public and private sectors with stakes in the most important policy areas. In the public sector, most interviews focused on the Ministry of Agriculture, Livestock, and Fisheries —including ministers and secretaries—but also involved the Commerce Secretariat of the Ministry of Economy and Finance, the Central Bank of Argentina (BCRA), and members of Congress. In the private sector, I sought to balance coverage across the three links of the value chain: input suppliers, agricultural producers, and traders. Additionally, three types of corporate profiles were included: institutional representatives (directors and presidents of sectoral associations), managers, and technical advisors or consultants. This diversity responds to the need to understand both political strategies and government relations, as well as the concerns and particularities of economic activity in each link. In all cases, I identified the public and private actors involved in the episodes where agendas were set and policies decided.

1.3 Organization of the Book

The book is organized as follows. Chapter 2 introduces the theoretical framework and the main concepts of business power that underpin the analysis. This theoretical foundation draws primarily on two major bodies of literature: on one hand, recent comparative politics literature that distinguishes between instrumental and structural power of business elites; on the other, various approaches that have sought to conceptualize the political activity of multinational corporations in Latin America.

Chapter 3 aims to analyze the ways in which the power of agrarian elites in Argentina has been conceptualized from the early twentieth century to the present, situating my contribution by identifying the analytical limitations of the most recent literature. Chapter 4 describes the structural conditions and recent transformations in the export agriculture value chain in Argentina.

Chapters 5 to 7 provide an analysis of the central arguments through a detailed reconstruction of policy episodes that influence distributive outcomes, the appropriation of revenues generated by the commodity boom, and the government's capacity to advance its objectives in each of the three policy areas (intellectual property, trade, and environment). Each of these chapters follows a common structure consisting of three parts: first, a summary of the specific argument for the policy area; second, a description of distributive and policy outcomes; and third, a reconstruction of the decisive episodes that led to those outcomes.

Finally, I present findings including a summary of the contributions, the main argument, and the theoretical implications of the book.

CHAPTER 2

Perspectives on Business Power

Power relations are fundamental to explaining both policymaking processes and the outcomes of distributive conflicts. Business power is particularly relevant in the debates on the political economy of development. Nevertheless, its study has been discouraged by the methodological difficulties to empirically capturing its effects, which have somehow prevented a better understanding of its role in politics. It is only recently that this situation has begun to change, thanks to conceptual and methodological innovations that have allowed for a more precise understanding of business power mechanics.

Over the past few decades, two major theoretical strands have emerged regarding business power, both of which inform this research. On one hand, comparative politics studies that distinguish between instrumental and structural business power. On the other, various approaches have sought to conceptualize the political activity of multinational corporations (MNCs) in Latin America.

This book engages with—and seeks to contribute to—ongoing debates, with particular emphasis on the structural power of multinational firms. In this regard, recent conceptual innovations, especially those that highlight the variable, relational, and strategic nature of structural power, are essential to advancing this field. Drawing on interview-based fieldwork, the analysis also underscores the importance of public officials' and policymakers' perceptions in understanding how structural factors

J. O'Farrell, *Business Power in Agriculture Value Chains*, Latin American Political Economy, https://doi.org/10.1007/978-3-032-06589-6_2

translate into political influence. A key conceptual contribution of this book lies in combining the notion of structural power with the global value chains (GVCs) framework, as well as with the broader literature on multinational corporations. This articulation deepens our understanding of both the power of multinational firms and the power dynamics that characterize global value chains.

This chapter presents the conceptual framework of the book. The first section systematizes the discussion on business instrumental and structural power, and clarifies where this book fits in ongoing academic debates. The second section analyzes how the power of multinational corporations has been studied in Latin America. The third section argues for the advantages of combining these theoretical approaches and summarizes the book's main conceptual contributions.

2.1 Instrumental and Structural Business Power

2.1.1 Background and Definitions

A classic approach to the study of business power rests on the distinction between instrumental power and structural power. In its original formulation, instrumental power encompassed mechanisms of *direct* influence, such as lobbying, the appointment of business leaders or sectoral leaders to positions of political influence, and the financing of electoral campaigns. Structural power, by contrast, was understood as an *indirect* form of influence stemming from control over production and investment decisions (Block, 1977; Lindblom, 1982).

Sources of instrumental power can be divided into those based on *relationships* and those based on *resources* (Fairfield, 2015). Relationship-based sources refer to the degree of business actors' access to the policymaking process. These include partisan ties—when a firm belongs to a party's voter base or broader political network (Gibson, 1996)—, institutionalized consultation or concertation through regular meetings with Executive or Legislative officials (Schneider, 2010), the appointment of business representatives (direct or indirect) to government posts, access to elected office (particularly in Congress), and informal political ties.

Instrumental power based on resources is also diverse. First, it depends on the cohesion or ability of economic elites to form and maintain a united front and engage in collective action—either across sectors or within a single sector. This cohesion enhances legitimacy, strengthens lobbying efforts, and increases the political cost of "divide-and-conquer" strategies by the government. The most important factor enabling cohesion is the existence of an *encompassing* organization. Second, *expertise* can be a prerequisite for gaining access to officials. The legitimacy earned by elites through technical knowledge depends, in turn, on the level of expertise held by public officials. Third, access to mass media strengthens the ability of business actors to shape public opinion. Finally, financial resources allow firms to fund organizational capacity, acquire technical expertise, hire lobbyists, gain media access, buy votes, and make campaign contributions.[1]

Initial contributions to the concept of structural power came from two critical traditions. In his critique of Marxist theories portraying the state as a mere instrument of dominant classes, Block (1977) argued that the state serves capitalist interests even without conscious or direct intervention by business elites, since those managing the state apparatus need to maintain a reasonable level of economic activity to stay in power. On the other hand, Lindblom (1982), in a critique to pluralist theories, argued that the ability of business to influence key economic variables—such as growth, investment, and employment—makes them privileged political actors. This is because they possess an "automatic punishment" mechanism that is triggered when their interests are negatively affected. This form of power is structural because it is exercised in an automatic, apolitical manner, with no intentionality or conspiracy. The business sector's main advantage over other social actors lies in its capacity to *exit*, that is, to relocate to another province or country if a policy harms its profitability.

2.1.2 Structural Power: Recent Conceptualizations and Attributes

One major issue with this classical conceptualization of structural power is that it tends to overestimate business influence, treating structural power as a constant and failing to explain why businesses sometimes *lose* (Bell, 2012; Hacker & Pierson, 2002). Moreover, it pays insufficient attention to government actors, which makes it less suitable for comparative analysis (Hacker & Pierson 2002; Fairfield 2015). The inability of early structuralist arguments to account for these dynamics has led many

[1] This way of conceptualizing instrumental power is systematized by Fairfield (2015). Earlier works within this theoretical framework include Schneider (2010, 2015).

scholars interested in explaining policy variation to turn to instrumentalist approaches—or to abandon the power framework altogether (Hacker & Pierson, 2002: 281).

It is necessary to advance a conceptualization of structural power incorporating the following attributes: (1) structural power is a variable, (2) it is relational, (3) it is influenced by policymakers' perceptions, (4) it can be expressed both automatically and deliberately, and (5) it feeds back into instrumental power.

2.1.2.1 Structural Power Is a Variable

Structural power should be understood as a variable (rather than a constant) that depends on the credibility of the disinvestment threat (Hacker & Pierson, 2002). This credibility, in turn, is conditioned by various factors identified in the literature, such as the economic and institutional context, the visibility of the issue on the public agenda, the electoral incentives of public officials, the level of popular mobilization, and the specificity of assets or sectoral characteristics.

Regarding the economic context, it has been shown that business actors exert the greatest influence during intermediate phases of the economic cycle (Vogel, 1987). During prolonged economic downturns, it becomes more difficult for firms to sustain the narrative that preserving an "investment climate" is essential. For instance, if unemployment reaches 25%, the threat of job losses due to lack of investment becomes less persuasive, and businesses may even be blamed for the crisis. Conversely, during economic upturns, business influence also weakens, as policymakers tend to take corporate complaints about state intervention less seriously.

This book is based on the premise that the economic cycle matters, but differs in its focus on the power of firms in specific sectors, rather than on the business community as a whole. Analyzing specific industries requires studying the particular elements of the economy beyond the general business cycle. For example, the power of firms involved in foreign trade stems from their ability to block the inflow of foreign currency; therefore, their structural power varies according to the economy's capacity to generate foreign exchange at a given time.

Second, structural power also varies according to the institutional context. One example can be found in federal systems: when subnational governments compete to attract investment, the power of firms increases (Hacker & Pierson, 2002). Firms may even seek to move negotiations to jurisdictions with more favorable institutions and attempt to influence those institutions in order to enhance their exit capacity. In other words, the institutional variable that shapes structural power can also be endogenous, resulting from the strategic actions of firms themselves—what some authors refer to as "structuring power" (Farrell & Newman, 2015: 534). Structural power also varies depending on the state arena where decisions are made: it tends to decrease in arenas involving multiple actors (Culpepper, 2010). In that regard, business power is generally lower in the Legislative Branch than in the Executive.

Third, when a given issue or reform gains public visibility, democratic governments have greater incentives to redistribute in favor of consumers or voters—especially in contexts of political competition and popular mobilization—, thereby diminishing business power (Fairfield, 2015b, Murillo, 2009; Post, 2014). On the other hand, the public and media are less likely to pay attention to technically complex issues, making politicians more prone to yield to corporate demands (Culpepper, 2010). In other words, Lindblom's theories (1982) hold true "when voters are not paying attention" (Culpepper, 2010). However, when issues become visible, "the structure of electoral democracy constrains firms more than the structural power of firms constrains democracy."

Fourth, structural power varies according to the specificity of firms' assets and their sectoral characteristics. Capital mobility—or the capacity for "exit"—is feasible for some firms but not for others, such as those involved in natural resource extraction or those with high sunk costs and assets difficult to relocate (Vogel, 1987). As will be analyzed later, much of the literature on multinational corporate power in Latin America assumes this position. However, this approach is often binary and static, reducing structural power to the question of whether a firm has exit capacity. In reality, structural power can operate without capital mobility, since even when assets are "sunk," the need to attract new investments can shape the policy options under consideration (Fairfield 2015). Even when sunk costs are low, disinvestment threats may be weak if they cannot materialize without significant costs to those making the threat.

2.1.2.2 *Structural Power Is Relational*

Another fundamental attribute of structural power is its relational nature, which implies that its analysis must consider not its absolute strength, but how it compares to the power of other actors—interest groups, other firms, and the state itself. Thus, the key question is not simply whether business actors are powerful, but rather how their power compares to that of other stakeholders within a given political and economic configuration.

One limitation of classical approaches to structural power is their insufficient attention to state actors (Bell, 2012; Culpepper, 2015). This is problematic because, just as governments depend on business investment decisions, firms are at least equally dependent on government decisions (Vogel, 1987). Traditional theories tend to conceptualize structural power in a unidirectional manner, overstating state subordination to the power of business and overlooking the existence of "reciprocal dependence": structural power creates mutual interdependencies between states and firms—dependencies that generate vulnerabilities on both sides (Culpepper, 2015). The key question from this perspective is not only how dependent the state is on private capital, but also: how costly is it for a firm to come into conflict with the government? From this viewpoint, structural power can be understood as a function of the level of firms' dependence on the domestic market. If a company generates sufficient revenue in other markets or sectors, it may be in a better position to ignore the threat of regulatory sanctions in a particular jurisdiction (Culpepper & Reinke, 2014).

Beyond the relationship with the state, intra-business relations are also crucial. Classical approaches often assumed that structural power was a collective attribute of the "business class," neglecting internal divisions or competing interests. In reality, structural power can be exercised by one firm or group of firms against other companies or against the state (Culpepper, 2015, Farrell & Newman, 2015). Therefore, a key analytical challenge lies with identifying how the structure of capitalism generates advantages for some firms (and not others) *vis-à-vis* the state, while simultaneously enabling some states (and not others) to leverage that structure to spark confrontation among businesses (Culpepper, 2015).

2.1.2.3 Structural Power Is Shaped by Perceptions

Classical interpretations of structural power tend to portray it as an objective and observable phenomenon, measured through indicators of a sector's contribution to the economy or through attributes defined in binary and static terms, usually focused on capital mobility. However, this perspective overlooks the considerable uncertainty surrounding how market actors may respond to changes in public policy (Fairfield, 2010; Fairfield 2015). In practice, policymakers and analysts often disagree in their forecasts about how business actors will react to measures such as tax increases, for instance. This suggests that there is no unequivocal measure of structural power: its influence is always, at least partially, shaped by the perceptions and interpretations of those making policy decisions. As noted by Blyth (2003) in his critique of rational action theories, "structures do not come with an instruction manual." Therefore, capturing the evolution in structural power over time, across countries, policy areas, and economic sectors requires integrating the structural foundations of the concept with policymakers' perceptions and their anticipatory responses (Fairfield, 2015).[2] Also, if business power depends on how it is perceived by government officials, then it becomes essential to understand how policymakers' ideas influence their actions, and how they create the perception that a firm or sector poses a threat to the government (Bell, 2012).

This has important—and advantageous—methodological implications. One way to detect whether structural power is strong, or has had an impact, is to identify evidence that policymakers perceived a credible (even if implicit) threat that a given reform would lead to reduced investment with negative economic consequences. In this way, perceptions serve as empirical traces of structural power and help identify to which extent it influences policy decisions (Fairfield, 2010; Fairfield, 2015).

This way of operationalizing structural power demands rigorous empirical work, with interviews with policymakers playing a central role. If the goal is to predict policy outcomes across a large number of countries, it may be more practical to use a more easily measurable variable, such as capital mobility. However, if the aim is to explain policy decisions in specific and relevant cases, one cannot disregard the role of policymakers' perceptions and their anticipatory responses (Fairfield, 2019: 176–177).

2.1.2.4 *Structural Power can be Automatic or Deliberate*

The area that has generated the most disagreement in recent literature is the debate between those who argue that structural power only manifests itself automatically—through individual market decisions (Hacker and Pierson, 2002; Fairfield, 2015, 2019)—and those who maintain that it can also be expressed strategically, deliberately, and with the explicit aim

[2] Perceptions are also an important attribute—although less developed—in Hacker and Pierson (2002), who also understand structural power as an automatic, anticipatory mechanism, and highlight the importance of the credibility of the disinvestment threat, which typically depends on capital mobility.

of influencing public policy (Bell, 2012; Culpepper & Reinke, 2014). This work leans toward the latter position.

Partly due to the influence of Lindblom's definition of structural power as an "automatic punishing recoil," most studies[3] have adhered to the first conceptualization. From this perspective, structural power differs from instrumental power in that it is rooted in individual business decisions and manifests through market coordination rather than organized collective action (Fairfield, 2015). In this view, most disinvestment threats are often implicit. Conversely, if there is political coordination of disinvestment, this implies a degree of organization and is therefore classified as instrumental power. The logic behind this stance is that since deliberate coordination of disinvestment or halting production with an explicit political goal—what is often termed a "capital strike" or business protest[4]—entails costs, such actions do not aim at maximizing profit and thus fall into a different category.

I argue, however, that structural power can be used as a strategic resource. The label "structural" has biased the conversation and diverted attention from business agency (Culpepper & Reinke, 2014). With the exception of Block and Vogel—who do consider the possibility of coordination—Lindblom and virtually all works since the 1990s (Hacker and Pierson, Winters, Swank, Smith) have limited structural power to automatic mechanisms. Yet insisting that structural power only exists as an automatic reaction within policymakers' minds is untenable, as it implies that businesses cannot actively invoke it during negotiations.[5] In practice, when a firm seeks to block a government initiative by leveraging structural power as a negotiating tool, that power must be explicitly invoked.

This also offers a methodological advantage, since its use can be empirically traced and observed in negotiations between government and businesses. A "capital strike" involves political coordination among firms, but it still constitutes structural power because it flows directly from

[3] To the exception of Block and Vogel, according to Culpepper and Reinke (2014).

[4] For a discussion on the theoretical definition of "business protests", *see* Fairfield 2011.

[5] To support this argument, Culpepper and Reinke (2014) show that the policies implemented after the 2008 financial crisis cannot be explained without taking into account the explicit threats made by banks to regulators during negotiations. Along similar lines, although without defining it as structural power, Mahon (1996) analyzes instances in which capital movements are deliberately used to exert pressure and can therefore be considered "political."

their role as owners of capital within the economy, rather than from investments in lobbying or business associations (Culpepper & Reinke, 2014).

In short, if businesses leverage their market power via threats that invoke such position, that would constitute structural power. Ultimately, the key analytical question is whether market coordination or political coordination predominates.

2.1.2.5 *Structural Power Operates in both Agenda Setting and Policy Design*

Another area of debate in the literature concerns the stage of the policy-making process in which structural power operates. Some authors argue that structural power is confined to the agenda-setting phase (Hacker & Pierson, 2002). From this standpoint, structural power does not dictate specific policies; rather, it acts as a signaling device that helps to define or exclude certain options from the agenda. It is ultimately the government that decides which policies to pursue in order to boost investment. Accordingly, attention must be paid to how the agenda is shaped—what alternatives are under consideration, how that set of policy options is constructed (which proposals make it onto the agenda and which are excluded from the outset), and whether this process reflects indirect sources of influence (Hacker and Pierson 2002: 285). This distinction is important because business influence during the agenda-setting phase can, in some cases, prove even more decisive than influence exercised after the government initiates a reform proposal (Fairfield, 2015: 10–11).

However, if structural power can be exercised strategically and deliberately, then it can shape not only the definition of the agenda but also specific legislation content (Culpepper & Reinke, 2014). Even some authors who understand structural power as an automatic and anticipatory resource acknowledge that it can operate at both the agenda-setting stage and later in the policymaking process, once a proposal has been introduced (Fairfield, 2015). For example, legislators may perceive strong structural power even if the drafters of a bill within the executive branch did not anticipate negative investor reactions.

Similarly, instrumental power can also play a role during the agenda-setting phase, through the anticipatory reactions of policymakers who may rule out certain policy options upon recognizing that business actors have the political resources to obstruct or complicate the approval of legislation.

2.1.2.6 *Feedback between Instrumental and Structural Power*

The points discussed above highlight the frequent difficulty of clearly distinguishing between structural and instrumental power. One of the main analytical challenges lies in understanding the relation between the two. To begin with, they reinforce each other (Fairfield, 2015). Structural power can enhance instrumental power, for instance when governments—concerned about potential market reactions—grant businesses greater access to decision-making arenas. Conversely, instrumental power can also strengthen structural power: firms may leverage their resources—lobbying, media access, and technical expertise—to heighten policymakers' concerns about investment risks or to shape regulatory frameworks in ways that entrench favorable market conditions over the long term. Technical expertise is one of the most effective resources for increasing a firm's structural power, as it confers both authority and legitimacy. This is particularly relevant in policy areas involving technical complexity, where government officials or politicians may lack the capacity to independently assess the potential impact on investment (Fairfield, 2015). Similarly, when journalists lack deep subject knowledge, they are more likely to rely on experts from the business sector, who thereby gain greater influence in shaping public opinion through issue framing. In the legislative sphere, the training and technical understanding of lawmakers also significantly affect the degree of influence that business actors can exert in Congress (Hertel-Fernandez, 2014).

2.2 The Power of Multinational Corporations in Latin America

Multinational corporations (MNCs)[6] hold an increasingly central role in Latin American economies. Since the early twentieth century, they have made significant investments in the region—initially in raw materials and railroads, later expanding into infrastructure and public services. During the import substitution industrialization (ISI) period, their focus shifted to manufacturing, and then again to infrastructure, services, and finance during the market reforms of the 1980s and 1990s (Schneider, 2013).

[6] In this work the term multinational corporations is used interchangeably with transnational corporations. Some authors prefer the term *transnational* because nearly all of them are controlled by capital from a central country (Evans, 1979).

By the early twenty-first century, MNCs accounted for between 30% and 40% of the total sales of the region's 500 largest companies.

Argentina represents "an extreme case of MNC-driven acquisitions and near complete denationalization of large firms" (Schneider, 2013: 78). By 1993, 60% of the sales of the largest firms came from MNCs (compared to 43% for Brazil), and by 2003 MNCs accounted for a remarkable 82% of sales and a similar share of exports (Chudnovsky & Lopez, 2007, cited in Schneider 2013). As explored in greater detail in Chapter 3, MNCs also play an increasingly important role in agriculture, integrating vertically from input provision to exports, and establishing increasingly asymmetrical relationships with local producers.

Despite their undeniable economic weight, there remains a substantial gap in both the conceptualization and empirical evidence regarding the sources of MNCs' power and strategies. Studies on business politics in Latin America and Argentina tend to focus more on the political activity of domestic firms than on that of foreign capital.[7] At the same time, more recent approaches emphasizing the role of MNCs in development—such as varieties of capitalism or global value chains—often sidestep the question of power.

This subsection addresses this gap through a review of the literature, guided by the following questions: What influence do MNCs have on domestic political processes in these countries? How has this power evolved over time in relation to states and other internal actors? What factors shape the balance of power between these actors?

2.2.1 *The Power of MNCs in Latin America in the 1960s and 1970s*

The question of the power of multinational corporations (MNCs) in developing countries drew significant attention during the 1960s and 1970s. Both the "dependent development" approach[8] (Evans, 1979;

[7] For a review of the literature on Latin American business politics, *see* Schneider (2004, 2010).

[8] Building on the general premises of classical dependency theorists, but also introducing substantial critiques and contributions, a group of authors in the 1970s characterized the development model of the more advanced Latin American countries as "dependent development" (Evans, 1979; Cardoso & Faletto, 1979; Gereffi, 1978; Gereffi & Evans, 1981). For a *situation of dependency* to exist, two consequences of MNC control must be identified: (1) an unequal distribution of benefits that favors MNCs more than the host country, and (2) at the level of domestic policymaking, a clear restriction on government

Cardoso & Faletto, 1979; Gereffi, 1978) and the "negotiation power balance" approach—associated with the concept of the *obsolescing bargain* (Vernon, 1971; Moran, 1975)— started from the premise that the distribution of revenues between MNCs and governments is determined by the outcome of negotiations and the balance of power between the two. While the former emphasized the dominant role of MNCs, the latter reached the opposite conclusion, highlighting their vulnerability to statist initiatives by governments in the region.

In both perspectives, the source of MNCs' power lies in their investment capacity and, above all, in their flexibility to divest—in other words, their ability to *exit*. This corresponds to a form of power that stems from their privileged position within the economic structure. From the perspective of international business (IB) studies, it has been argued that this positioning influences the political resources that MNCs can later mobilize. Since investing abroad entails high costs, MNCs only do so if they possess advantages over local firms in terms of access to financing, technology, capabilities, or other resources (Dunning, 1992; Levy & Prakash, 2003). As a result, they tend to position themselves in imperfect or oligopolistic markets, which not only grants them market power but also increases their ability to limit governments' policy options. Added to this are the inherent advantages of their transnational structure, superior organizational capacity, and their ability to evade state monitoring mechanisms.

One important contribution of these approaches is that they do not view structural power as static, but as a resource influenced by multiple factors.[9] The first such factor is the type and characteristics of the sector in which they operate. In certain industries, the capacity to divest is low, which reduces MNCs' *exit* ability and their power along with it. Thus, they are in a more vulnerable position when their projects require

policy options, as these may conflict with the global priorities of the corporations (Gereffi, 1978: 241).

[9] For a recent systematic review of negotiation theories between governments and MNCs, *see* Mullner and Puck (2018). They find that the bargaining power of MNCs is strengthened by a range of factors, including technological advantages (specific capabilities, technology intensity in production), product differentiation, efficiency in communication and transportation, local allies, legal instruments (contracts, international laws, trade agreements), financial instruments and borrowing capacity, international competition among countries/states (globalization), and the likelihood of future investments (intertemporal dynamics and repeated-game settings).

large upfront capital investments and stable technologies, as is the case with extractive industries (Evans, 1979; Moran, 1978). In these capital-intensive industries, once the investment has been made and time passes, the balance of power tends to shift in favor of the state (Moran, 1975; Vernon, 1971). The expropriations that took place in the 1970s in natural resource sectors show that multinationals are not always the dominant actor. Conversely, in industries with low fixed costs, adaptable technologies, strong product differentiation, and a focus on marketing and advertising, MNCs tend to hold greater bargaining power, and the threat of nationalization becomes less credible.

In the same vein, the level of technology and knowledge controlled by MNCs is a key factor in understanding the balance of power between them and the state. An MNC's position is never as strong as when it arises from the monopolistic control of new knowledge (Evans, 1979: 200). For this reason, MNCs prefer to operate in sectors with universally applicable and rapidly changing technologies, which cannot be obtained on the open market. They seek to standardize consumption patterns across as many markets as possible while concentrating research and development (R&D) in their headquarters, located in central countries. This logic is even more relevant today, given the expansion and centrality of the knowledge economy, and—as shown in Chapter 4—is particularly important in the case of agricultural biotechnology.

The second group of factors refers to the characteristics and conditions of the domestic economy. Domestic market size and growth rate increase the attractiveness of foreign investment and thus strengthen the state's bargaining position (Moran, 1978). Similarly, the power of MNCs diminishes when a country has valuable natural resources (Evans, 1979; Gereffi, 1978). A strong industrial sector also increases the credibility of nationalization threats and reduces the opportunity cost of a failed nationalization strategy (Moran, 1978). Lastly, greater access to commercial credit or high domestic savings rates reduces dependence on foreign direct investment and thus enhances the power of the state (Haggard, 1989; Kohli, 2009).

The third group of factors includes the capacities and characteristics of the state bureaucracy. Government power increases when officials possess technical expertise, information control, and administrative capacity. Conversely, internal priority conflicts, weak regulatory or oversight capabilities, and corruption enhance the relative power of MNCs (Haggard, 1989).

Finally, attention must also be given to the political advantages of local capital. Although MNCs have technological advantages, they are often at a political disadvantage compared to domestic capital (Moran, 1978). Local actors possess two key resources: legitimacy and access—both formal and informal—to government officials and politicians. This may constitute an incentive for MNCs to share control with segments of local capital, either to facilitate bureaucratic access or to enhance their legitimacy. In many cases, particularly in extractive industries, governments are reluctant to grant concessions to foreign firms without local partners (Moran, 1978). In others, it is MNCs themselves that seek partnerships with national business elites to improve their access to government.[10]

Despite the continued relevance of many of these arguments in explaining the power balance between states, MNCs, and domestic actors, the structuralist approach of dependency theory has largely neglected the role of domestic political institutions (Haggard, 1989, 1990). This is problematic, since many countries similarly situated in the international context have adopted different policies in response to external pressures. To understand these differences, it is necessary to develop theories that take into account the incentives of political actors and the dynamics of domestic institutions. Since bargaining resources do not automatically translate into control over outcomes, the key question is how decisive the "structural" characteristics of the relationship between governments and MNCs truly are. Answering this question requires greater attention to the political institutions and processes that shape corporate behavior (Haggard, 1990).

2.2.2 *Decreased Interest in Business Power in the Context of Globalization*

Academic interest in the power balance between MNCs and states began to wane in the 1980s. The limited scholarly production on the political behavior of MNCs is paradoxical, given that it was precisely in this period that these firms came to play a central role in the global economy (Strange, 1989), while Latin American countries underwent a sustained

[10] For example, upon realizing that its subsidiary in Mexico was not growing and that it was partly due to the lack of alliances, Monsanto decided to partner with Mexican investors and create a new company, retaining 38% ownership but under the control of a Mexican holding company (Evans, 1979: 299).

process of foreign acquisition of their major companies (Schneider, 2013). During the 1980s and 1990s, the room to maneuver of regional governments shrank considerably, and market-oriented reforms and policies favorable to international capital were implemented—even by populist governments or left-wing parties with labor union support (Campello, 2015; Etchemendy, 2014; Mahon, 1996).

This lack of academic attention to MNC power is even more striking considering the profound structural and institutional transformations that strengthened that power over that period. First, the trade agreements signed since the 1980s expanded investor rights and curtailed the capacity of countries to regulate capital according to social or redistributive goals.[11] Second, the strengthening of intellectual property rights made access to key technologies more expensive and hindered their adoption in developing countries. Third, new export-oriented development models reinforced the role of MNCs as privileged channels for access to international markets, capital, and technology. Fourth, capital flows liberalization favored multinational corporations, which have greater mobility, whereas national firms remain more dependent on the economic conditions of their countries of origin (Gill & Law, 1989).

As a counterweight to these trends, there is nonetheless some room for countries to defy trade agreements (Post, 2014), as well as intellectual property rights (Shadlen, 2017). This holds true in industries with high sunk costs, such as public utilities and infrastructure, where the wave of property rights strengthening at the international level in the 1980s and 1990s failed to shield multinational corporations (MNCs) from the *obsolescing bargain* (Post, 2014). This is partly explained by the fact that the sanctions imposed through international arbitration were less burdensome than the economic challenges faced by governments in developing countries—challenges that prompted them to revise existing contracts. In many cases, contract renegotiation turned out to be more advantageous for domestic firms than for MNCs. Moreover, in sectors dominated by national companies—in terms of market share—MNCs tend to exert more limited influence (Shadlen, 2017). A telling example is Argentina, where domestic pharmaceuticals succeeded in delaying and restricting reforms promoted at the international level, such as the World Trade

[11] There is evidence indicating that—unlike in OECD countries—in developing countries, trade openness and trade dependence are correlated with lower welfare efforts (Wibbels, 2006).

Organization's intellectual property agreement (TRIPS: Trade-Related Aspects of Intellectual Property Rights). The case of genetically modified seeds, analyzed in this book, provides further evidence of the room to maneuver within the intellectual property regime to favor local actors.

Another factor that has undermined the position of MNCs since the 2000s is the rise of new actors, notably NGOs and the so-called "global civil society." These actors, despite often lacking material resources, have been able to exert influence through coordinated lobbying strategies, information dissemination, and appeals to moral principles and social legitimacy (Levy & Prakash, 2003). As discussed in the chapter on seeds intellectual property rights, this type of dynamic weakened the bargaining position of biotechnology firms in Argentina. Finally, a key point raised in the literature—and relevant to the context of this book—that helps explain variation in the power of traders is that periods of rising commodity prices or low international interest rates tend to increase the autonomy of governments in the region. In such contexts, governments become less dependent on external financing and more able to resist pressure or market-friendly policy recommendations (Campello, 2015; Murillo et al., 2011).

2.2.3 *The Growing Role of MNCs in the Organization of Production*

Recent literature recognizes the increasingly central role played by MNCs in structuring the economies of developing countries (Doner & Schneider, 2016; Gereffi & Korzeniewicz, 1994; Schneider, 2013). However, the focus has shifted from conflict between states and MNCs to the collaboration between them, giving way to other concerns such as the role of MNCs in the reorganization of production through global value chains (Gereffi & Korzeniewicz, 1994), the contributions of foreign investment to development, and the state capacities needed to foster such development (Amsden, 1989; Evans,1995; Johnson, 1982; Wade, 1990).[12]

[12] The literature from the 1980s and 1990s delved into one of these dimensions: state capacity and its importance in driving development processes. Notable works include Johnson's (1982) study on the role of MITI in Japan's industrialization, the analyses by Wade (1990) and Amsden (1989) on the role of autonomous agencies in the late industrialization of Korea and Taiwan, and Evans' (1995) work on embedded autonomy. Amsden (1989) points out that in Korea, Japan, and Taiwan, the state was more effective

MNCs have played a dominant role in the restructuring of production and trade toward the end of the twentieth century, according to the literature on Global Value Chains (GVCs) (Gereffi et al., 2005). However, this body of work has gradually moved away from its original structuralist perspective—centered on hierarchies and inequalities—toward an emphasis on the capabilities of firms or countries to insert themselves in GVCs or to move into higher value-added links (*upgrading*) (Bair, 2005; Fernández, 2015; Levy, 2008). This trend has been described by some as a form of "developmentalist illusion" (Bair, 2005). Although power is a central concept within this perspective, it is rarely defined explicitly or analyzed systematically (Dallas et al., 2019: 667). An additional shortcoming of current GVC approaches is their insufficient attention to the conflicts of interest among different actors in the chain, and between national states over whose territories the chains unfold (Santarcángelo et al., 2017).

Multinational corporations (MNCs) also play a central role in the characterization of Latin American capitalisms as "hierarchical market economies" (HMEs), as proposed by the literature on varieties of capitalism (VoC) (Schneider, 2013).[13] Interestingly, the proponents of this position argue that, as a legacy of the import substitution industrialization (ISI) period—and further intensified by the wave of privatization, economic concentration, and the rise in foreign direct investment (FDI) during the 1990s—MNCs, alongside diversified business groups, became key channels for organizing access to capital, technology, and markets.

This "Coasian onslaught"—a pervasive strategy by large firms to expand corporate hierarchies through mergers and acquisitions—helps explain that "in an oversimplified sense, economic activity in Latin America is still largely subject to planning, rather than to the spontaneous free play of market forces, but the planning shifted after the 1990s from ministry offices to corporate boardrooms" (Schneider, 2013). From

than in other late-industrializing countries because it had the power to discipline large firms.

[13] Nölke and Vliegenthart (2009) offer a similar characterization of the role of MNCs in Eastern Europe, where hierarchy is the main coordination mechanism. There are institutional complementarities between the transfer of technological innovations within transnational corporations, the provision of capital through FDI, and low-wage skilled labor. Inspired by Evans's (1979) work on Latin America, they call these "dependent market economies" (DMEs).

this perspective, MNCs fulfill essential functions at four levels: finance, infrastructure, technology, and trade (Schneider, 2013).

However, like most studies on VoC, Schneider's work emphasizes the economic-institutional organization of MNCs while political analysis takes a back seat. When it does address the political dimension of MNCs, it focuses primarily on their instrumental power and portrays their political engagement as passive. This political passivity—particularly in electoral contexts—creates room for large domestic business groups, which tend to hold an advantage over MNCs in terms of domestic political influence. Moreover, since they enjoy advantages in markets where their exit alternatives are better, they tend to exhibit weaker preferences regarding national development strategies (Schneider, 2013: 87–88).

2.2.4 Complementarities: The Structural Power of Multinational Corporations

The dialogue between these conceptual frameworks offers a more comprehensive understanding of key aspects of business politics than either one could provide on its own. This section delves into the complementarities between these approaches and explains how this articulation informs the book's contributions. It also summarizes how the insights generated by the book inform the conceptual discussion developed in this chapter.

First, this book draws on the complementarity between structural power theories and the global value chains (GVC) approach. Most studies on business politics—including recent structural power theories—tend to focus on the relationship between business actors and governments (or the state). In contrast, the GVC framework sheds light on the importance of relationships between private actors within the chain itself, rather than just with the state. One of the original contributions of this book is to show that distributive conflicts between private firms are also central to the discussion of power, as they often involve struggles to exert greater influence over the state and public policy decisions that determine winners and losers. A compelling example is the political use of technology licenses by biotechnology firms to align seed companies' interests with their own during negotiations with the government. This form of power deployed in inter-firm negotiations represents a promising and underexplored research agenda.

Conversely, the literature on value chains and on varieties of capitalism (VoC) can benefit from recent conceptual developments in the study of business power, particularly in response to criticisms regarding its functionalist or economistic bias and its limited treatment of power. While the GVC and VoC literatures offer insights into the functions that MNCs perform within Latin American capitalism, they provide less clarity on how such functions translate into influence—or not. The literature on structural power (Culpepper & Reinke, 2014; Fairfield, 2015; Hacker & Pierson, 2002) provides valuable conceptual and methodological tools to overcome this limitation. These contributions help trace the actual impact and activities of MNCs in concrete policymaking processes. In other words, once we identify the structures, functions, and roles that MNCs play in a given economy, the crucial question becomes: through what mechanisms do these privileged positions translate (or not) into influence? Since a privileged position does not necessarily entail control over outcomes, the key issue is how constraining the "structural" features of the relationship between governments and MNCs truly are.

Second, another issue identified in this chapter is that the literature tends to conceptualize structural power mainly in terms of disinvestment or *exit*, overlooking the power derived from the ability to block local actors' access to export markets and technology. This is a central yet underexplored form of structural power. A global value chains (GVC) perspective can contribute to the literature on business power by improving our understanding of the relationships between domestic actors (firms and governments) and the companies that control these global chains. Similarly, the literature review on multinational corporations (MNCs) sheds light on the commercial and productive structures through which they engage with domestic actors. These approaches highlight resources beyond *exit* that contribute to MNCs' structural power. In the case of Argentina's export agriculture, the role of technology and the capacity to influence exports stand out. This is explained by the sector's size, which makes *exit* a costly option for firms and therefore less frequently used. The empirical chapters provide concrete examples illustrating how these dynamics have influenced public policy.

Another conceptual innovation of this book regarding technology as a source of power is to show that, in some cases (such as biotechnology), power depends on the capacity to legally protect technology or knowledge. This strengthens the ability to exclude other actors from using that technology, thus enhancing the capacity to shape outcomes in distributive conflicts and policymaking. In this regard, the book's structuralist perspective emphasizes the role of legal structures alongside economic, productive, and technological ones.

Shifting the focus from MNC *exit* to local actors' access to markets and technology also contributes to discussions regarding the impacts of globalization on the political economy of developing countries. While the literature suggests that globalization has increased corporate power by facilitating firms' exit options, this book argues that globalization has enhanced some MNCs' ability to affect countries' access to international markets, and that policymakers consider this capacity when analyzing decisions that may affect these firms' interests.

Third, this book offers a conceptualization of structural power that admits the possibility of coordination and deliberate action. As noted above, some scholars argue that structural power manifests only indirectly, through market decisions, while others contend that it can also be expressed strategically through political and deliberate choices. This work supports the latter view and presents concrete instances where structural power is exercised strategically. For example, biotechnology firms make explicit threats not to introduce new technologies or to shut down R&D programs in the country. Likewise, traders, in addition to withholding exports awaiting devaluation (a market decision), also engage in coordinated, deliberate political action to obtain concessions from the government. It is yet worth noting that empirically distinguishing when such actions are deliberate poses a significant methodological challenge.

Fourth, the literature on structural power reviewed in this chapter is largely insensitive to how the context and specific characteristics of national economies affect corporate power. The empirical chapter shows that the structural power of firms depends on the country's context, and attempts to propose a notion of structural power sensitive to Argentina's reality. A key feature of the Argentine economy is the recurrent balance-of-payments crises, which makes policymakers especially concerned about corporate actions that might jeopardize foreign exchange flows—more so than in countries less vulnerable to such crises. This is particularly relevant for firms in the export agriculture sector, given their heavy reliance on agricultural commodity exports.

Fifth, power appears to vary across different policy areas; certain sources of power may prove effective in one policy domain but not in another. This perspective departs from the studies reviewed in this chapter, which tend to compare power between countries within the same policy area or sector. For example, the power of banks in the United States and Great Britain (Culpepper & Reinke, 2014), the power of business actors in fiscal policy in Argentina and Chile (Fairfield, 2015a), or social policy in the United States across different periods (Hacker & Pierson, 2002). This also represents an innovation relative to studies that have analyzed the structural power of business actors in Argentina but based on alternative conceptualizations of power, such as Etchemendy's (2014) work comparing the role of power in market reforms across countries, or Shadlen's (2017) analysis comparing the power of pharmaceutical companies in different countries.

Finally, this work can contribute to the conceptualization of development and dependency. The dialogue between the approaches reviewed here can enrich the concept of dependent development, defined as a growth process characterized by a distribution of benefits that favors MNCs over local actors, and by a clear restriction on government policy options at the domestic level (Gereffi, 1978). A recurring critique of dependency theories is that they lost relevance because they failed to specify the political and economic mechanisms through which dependency operates, and did not offer causal arguments suitable for empirical evaluation (Stallings, 2020, Wibbels 2009). The conceptualization of business power presented here allows us to identify the actors (multinational companies, officials, politicians, voters), their preferences, and the constraints under which they operate, which result in varying degrees of dependency.

CHAPTER 3

The Political Economy of Agriculture in Argentina

The aim of this chapter is to analyze the various conceptualizations of the power of agrarian elites in Argentina from the early twentieth century to the present. The chapter also seeks to position this book's contribution within this field by identifying the analytical limitations of recent literature and outlining how these limitations will be addressed. The review and analysis are organized around the theoretical framework on instrumental and structural power presented in Chapter 1.

The first section reviews the literature focused on the twentieth century, arguing that the studies examining the politics of the sector during the early agro-export model pointed to the dominant role of agrarian elites, whose structural power stemmed from land ownership and control over the majority of exports. Even analyses that highlighted the sector's weak partisan and electoral presence acknowledged the influence these elites wielded due to their privileged position within the agro-export system. The notion of a structurally powerful sector is common to most works that examined the Peronist governments and the period of import substitution industrialization (ISI). In policy terms, this translated into the failure to implement a land reform and the challenges faced by successive governments in attempting to modernize the sector. Some studies also noted the dominant role, from early on, of foreign processing and exporting companies, while input-supplying firms did not emerge as influential actors until the twenty-first century.

J. O'Farrell, *Business Power in Agriculture Value Chains*, Latin American Political Economy, https://doi.org/10.1007/978-3-032-06589-6_3

The second section analyzes the literature addressing agrarian elites in the twenty-first century—the period analyzed in this book—marked by the commodity boom and three successive administrations with redistributive and statist policy objectives. In this context, the literature is sharply polarized between, on the one hand, comparative politics studies with an institutionalist approach that conclude that agrarian elites are politically weak, and on the other, structuralist sociological analyses that maintain they remain a dominant actor in Argentine politics.

The third section seeks to organize the underlying reasons behind these polarized conclusions, arguing that the apparent contradiction between viewing the sector as weak versus dominant arises from differing definitions of (i) the business actors in agriculture, (ii) their sources of power, and (iii) the policy areas in which they have vested interests. In relation to the comparative politics literature, this study argues that any analytical attempt to understand the sector's power must necessarily incorporate multinational corporations (MNCs) that control exports and the provision of inputs. It also emphasizes the need for a systematization of the mechanisms through which structural power is translated into influence, and for broadening the analytical scope beyond export taxes to include other regulatory dimensions relevant to the political economy of development. The recent advances in the conceptualization of business power presented in Chapter 1 of this work offer valuable tools for addressing these analytical gaps.

3.1 The Power of Agrarian Elites in the Twentieth Century

Throughout the twentieth century, Argentina's agrarian elites attained varying degrees of success in influencing politics. The literature on the power of these elites—comprised of large landowners and grain and livestock producers—suggests that their influence stemmed more from the privileged position they held in the country's economic development than from their institutional political resources. Their control over vast tracts of land and their role as the main contributors to national exports enabled them to resist redistributive policies and to influence the course of the national economy. However, this privileged access to decision-making spheres also discouraged the development of party-based political organization, leaving them in a position of relative electoral weakness. As a result, they were vulnerable to successive governments imposing high tax burdens on the sector.

3.1.1 *Landowners as a Dominant Class in the Early Twentieth Century*

A very influential argument on agrarian elite politics is that these elites represented a major obstacle to democratization processes (Acemoglu & Robinson, 2006; Albertus, 2015; Moore, 1966).[1] In the same vein, many studies on Latin American landed elites argue that they opposed democracy and supported coups whenever their interests were threatened, thereby delaying the modernization of the economy.

Argentina stands out as a case of notable agrarian elite influence at both regional and international levels (Albertus, 2015). A considerable portion of historiography argues that, due to their economic and political dominance in agricultural production, large landowners had the capacity to decisively influence the national economy—an interpretation that persists today. Accounts of the dominant character of Argentina's landowning elite often cite the fact that, along with Uruguay, it was the only Latin American country where these elites managed to block land reform initiatives (Albertus, 2015).

In the early twentieth century, Argentina's agrarian structure was characterized by land concentration, the absence of a strong peasantry, a significant but subdued number of small and medium farmers, and the monopolistic presence of foreign companies in strategic sectors such as foreign trade, transportation, and meatpacking (O'Donnell, 1977; Hora, 2015; Pucciarelli, 1986; Sábato, 1988).

The concentration of land and income by Argentine landowners at the beginning of the twentieth century finds no parallel in the agricultural histories of the United States, Canada, or Australia (Hora, 2015:109). A second key feature was that, unlike other Latin American economies organized around *haciendas*, enclaves, or plantations, Argentine land was controlled by an emerging local agrarian bourgeoisie that coexisted with a growing commercial and incipiently industrial urban sector (O'Donnell,

[1] Since land is a fixed asset, landowners are an easy target for taxation or expropriation. As a result, democratization is more threatening to landowners than to other economic elites, and the greater the inequality in land ownership, the stronger the incentives for landowners to oppose democracy.

1977). The power of this Argentine agrarian bourgeoisie was greater than that of its counterparts in the region due to its "international homogeneity"—meaning that areas not directly incorporated into the global market (such as subsistence peasants and non-exporting sectors) carried far less economic and demographic weight. Unlike in enclaves where production was actually controlled by foreign companies, Argentina's dependence stemmed from European control over ports, transportation, financing, and commercialization (O'Donnell, 1977).[2]

What role did foreign companies play in this structure? While their main investments—particularly British—were concentrated in the railway system, foreign capital also monopolized essential services, trade, finance, and a large portion of the agro-industrial sector. The clearest examples of this "privileged position" in the national economy are the monopolies in meatpacking and in the commercialization of unprocessed commodities.[3] Positions held by agricultural producers in relation to the tensions with these foreign companies varied depending on the size of their operations. Across the board, small and medium producers were typically the first to voice opposition to foreign capital, more so than large landowners.

The structural power of landowners ensured them a prominent role in shaping the social and economic order, yet it did not automatically translate into effective access to political power as a group, nor into decisive influence over party politics (Figueroa & Leiras, 2014; Gibson, 1996; Hora, 2009, 2015; Losada, 2009). Even during the conservative order, large landowners were the most influential political actors, though they never achieved full hegemony. Their power rested primarily on their strategic position within the agro-export model and their social prestige, rather than on direct control over political institutions.

This conclusion is partly drawn from a comparative analysis. In most Latin American countries, the process of party formation before the advent of mass politics mimicked that of Europe, where the rural-urban cleavage gave rise to parties representing rural elites ("conservatives") and urban commercial-industrial elites ("liberals"). In Argentina, however,

[2] The homogeneity and economic and wealth concentration, in addition to securing the group's hegemonic role at the political level, negatively affected the course of the economy, particularly due to the priority given to the availability of money over the use of capital for productive purposes (Sábato 1988:143).

[3] Smith (1968) proposes a similar argument, focusing on the tensions between livestock producers and foreign meatpacking companies.

party formation did not follow the same logic. While the *Partido Autonomista Nacional* (PAN) represented many agricultural landowners, and the *Unión Cívica Radical* (UCR) found support among segments of the rural middle class and tenant farmers, no political parties emerged that were explicitly agrarian or organized around the interests of the agricultural sector.[4]

The privileged position that landowning classes held within the agro-export model discouraged the development of their own partisan organization. Since the governments of the time had strong incentives to implement policies favorable to agricultural exports, large landowners saw little need for direct or sustained engagement in the political system; as a result, the "cost of political indifference" was low (Hora, 2015:132). Another key explanation for the absence of a unified conservative party lies in the predominance of regional cleavages over the rural-urban divide (Gibson, 1996). This regional divide reflected divergent interests among rural elites: while landowners in the Pampas supported the agro-export model, economic elites in non-central provinces—particularly Mendoza, Tucumán, and Salta—advocated for a domestic market-oriented model that protected regional industries, especially wine and sugar production.[5]

Additional factors that discouraged landowners from engaging in partisan politics included the lack of perceived threats from subordinate rural sectors against their interests—as occurred in Mexico (Hora, 2009, 2015)[6]—and the specific social structure of the Pampas, which made it difficult for landowners to build a social base they could mobilize in their favor (Figueroa & Leiras, 2014; Losada, 2009).

[4] Studies such as that of Lupu and Stokes (2009), which examine the social bases of political parties in Argentine history, confirm that agrarian interests were represented by different parties over time, without this implying that their interests were predominant or constituted the main ideological backbone of any particular party. In one section of their work, they inquire about the relevance of the rural-urban cleavage, but they do not find it to have been significant.

[5] Gibson (1996) thus presents the oligarchic regime that emerged after 1880 as a way to overcome and stabilize (an "institutional solution") the conflicts between the elites of Buenos Aires and those of the interior. This bears similarities to Natalio Botana's description of the "conservative order" as a system designed to maximize oligarchic power and minimize interregional conflict.

[6] In Argentina, "the rural poor never offered sustained support for democratic reform programs targeting the rural order—aimed at limiting land concentration and the privileges of large landowners—occasionally promoted by Sarmiento and other members of the urban political elite" (Hora, 2009).

But this does not mean, as some approaches suggest, that landowners' wealth automatically guaranteed their political success. Their power was not expressed purely in structural or material terms. Landowners influenced the direction of the country primarily through ties with the state apparatus rather than through partisan organizations and elections. In this sense, another disincentive to forming partisan organizations lies in the fact that landowners simply did not need them to access the state apparatus. Although no member of the landowning families became president, several held ministerial and legislative positions. Moreover, landowners belonged to the same social circles as the main political leaders of the period (Losada, 2009).[7] The wealth derived from agriculture enabled landowners to exert political influence, granting them access to elite social spheres that facilitated their incorporation into established political parties. Those landowners most integrated into elite sociability had a higher probability of accessing political office and, once elected, legislated in line with their economic interests (Figueroa & Leiras, 2014).

3.1.2 *The Power of the Agrarian Sector as a Barrier to Agrarian Reform during the First Peronist Government*

The first Peronist government brought along a significant decrease in the presence of the agricultural sector in the state, as the shift in the development model prioritized the domestic market and manufacturing industry over agriculture. Nevertheless, and despite the decline in its contribution to GDP, the agrarian sector retained significant defensive and resistant power, anchored in its role as the main source of foreign currency inflows.

Peronism took measures against the interests of the rural export elites. Although these elites succeeded in protecting their property rights and keeping off the agenda any attempt at agrarian reform, their ability to influence tax and exchange rate policies was significantly reduced (Fernández Milmanda, 2019b: 15). Moreover, as other types of producers (smaller or regional) began to organize, the fragmentation of interests strengthened the relative power of the state (Manzetti, 1992).

[7] Gibson (1996) proposes a similar explanation to account for this political weakness of the wealthiest or the lack of a conservative party: "In the uninstitutionalized context of Argentine conservative party politics, when opportunities exist for direct access to state power or policy making, conservative politicians will tend to neglect or retreat from party building efforts."

In light of the apparent weakness of large landowners during this period, the question of why land reform was not implemented under Peronist governments becomes even more relevant. Although there are several answers to this question, they seem to converge on the structural importance of agriculture. According to Hora (2018), Perón faced a dilemma: either pursue land reform or ensure a minimum level of grain production—and he opted for the latter. At the time, Peronist sectors advocating for reform argued that official reticence was due to fear of an "oligarchic sabotage," namely a deliberate reduction in production (Hora, 2018: 134).

Other interpretations point to the role of the export-oriented agricultural sector as a source of foreign currency in a context of external imbalance. Gerchunoff and Llach (2003) argue that "in the Peronist economic model, the agricultural sector had the very important role of providing the foreign currency inflows needed to import inputs and machinery not yet produced locally. This could be the reason behind the cautious land reforms carried out under Peronism. Although many party leaders were not satisfied with the freeze on rental prices and advocated for land reform to end large estates, the government was unwilling to risk further deterioration of a balance of payments situation that was already beginning to worsen" (p. 192). Other authors even highlight the "social power" retained by landowners.

The 1943 Agricultural Lease Act (*Ley de Arrendamiento Rural)* was the closest Argentina would ever come to a land reform. According to Hora (2015), the legislation increased the share of landowners over tenants, reduced the average size of rural properties, and drove a profound change in the relationships between owners and tenants, gradually but irreversibly eroding the concentration of land ownership consolidated a century earlier (pp. 299–230). This transformation—coupled with the disorganization and passivity of subordinate rural classes (Hora, 2015: 296)—may help explain the absence of stronger demands for land reform as seen in other Latin American countries, partly because the process of change was already underway (p. 230). Over time, former tenant farmers adopted increasingly conservative positions and gradually aligned with the large landowners (p.301).

The Peronist government did manage to advance in key areas such as foreign trade regulation, the nationalization of ports, and the creation of the *Estatuto del Peón Rural* (Rural Laborer Statute).

3.1.3 *The Agrarian Elites as a Barrier to Modernization during the 1960s and 1970s*

Studies focusing on the period between the first Peronist government and the 1976 coup agree that agrarian elites—landowners and large producers—retained considerable defensive power, which in some cases worked as an obstacle to modernization initiatives. O'Donnell (1977) argues that Argentine agriculture could have been modernized "through policies that forced structural change," such as initiatives to tax land differentially—measures that repeatedly failed. This situation contrasts with other Latin American countries where the state, driven by and aligned with the national bourgeoisie, succeeded in imposing modernization processes on rural regions and landowning elites (p. 541).

According to O'Donnell, the particular power of Argentina's agrarian bourgeoisie stems from its weight in total exports. Thus, attempts to restructure agriculture through fiscal tools had a direct impact on the balance of payments. In contrast, in other countries in the region, the dominant classes "were essentially regional and none had the weight of the Pampean bourgeoisie, so that a potential temporary drop in production would not have as much impact." There, the state was able "to subordinate those classes and the regional states under their control, without compromising the main circuits of capital accumulation or seriously harming the balance of payments" (O'Donnell, 1977: 541). Another specific feature of the Argentine economy that endows the agrarian bourgeoisie with structural power is the nature of its main export commodities—grains and beef—which are among the most salient wage-linked goods for popular sectors. Thus, policies aimed at ensuring food supply and regulating food prices also have direct implications for the balance of payments.

Subsequent studies, such as those by Carlos Acuña, have reinforced this argument by highlighting the state's weakness and dependence on the agricultural sector. Acuña describes this power as the capacity to "disinvest": "States like Argentina's, which depend on the capitalist agrarian sector for foreign exchange, find themselves in a relatively weaker position than states that control the production/extraction and commercialization of a society's main export goods. In this sense, the disinvestment power of the Pampean bourgeoisie places the Argentine state in a situation of far greater dependence than that which, for example, characterizes the Chilean or Venezuelan state *vis-à-vis* local capitalist groups" (Acuña, 1990: 8).

During authoritarian governments in this period, agrarian interests were historically represented through personal networks: associations in the sector had direct access to the highest levels of government and exercised considerable control over the Ministry of Agriculture (Schneider, 2004). Given the instability of the party system and the weakness of institutional rules for participation and conflict resolution in those years, both the agrarian and industrial bourgeoisies developed meta-institutional behavior, operating independently of political party structures (Acuña, 1995). By directing their demands toward and exerting pressure upon the Executive, they structured their organizational logic around the only relatively stable space of institutional power.

3.1.4 Return to Democracy and Economic Liberalization (1983–2003)

Since 1983, agricultural policy in Argentina has been shaped by two major transformations: a political shift—the return to democracy—and an economic one—the liberalization of markets and the sector's technological transformation.

The introduction of electoral competition and regular legislative politics posed a significant challenge for a sector historically accustomed to exerting influence through non-democratic channels. Yet, informal access to power remained a key avenue of influence even after the country's return to democratic rule (Fernández Milmanda, 2024).[8]

During the administrations of Raúl Alfonsín (1983–1989) and Carlos Menem (1989–1999), when informal access to the Executive was limited or nonexistent, rural organizations successfully resorted to protest as a form of political leverage (Acuña, 1990; Fernández Milmanda, 2024).

[8] For a regional analysis of the challenges posed by the democratic context to landowners, *see* Fernández Milmanda (2019). As the author explains, the notion that landowners are a constraint on democracy presents a challenge for understanding the stability of the political system in the region since the third wave, despite the persistence of land concentration and inequality in land access. With the return of democracy, landowners developed strategies to protect their interests from redistribution, such as building conservative parties (Chile and El Salvador), investing in multiparty representation through congressional caucuses (Brazil), or resorting to protest (Argentina and Bolivia).

Under Alfonsín's presidency, the four most prominent entities—the *Sociedad Rural Argentina* (SRA), *Confederaciones Rurales Argentinas* (CRA), *Confederación Intercooperativa Agropecuaria* (CONINAGRO), and *Federación Agraria Argentina* (FAA)—organized a series of commercialization stoppages and demonstrations between April and September 1986. As a result, the government conceded to several demands: it appointed a minister of agriculture aligned with the sector, reduced export taxes, abandoned a proposed tax on unimproved land, and eased price control mechanisms on agricultural products (Acuña, 1990: 37–39).

During Menem's administrations, institutional weakness did not prevent the SRA from exerting considerable influence over government policy (Caligaris & Trento, 2018; Fernández Milmanda, 2024; Heredia, 2003). Many of the association's long-standing demands were implemented: price controls were lifted, commercialization restrictions were removed, import tariffs on capital goods were reduced, and export taxes were first reduced and then eliminated. Despite its traditional opposition to anti-export policies, the SRA accepted—and even supported—the fixed parity between the peso and the dollar as a necessary means to achieve monetary stabilization.

However, the sector's structural power weakened under the convertibility regime due to the features of the prevailing economic model. This model reduced the state's and the economy's reliance on foreign currency, food prices, and the agricultural sector's fiscal contribution—historically the foundations of the agro sector's structural power. The liberalization of the domestic market and exchange rate stability diminished the impact of agricultural prices on the population's standard of living. Likewise, a new structure with higher tax consumption rates reduced the state's dependency on revenue from producers in the Pampas region. Lastly, the diversification of exports lessened the weight of agricultural products as the country's primary source of foreign exchange (Lattuada, 1996; Heredia, 2003). Within this economic framework, the sector underwent profound changes, marked by a sharp decline in the number of farming establishments caused by the bankruptcy of hundreds of thousands of small producers.

3.2 The Power of Agrarian Elites during the Commodity Boom (2003–2015)

The rise in global agricultural commodity prices beginning in the early 2000s—along with the 2008 conflict between the government and rural employer associations—revitalized scholarly interest in the politics of the agrarian sector. This renewed focus led to significant advances in theorizing the sector's relationship with electoral politics and political parties (Fairfield, 2015; Freytes, 2015; Fernández Milmanda, 2019b, 2024; Mangonnet et al., 2018), the representation of producer associations (Fairfield, 2015; Gras & Hernández, 2016; Lattuada, 2006; Richardson, 2012), protests and commercialization stoppages (Anchorena, 2017; Fairfield, 2011; Hora, 2010; Mangonnet & Murillo, 2017), distributive conflicts among actors within the agricultural value chain (Freytes & O'Farrell, 2017), the negative institutional consequences of the boom (Mazzuca, 2013), regulation of new technologies (Amin Filomeno, 2013; Arza & Van Zwanenberg, 2014; Newell, 2009; Poth, 2019; Perelmuter, 2018), and socio-environmental conflicts (Arancibia, 2013; Lapegna, 2019; Svampa, 2013).

The question of the agrarian sector's political power runs through many of these studies. However, interpretations are significantly polarized: some portray the sector as politically weak, unable to halt a hostile government's policies, while others depict it as a dominant or hegemonic force capable of dictating government decisions. They also propose opposing views on the other side of the spectrum: on the one hand, the image of a populist government overpowering a private sector unable to defend its interests; on the other, the view of a government lacking autonomy, co-opted by private interests.

As analyzed below, this polarization is largely shaped by disciplinary lenses: institutionalist approaches in political science tend to underestimate the power of the agricultural sector, while structuralist sociology often overestimates it.

3.2.1 *The Power of Agrarian Elites from the Perspective of Comparative Politics*

Comparative political science generally begins by noting that Argentina imposes higher taxes on agriculture than similar countries. These studies tend to present the paradox of a sector that is economically powerful—mainly due to its capacity to generate exports—yet politically weak. Below, I systematize the main findings of this literature and evaluate its strengths and limitations, using three key dimensions of power: institutional, collective action, and structural.

3.2.1.1 The Political-Institutional Weakness of Agricultural Producers

In line with previous studies on earlier periods (Heredia, 2003; Lattuada, 2006; Manzetti, 1992), the literature focusing on the commodity boom converges in pointing out the weakness of Argentine agricultural sectoral associations (Fairfield, 2015; Richardson, 2012). These organizations are characterized by a high degree of fragmentation and limited resources to engage in lobbying, finance electoral campaigns, carry out media initiatives, or pursue other strategies to promote their interests (Richardson, 2012).[9]

There is also broad consensus regarding the limited participation of sector representatives in key decision-making arenas during the administrations of the *Frente para la Victoria* (FPV) (Fairfield, 2015). Producers' ties with the Secretary of Agriculture were weak, and the fiscal urgency of the period granted greater relative authority to the Ministry of Economy—particularly to the Secretariat of Commerce—which rendered these informal links with the Secretary of Agriculture even less effective. The Ministry of Agriculture was institutionally under the orbit of the Minister of Economy and, in practice, to the then-Secretary of Commerce, Guillermo Moreno. Institutionalized consultation spaces were scarce, and although some agricultural representatives were able to secure meetings, the outcome of such interactions was subject to the discretion of officials, with no real expectation that they would translate into concrete policy decisions. In addition to the low institutional rank of

[9] Richardson (2012) contrasts this weakness with the strength of the sector in Brazil. He attributes the differences to the structures of agricultural markets and how they promote—or fail to promote—political organization. The explanation for the lack of incentives to invest in associations is that—unlike in Brazil—Argentina developed a more flexible form of agricultural production based on the outsourcing of services which allows Argentine farmers to move or adapt more easily upon the implementation of unfavorable policies. In Brazil, farmers incur higher sunk costs when setting up agricultural operations and it is precisely that limitation on moving invested capital in Brazil that has led farmers—especially those in the country's center-west region—to invest in party-building efforts.

the spaces in which they participated, interlocutors changed frequently, making it difficult to sustain a policy agenda over time (Fairfield, 2015).

The lack of cohesion among different types of farmers enabled the government to deploy a "divide and conquer" strategy, using selective compensations and sanctions such as exclusion from meetings, suspension of benefits, and other mechanisms to raise the cost of protest (Fairfield, 2015; Freytes, 2015; Freytes & O'Farrell, 2017; Mangonnet & Murillo, 2017). This sector's fragmentation—both regional and socio-economical—results in a large number of associations with often contradictory policy preferences. The sector thus lacks a unified voice, and no political party in the country consistently represents the interests of agrarian elites (Fernández Milmanda, 2024).

The institutional weakness of the sector is also evident in the partisan and electoral arenas (Fairfield, 2015; Fernández Milmanda, 2024; Freytes, 2015;). Focusing on electoral and legislative representation, Freytes. (2015) argues that agricultural producers in Argentina lack institutionalized political resources in these domains, which prevents them from blocking policies that negatively affect their sectoral interests.[10] This deficiency stems from the geographical distribution of export-oriented agriculture and the country's electoral rules.[11] Fernández Milmanda. (2024) supports the idea of agrarian elites' electoral weakness in Argentina, but attributes it to the absence of existential threats—such as land reform initiatives—experienced by agrarian elites in other countries of the region.

The lack of electoral resources left agricultural producers somewhat defenseless against FPV administrations, which explains why, in 2008—lacking both formal and informal access to government ministries—they resorted to protest as their primary political strategy (Fairfield, 2011).

[10] Farmers have territorial power that they can mobilize for protest, but doing so is highly demanding and cannot be sustained indefinitely. In contrast, institutionalized political resources provide continuous influence in policymaking (Freytes 2015).

[11] On the one hand, in Argentina, agricultural production is located in metropolitan provinces that also host large urban populations, which forces producers to compete with urban interests for political representation. On the other hand, proportional representation with closed party lists means that political parties retain control over the selection of candidates. Finally, the overrepresentation in Congress of peripheral provinces—where agriculture is typically less relevant—also undermines the representation of metropolitan agrarian interests. These three factors constrain independent strategies to include sectoral or interest group representatives on electoral lists. Moreover, congressional seats are considered a party asset, and those who occupy them are expected to adhere to party discipline (Freytes 2015).

3.2.1.2 Collective Action: Causes and Effects of the 2008 Conflict

Export taxes were reintroduced in Argentina in 2002, in the context of a severe economic crisis and following a sharp currency devaluation. In the following years, the Kirchnerist government (*Frente para la Victoria*, FPV) repeatedly increased the rates as international commodity prices rose: by January 2007, the soybean export tax rate had reached 27.5%, and in November of that year it was raised to 35%. A new increase in March 2008, which introduced a system of variable export duties with an effective rate of 44%, triggered an unprecedented wave of protests. The conflict only began to subside after Congress rejected the measure proposed by the Executive. The 2008 conflict and its aftermath largely mark the starting point for the most recent reflections on the political power of the agrarian sector.

As previously noted, the 2008 protest was largely a reaction to the lack of institutional channels available to agricultural producers, who, in the absence of structural or instrumental power, turned to collective mobilization. While they achieved their immediate goal—blocking the proposed increase in export duties—the protest did not significantly reduce the sector's overall tax burden.

Commercialization stoppages are part of the Argentine agrarian sector's traditional toolkit of protest, used with varying success since at least 1922, when the *Sociedad Rural Argentina* led a farm gate boycott against major meatpacking firms (Hora, 2010:83). The 2008 protests stood out for their length—four months—and for the broad support they garnered, not only from urban sectors but also from opposition parties that had recently suffered a resounding defeat in the 2007 elections. Tensions between the government and the agricultural sector had been building since 2006 due to increasing state intervention and growing fiscal pressure on rural production.

A key factor in understanding the magnitude and persistence of the protest was the design of Resolution 125, which established a variable tax rate that could reach up to 95% if soybean prices exceeded US$600. This created substantial uncertainty and undermined future profit expectations (Fairfield, 2011). Following the announcement of the measure, regional agricultural associations—particularly CRA—played a critical role in coordinating protest actions (Mangonnet & Murillo, 2017).

After four months of mobilization—interrupted by a few significant ceasefires—pressure from the sector led the Executive Branch to submit the resolution to Congress, where it was ultimately rejected in the Senate.

Producers and their allies exerted intense lobbying efforts on lawmakers, resulting in 28 representatives, 10 senators, and, in a politically momentous move, the Vice President himself, breaking ranks with the ruling party to vote against Resolution 125. Voting patterns clearly reflected the relative importance of agriculture in each province: stronger rejection came from districts with strong agricultural interests, while support was higher in areas where the sector is marginal (Fernández Milmanda, 2019b:27; Freytes, 2015:232–233).

Against this backdrop, it is worth asking whether the effectiveness of the protests stemmed primarily from their scale, visibility, and political repercussions—immediate, through roadblocks, and long-term, through electoral outcomes—or rather from the economic harm caused by halting a sector that is key to generating foreign currency, i.e., the activation of the sector's structural power.

Existing studies agree that the boycott caused significant economic disruptions, such as inflation, food shortages, and reductions in fiscal revenue and foreign exchange inflows. However, these effects are rarely the subject of systematic analysis, and the literature does not yet offer a clear assessment of which mechanisms had the greatest influence on the government's decision-making. Some authors suggest that local-level economic disruptions contributed to the outcome of the following year's mid-term elections (Mangonnet et al., 2018). Yet important questions remain: Which of these factors weighed more heavily in the government's decisions? Were there divisions within the Executive regarding the perceived threat? Was the main concern the economic cost, or was the conflict primarily about controlling public opinion and the potential electoral impact? Considering that the agricultural sector's power has historically been exercised through the interruption of foreign exchange flows, how did the government perceive the effectiveness of grain hoarding as a pressure tactic?

Another central dimension in analyzing the effectiveness of the protest is social power—or the sector's legitimacy in the eyes of the public. A distinctive feature of the 2008 protests was the ability of agrarian actors to gain visibility not only along rural roads but also in major cities. Agrarian organizations succeeded in appealing to new audiences and reshaping public perceptions of their contribution to the economy. As previously discussed, the sector's image and legitimacy have evolved over time: it enjoyed high prestige in the early twentieth century, but from the 1930s onward a more critical view took hold, portraying agricultural elites as urban rentiers settled down in Buenos Aires and away from their land (Hora, 2015). According to Hora (2010), this negative image began to fade in the 1990s as agriculture overcame the image of a technologically backward, socially unjust sector that did not create employment, to be seen as a modern, dynamic sector—especially as the industrial sector and domestic market lost consensus as primary drivers of growth. This modernization strengthened the sector's identity and bolstered its organizational and mobilization capacities (Hora, 2010). The growing legitimacy of agriculture as a "driver of development" and the communication strategies deployed by its leaders reflect what has been described as a "renewed hegemonic ambition" (Hora, 2010:104). During the conflict, some media outlets reinforced the image of a dynamic rural business class (Hernández, 2007), associated with values such as honesty and apolitical professionalism, in contrast to clientelism, the erosion of the "culture of work," political opportunism, and corruption (Anchorena, 2017). The relative importance of these symbolic and opinion-related issues—compared to economic and structural factors—in the resolution of the conflict remains an open question in the literature.

Political parties viewed the conflict as an opportunity to reposition themselves and incorporated agrarian figures into their electoral lists—the so-called "agro-deputies" (Freytes, 2015). In 2009, 15 candidates with ties to the sector ran for office, of whom 11 were elected, primarily on the tickets of the *Coalición Cívica* and the *Unión Cívica Radical* (UCR). However, their weak coordination in Congress hindered substantial progress on pro-agricultural legislation, which helps explain the decline in farmer participation in the 2011 and 2013 elections: most of those elected in 2009 failed to secure reelection (Freytes, 2015: 235–240).

The results of the 2015 presidential election, which brought Mauricio Macri to power under the *Cambiemos* coalition, could have been a turning point in the political empowerment of the agricultural sector. *Cambiemos* was seen as the first electorally competitive party with structural ties to agrarian interests (Mangonnet et al., 2018; Vommaro, 2019). While the commodity boom had previously bolstered the FPV's reelection in 2007, the 2008 protests brought the redistributive nature of export taxes to the spotlight. Indeed, there is a strong correlation between soybean production by district and the vote for Macri in 2015 (Mangonnet et al., 2018). Although the agricultural sector was not the core of *Cambiemos*' electoral base, numerous indicators point to a strong affinity between the coalition and agrarian actors (Fernández Milmanda, 2024).[12]

3.2.1.3 *Structural Power in Argentine Agriculture during the Commodity Boom*

As I showed in the reconstruction of agricultural policy throughout the twentieth century, the role of the sector as a provider of foreign currency has historically been one of the main sources of power for landowners and agricultural producers. Institutional weakness was offset by its position as the country's primary export sector and its formal and informal access to decision-making. Despite this consensus, the recent comparative politics literature on agriculture during the commodity boom assigns only a secondary role to structural power. With the sidelining of structural power, there has been little progress toward a deeper understanding.

The only work that systematizes the analysis of the structural power of farmers and the mechanisms through which this resource translates into influence is Fairfield's (2015). As discussed in Chapter 1, her conception of structural power is operationalized as policymakers' perceptions of the credibility of disinvestment threats, which in turn depends on the impact of a reform on profitability. In this line, she argues that producers' structural power from 2002 to 2008 was weak, since it was not credible that increased export taxes would disincentivize agricultural investment. This view is shared by other authors, who note that in Argentina, the high profitability generated by the 2002 devaluation and high international prices made the threat of disinvestment largely unconvincing (Anchorena, 2017: 64).

Fairfield's (2015) is also the only study that explicitly analyzes the structural power of multinational corporations controlling foreign trade. She argues that the structural power of traders in the early 2000s manifested itself through credible and occasionally realized disinvestment threats, coordinated through the market. According to her, these companies held strong structural power after the 2001 crisis because the state owed them US$ 800 million in VAT refunds. Moreover, in a context

[12] Among others, Fernández Milmanda (2024) notes that the sector was involved in designing campaign policies during 2014 and 2015; the associations contributed their territorial presence to the PRO's national expansion—the main party in the coalition; representatives from the sector later occupied key agricultural posts; and the majority of producers voted for the PRO.

of sovereign default and capital flight, the State was more dependent on them for foreign currency. Traders periodically suspended operations in 2002 and demanded repayment of the VAT debt in exchange for foreign currency through export settlements (Fairfield, 2015).

Some studies draw on Bates (1981, 2014) and argue that the economic weight of the sector is not politically capitalized due to the high degree of fragmentation and territorial dispersion, two factors that hinder collective action (Freytes, 2015). Richardson (2012) also supports the idea that producers are structurally weak due to the fragmentation of production: "Farmers typically lack both structural and instrumental power. [...] Agricultural production—even in its contemporary, large-scale form—is fragmented, and it is individually rational for farmers to try to produce as much as possible. While farmers may loudly complain that a given tax policy will destroy the agricultural sector, it seldom does; some farmers individually may be forced to exit production, but others will take over."

In another widely cited work, Richardson (2009) presents an argument with a strong structural component, showing a decline in the structural power of meat and wheat producers in Argentina during the commodity boom. His analysis suggests that as the economy became less dependent on these traditional crops, it became possible to increase taxes, particularly on soybean exports. The emergence of soybeans—a commodity not consumed domestically—and their dominance in agricultural exports increased the government's capacity to raise taxes without triggering balance-of-payments crises. As the economy became less dependent on so-called wage goods (wheat and meat), Argentina broke the cycle of recurring crises associated with such goods and expanded the range of possible economic strategies. Breaking the historical dynamic depicted by O'Donnell (1977), Argentina was able to carry out an export-oriented populist experience and even ban meat[13] and wheat exports without incurring a trade deficit or balance-of-payments crisis. Since the economy no longer relied on a single commodity to generate foreign currency and secure food for urban populations, the cycle of recurrent crises tied to

[13] "In one key episode, the Kirchner government announced in March 2006 a 180-day embargo on beef exports to increase the supply of beef to the domestic market. Consequently, beef prices at the Liniers Market in Buenos Aires fell 15–31% over the next few months, eliminating the price gains of the past year. Not surprisingly, this move provoked a sharp reaction from cattle ranchers, but given the small share of export revenue generated by beef, the government was not pressured by the prospect of a trade imbalance" (Richardson 2009).

wage goods was disrupted, allowing for a broader range of economic strategies.

Structural power is also analyzed in the work of Fernández Milmanda (2019, 2024), although her main focus is on instrumental power. She argues that technological advances, rising prices, and increased demand strengthened the structural power of the agricultural sector, as it became more central to the economic development strategies of the region's countries.[14] These new structural conditions, she suggests, may have discouraged left-wing governments from pursuing land redistribution policies.

While acknowledging the importance of these structural changes, Fernández Milmanda (2019, 2024) emphasizes the role of political organization. She argues that in countries where landowners did not organize electorally—such as Argentina, Bolivia, and Peru—governments were able to advance further in redistributive policies. Economic weight, therefore, matters only insofar as it is leveraged through organization and electoral influence (Fernández Milmanda, 2019).

An important point is that, in downplaying the predictive power of structural explanations, Fernández Milmanda references the classical conceptualization of structural power, rather than more recent approaches. This leads her to assume that increasing economic weight should automatically translate into political influence: "Structural accounts of the political power of business would predict that the augmented economic power of agrarian elites would translate directly into greater policy influence across countries, without requiring political organization efforts (Block, 1977; Lindblom, 1977)." According to the author, the evidence reveals discrepancies in the policies implemented by the different countries and administrations, which would rebut any predictions based on structural power approaches: "A quick look at contemporary Latin American democracies, however, proves this prediction wrong. As we have seen, the ability of agrarian elites to influence sectoral policies, such as tax rates, subsidies to producers, or environmental regulations, varies greatly across countries and administrations" (Fernández, Milmanda, 2019).

I find this argument problematic for two reasons. First, I believe that landowners are no longer the agrarian elites: as explained in Chapter 3,

[14] From 1980 to 2010 the area used for agriculture in the region grew by 35% (Fernández Milmanda 2019).

the economic and political transformations since the 1990s have made technology and market access play a far more important role in the structure of production and commercialization. Since then, power has shifted toward the actors who are able to control these factors, rather than land itself. In this sense, it is not analytically useful to treat the economic weight of agriculture as a uniform whole and attribute it to a single type of actor (i.e., landowners). A more useful approach may result from disaggregating the components of economic weight into different factors and analyzing which actors are capable of controlling them. Second, the criticisms made of the structural power perspective are valid when applied to its classical conceptualization, but not to more recent formulations. While classical versions struggle to explain variation in outcomes, more recent works—such as those reviewed in Chapter 1—provide conceptual and methodological tools to address this limitation.

Finally, an ongoing debate in the literature concerns whether commercialization stoppages (lockouts) are an expression of structural or instrumental power. Fairfield (2015) and Freytes (2015), for example, consider them to be an instrumental power resource, since their effectiveness depends on a significant degree of coordination and organization. When the activity remains profitable—as was the case with soy production in Argentina during the boom—there is no objective threat of disinvestment that might deter the government (as the conflict is over rent appropriation, in the sense of extraordinary returns over the opportunity cost of capital). Thus, these actions do not constitute a credible threat of disinvestment unless they are organized (Fairfield 2015). Culpepper and Reinke (2014) criticize Fairfield's characterization and argue that a capital strike such as that of 2008 is an expression of structural power because it flows from the actors' role as capital owners. As discussed in Chapter 1, this work adopts Culpepper and Reinke's (2014) conception, according to which structural power is not limited to market decisions but can also be political and deliberate, therefore considering that lockouts like the one in 2008 are an expression of structural power.

3.2.2 *Sociological Perspectives: Agribusiness as the Dominant Actor*

At the other end of the spectrum in theories about the sector's power, some authors argue that agriculture remains a dominant economic and politically influential sector. These studies differ regarding which actor or group controls the sector: whether it is the traditional landed elite

(Azcuy Ameghino, 2016; Basualdo, 2008; Basualdo & Arceo, 2009) or a coalition of agricultural investment funds[15] and multinational corporations that emerged with new forms of production (Giarracca, 2009; Lapegna 2017; Newell, 2009; Turzi, 2010).

Economists such as Basualdo and historians such as Azcuy Ameghino maintain that large landowners remain the sector's protagonists and reject the narrative of the rise of agricultural investment funds which would entail a significant decline in the proportion of landowners controlling production and an increase in the proportion of rented land. Basualdo (2008) bases his argument in estimates showing that production control remains in the hands of traditional landowners: in 1988, landowners worked 90% of the productive land in the Pampas region, and by 2002 that figure still stood at 86%. This perspective argues that, from their position as landowners, they retain the economic power that has historically enabled them to "check" the political power of the state.

According to this view, in 2008 landowners from the Pampas succeeded in forming an unprecedented social alliance both within and beyond the sector, which allowed them to spearhead the demands of dominant sectors. This front included "other factions of the business elite, middle-class sectors, the media, and opposition political forces." It is argued that, in addition to winning the battle for "common sense" and the confrontation in the streets, they also won the Senate vote thanks to extremely intense social pressure exerted on Senators from the Pampas (Basualdo, 2008:47–53). From this standpoint—shared by many government officials and allied intellectuals—the 2008 conflict went beyond a sectoral response to a confiscatory tax. The landowners sought "to maximize their profits and position themselves at the center of the political and economic stage, shaping a model of capital accumulation in which both wage labor and industrial production would henceforth be subordinated to their own expansionary needs" (p. 48).

In contrast, other authors argue that the sector is now controlled by a new actor, commonly referred to as "agribusiness," composed of agricultural investment funds and export firms (Giarracca, 2009; Lapegna, 2017; Newell, 2009). This actor is not only characterized by distinct economic features but also by unique social and cultural ties with public universities, the media, and even the creation of its own annual exhibitions,

[15] In Argentina, commonly known as "*pooles de siembra*."

such as Expoagro. According to Giarracca (2009), by 2008 the traditional landowner of the Pampas was merely "a shadow" of what he once was, and the intellectuals aligned with the FPV government had attributed to the producers on the roads a hegemonic power they did not actually possess. Along with other authors, she also criticizes Basualdo's (2008) estimates on methodological grounds.

A significant contribution by Giarracca (2009) lies in her thorough analysis of the relationship between various segments of the agricultural sector and the government, grounded in a deep understanding of the complexity of the agro-industrial value chain. In contrast to perspectives that portray the agricultural sector as a homogeneous bloc, Giarracca emphasizes that, up until 2008, the so-called *agribusiness*—namely, the alliance between large-scale agricultural investment funds and exporting firms—enjoyed the support of the Kirchnerist government. This group was valued for its "innovative, entrepreneurial profile, linked to the knowledge society," and had privileged access to high-level executive officials, as well as the ability to shape laws, decrees, and resolutions (Giarracca, 2009).

Giarracca draws an important distinction between the agribusiness alliance and other agricultural actors. On the one hand, medium-scale producers maintained relatively fluid relationships with mid-level government officials—such as the president of the Agriculture Committee in the Chamber of Deputies or the head of the *Instituto Nacional de Tecnología Agropecuaria* (National Institute of Agricultural Technology (INTA))—yet achieved limited success, which partly explains their subsequent political alliances. On the other hand, members of the old landed elite, now subordinated to new centers of power, were formally distrusted by democratic governments "for their old sins" although they often remained socially close to many government officials, simply because they lived in the same neighborhoods or moved in the same social circles.

In line with broader critiques of extractivism (Svampa, 2013), these authors argue that new production dynamics have made the soybean model increasingly similar to extractive industries such as mining and oil. They also contend that the FPV administrations actively promoted this model through favorable public policies—particularly in the field of biotechnology. From this perspective, the 2008 events—especially the Clarín Group's media support to rural producers—are interpreted as a rupture within the hegemonic power bloc.

Lapegna (2017) offers a significant contribution to the analysis of the sector's complexity by focusing on those agricultural actors harmed by the prevailing production model. He argues that the FPV favored "global corporations and authoritarian governors" over small family farms.[16] According to Lapegna, in its early phase (2003–2007), the FPV incorporated social movements, including peasant and smallholder organizations, engaged in a discursive confrontation with agribusiness, disputed extraordinary rents with the elites. However, the FPV failed to address the material inequalities in the rural sector while favoring the expansion of agribusiness by supporting the adoption of agricultural biotechnology through alliances with global corporations. From this perspective, the 2008 conflict marks a turning point: an opportunity seized by agribusiness actors to challenge the hegemonic national-popular model. They successfully articulated a broad social coalition—bringing together the urban middle class, mainstream media, and middle- to upper-tier rural producers—under the self-proclaimed label of "*el campo*" ("the countryside") and managed to present their interests as those of "the nation." The 2008 crisis proved decisive: it sealed the fate of the government's cross-sectoral alliances, redefined the political balance among political forces, and revitalized the hegemonic capacity of the agribusiness sector. Interpreted through the lens of O'Donnell (1977), the conflict represents the reemergence of a "structural" cleavage between an offensive coalition—now led by agribusiness as a dynamic new actor—and a defensive, national-popular coalition.

Other studies on agribusiness hegemony point to the overwhelming influence of input providers over the Secretariat of Agriculture and the state agencies responsible for registering, regulating, and controlling production technologies. Newell (2009) argues the existence of a "biohegemony," sustained by an alliance between seed companies and grain traders, which successfully promoted the use of genetically modified organisms (GMOs) in Argentina through a combination of institutional, discursive, and—above all—material power stemming from their control over production and technology.

[16] It draws on Gramsci's concept of "passive revolution" to highlight both the continuities and the transformations in relation to the neoliberal period, emphasizing a top-down process of change in which the government granted some demands made by farmers while sidelining others.

This approach raises two key insights. First, by focusing on a different set of actors within the agricultural sector, Newell (2009) challenges the prevailing assumption in comparative politics that the agricultural sector lacks instrumental power. Second, despite underscoring the power derived from technological ownership, he does not fully reconstruct the mechanisms through which this resource translates into influence. Finally, his concept of biohegemony falls short of explaining why these companies, despite their power, failed to impose their own agendas—such as the amendment of the *Ley de Semillas* (Seed Law)—while succeeding in securing more flexible environmental regulations. The question then follows: why was their power effective in some regulatory areas but not in others, particularly those concerning intellectual property rights?

In sum, economic sociology reaches conclusions that diverge from those of comparative politics because it considers a broader range of power resources, including not only instrumental power but also structural and symbolic power—and, more generally, the associated capacity to build alliances with other social actors. Nevertheless, the notion of a dominant or hegemonic sector struggles to explain how, despite the political setback represented by the rejection of Resolution 125, Kirchnerism was able to sustain high levels of taxation on the agricultural sector and achieve a decisive electoral victory in 2011.

3.3 Discussion: How to Overcome the Analytical Shortcomings Identified

The literature review presented thus far urges caution against drawing sweeping conclusions about the power of the agricultural sector based on the analysis of a single policy area or a specific actor within the value chain. Broadly speaking, while comparative politics has emphasized that agricultural producers, lacking instrumental power resources, have been unable to resist the imposition of high export taxes, approaches that highlight the sector's dominance have focused on its influence to obtain flexible socio-environmental regulations.

A second, and crucial, point is that the apparent contradiction between a weak sector and a dominant one arises from divergent definitions of (i) agribusiness actors, (ii) their sources of power, and (iii) the policy areas in which they are engaged.

3.3.1 Actors: From Farmers to a Value Chain Perspective

Divergent conclusions regarding the power of the agricultural sector are, in many cases, tied to differences in the type of actor analyzed. This book proposes moving beyond the traditional focus on agricultural producers to adopt a value chain approach—one shifting the spotlight to actors long overlooked in political science research.

The political and economic transformations of recent decades have challenged the conventional depiction of producers (or landowners) as the "agrarian elite" and the primacy of their conflict with urban sectors. Since the 1980s, technological innovation, economic liberalization, and privatization have fundamentally reshaped agricultural politics in Latin America. These changes gave rise to new actors and expanded a bilateral distributive conflict—between agricultural producers and consumers—into a broader struggle that also involves input suppliers, traders, and communities affected by the expansion of the agricultural frontier.

In general, studies focused on farmers have tended to underestimate the sector's power, as they represent the weakest link in the value chain of export-oriented agriculture. Conversely, studies centered on multinational corporations (MNCs) tend to overestimate that power, as they concentrate on the most powerful and consolidated links in the chain.

Comparative politics has overlooked the links at the end of the value chain—input provision and commercialization—both of which are dominated by multinational corporations such as Monsanto, Bayer, Cargill, and Bunge. This omission is problematic, as these segments concentrate the economic weight often cited in the literature to explain the apparent paradox between the economic strength and the political weakness of the sector. It is the exporters who possess the capacity to generate foreign currency, and the input segment where most of the value added is concentrated.

This omission has acquired greater significance in recent years. As studies on the economic structure of the sector have shown, over the past two decades leading firms in these segments have integrated vertically—gaining control over multiple stages of the chain—and horizontally—through mergers and acquisitions. These processes have increased their market power, control over the value chain, and asymmetry in their relationship with producers (Anlló et al., 2013; Turzi, 2010). At the associative level, this structural shift is reflected in the growing influence of technical organizations with ties to input multinationals, such as

Asociación Argentina de Consorcios Regionales de Experimentación Agrícola (AACREA) and *Asociación Argentina de Productores en Siembra Directa* (AAPRESID), at the expense of traditional producer associations like the *Sociedad Rural Argentina* (SRA) (Gras & Hernández, 2016). In other words, a narrow focus on producers obscures those actors in the agribusiness sector who possess the greatest capacity to leverage political influence through control of foreign exchange—a historical source of the sector's power—and of new technologies, which, since the transformations of the 1990s, have become a key determinant of productivity and the dominant production model. By failing to incorporate this new structure and by interpreting the traditional producer associations as central players, many existing approaches overlook the fact that the center of economic power has shifted from land ownership to knowledge ownership.

This underscores the need to carefully consider which segment of the value chain is being analyzed, and to avoid extrapolating the power of one segment to the chain as a whole. One of the most important contributions of the literature on the commodities boom is the insight that, because producers lack structural power, under democratic conditions their only sustainable path to influence is through investment in electoral politics via political parties (Freytes, 2015). While this may hold true for one segment—producers—in other segments where structural power is more robust, MNCs have managed to maintain sustained influence without the need to invest in electoral politics.

Analyzing different actors is essential because the sector is far from homogeneous, and interests within the value chain often diverge. Intra-chain conflict limits the sector's ability to coordinate collective political action and provides governments with opportunities to fragment or neutralize that action (Freytes & O'Farrell, 2017). Examining these actors in isolation has the added drawback of obscuring internal conflicts of interest within the chain. To understand the outcomes of distributive conflicts, it is therefore necessary to incorporate an analysis of power relations among private actors themselves—not only between private actors and the state.

In short, the agricultural sector is heterogeneous and, since the 1990s, has undergone rapid transformation in its productive, technological, and commercial structure. These changes have brought forth new actors and a redistribution of economic power. Any effort to assess the political weight of the sector must take this heterogeneity and recent transformations into account.

3.3.2 Forms of Power: Incorporating Structural Power as a Variable

Recent literature on comparative politics has made significant progress in explaining the instrumental power of the agricultural sector—for instance, regarding the weakness of rural associations (Richardson, 2012), the sector's performance in electoral and legislative arenas (Fairfield, 2015; Fernández Milmanda, 2024; Freytes, 2015), and the use of mobilization as a political resource (Fairfield, 2015; Mangonnet & Murillo, 2017). However, it has largely overlooked the dimension of structural power,[17] a limitation that arguably extends to most of the literature on business politics in Argentina.

Due to the lack of a systematic analysis of structural power, we know little about the mechanisms through which the sector's economic weight translates—or fails to translate—into political influence. As a result, conclusions about its power remain ambiguous. In addition to this omission, the institutionalist bias prevalent in much of the literature has obscured other sources of influence, further underestimating the sector's power. By disregarding non-institutionalized forms of power, many studies have tended to equate organizational weakness with political weakness, as illustrated by one of the most cited authors on the topic: "A politically weak rural elite is another area in which contemporary Argentina contrasts with other countries at similar levels of economic development" (Richardson, 2012: 39).

In contrast, economic sociology—more attuned to capturing forms of structural and symbolic power—contends that agribusiness is a dominant sector in Argentine politics. However, with a few exceptions (Giarraca, 2009; Gras & Hernández, 2016), this perspective struggles to pinpoint where structural power actually resides, through what mechanisms influence is exercised, and why, despite this structural power and the sector's renewed symbolic prestige, it has failed to block policies that impose significant costs, such as high export taxes—at least on one segment of the value chain. One of the key limitations of this approach is the limited attention it pays to the mechanisms through which power resources are

[17] Fairfield (2015) constitutes an exception in this regard.

converted into political influence. Although economic sociology tends to emphasize the structural determinants of politics, it often does so in a static manner: many studies in Argentina rely on indicators such as the sector's overall size, market share, or hectares controlled. This approach does not allow us to understand variation in political outcomes—either over time or across different regulatory arenas. One of the advantages of shifting from a static to a relational conception of power—one that identifies concrete mechanisms of influence—is that it can help resolve the current debate over who constitutes the agrarian elite today: whether it remains in the hands of traditional landowners or has shifted to new technology-driven firms or MNCs. To answer this, we must empirically reconstruct the role that each of these actors plays in the resolution of the sector's distributive conflicts, examining both their capacity to influence the state and the balance of power they maintain *vis-à-vis* other private actors.

3.3.3 Policy Areas: Beyond Export Taxes

Many of the divergent conclusions about the power of the agricultural sector stem from differences in the policy area under analysis. Comparative politics introduced a bias by placing excessive emphasis on export taxes, while overlooking other critical policy areas, such as technology and environmental regulations, and disputes over control of foreign exchange revenues. In this sense, it is puzzling why the state succeeded in advancing export taxes but not in enacting regulations to mitigate the socio-environmental impact of agricultural production, to increase state participation in grain trading, or to promote local firms in the development and patenting of biotechnological innovations.

Choices over policy areas condition the conclusions drawn about the sector's power. Studies that focus on export taxes—an area where the state has made progress in pursuing its fiscal objectives—tend to emphasize the political weakness of producers. In contrast, those that examine the productive model or environmental regulations—domains marked by lax regulation or outright deregulation—conclude that the sector exerts uncontested influence over policy agendas and outcomes. This apparent contradiction is also evident when comparing other relevant areas, such as seed biotechnology intellectual property rights. Two of the most widely cited studies reach opposing conclusions regarding the power of the *Federación Agraria Argentina* (FAA): the one that focuses on export taxes asserts that the FAA is weak (Richardson, 2012), while the one analyzing the negotiations over the Seed Law finds the organization to be influential, highlighting Argentina as a distinctive case where FAA-affiliated producers successfully resisted the bill promoted by Monsanto (Amin Filomeno, 2013b). Rather than treating these regulatory domains in isolation, their comparison could offer a more robust explanation of the mechanics of these actors' power.

This type of analysis requires a broader and more nuanced understanding of the state's programmatic goals. Public policy is not limited to tax collection or the defense of consumers' purchasing power. Even if they receive less media coverage than disputes over export taxes, various government agencies are engaged in negotiations with private agricultural actors over issues that are central to economic development, from technology regulation to foreign currency flows.

The dominant fiscal lens has obscured concerns that were prominent in earlier waves of agrarian studies—particularly those focused on how structural power hinders the development prospects of semi-peripheral or Global South economies.

Expanding the focus to include these other areas challenges the notion of a state that in Argentina easily imposes its will on agrarian elites. Conversely, if we look beyond environmental regulation and the productive model, and consider the defeat of Monsanto's Seed Law proposal in Congress, the idea of the multinationals' hegemonic power also appears to be at least overstated.

Broadening the scope is also crucial because conflicts over taxes, trade, intellectual property rights, and the environment are not resolved independently of one another. What happens in one policy domain can affect the intensity of actors' preferences in another. For example, the government's decision to postpone the reform of the Seed Law can be interpreted as a compensatory gesture toward farmers, in the context of an ongoing dispute over the distribution of sectoral rents via export taxes (Freytes & O'Farrell, 2017).

Considering a wider array of negotiation arenas also helps us better understand how distributive conflicts among private actors are resolved. Most research has concentrated on state–business conflicts, but the resolution of distributive conflicts and the development of the sector also depend on inter-firm relations and struggles within the private sector.

This type of exercise also requires attention to the diversity of decision-making arenas. An actor may be influential in one ministry but not in another; or may wield power in Congress but lack access to relevant decision-making spaces within the Executive. As previously discussed, MNCs often succeed in low-visibility technical arenas within ministries but struggle in legislative spaces where electoral incentives and social legitimacy weigh more heavily.

Understanding the sources of variation in the power of agricultural actors across regulatory areas and decision-making arenas is essential. This requires identifying which regulatory domains are most relevant in terms of distributive conflicts.

Such an approach allows us to revisit a long-standing question that, despite having recently received less attention, remains nonetheless critically important—and arguably more so now than three decades ago: to what extent does the power of the agrarian elite constitute a structural obstacle to development? Answering this question demands moving beyond fiscalist approaches—which tend to argue that elites do not represent a constraint—and also beyond environmentalist accounts that present a one-dimensional image of dependence lacking nuance or historical variation.

CHAPTER 4

Recent Transformations in the Structure of Export-oriented Agriculture in Argentina

This chapter examines the structure of the export-oriented agricultural value chain under the administrations of *Frente Para la Victoria* (FPV) (2003–2015). Section 3.1 explores the role of this chain in the Argentine economy. It first highlights the country's structural dependence on agricultural production and exports, which frames the analysis within the specificities of a food-exporting country—a condition that shapes the nature of the emerging conflicts. Second, the chapter situates the discussion within the global commodity price cycle, marked by an upward trend from 2002 to 2010 followed by a decline beginning in 2011. This cycle gave rise to significant windfall rents, which triggered a series of distributive conflicts.

The second part of the chapter analyzes the structure of the agricultural value chain, focusing on the key actors involved, their interests, and the economic relationships among them. This structural analysis supports the argument that recent productive and organizational transformations have added new layers of conflict to those traditionally observed—namely, the conflict between producers and consumers, and the fiscal tensions between the state and producers (O'Donnell, 1977). Specifically, new intra-chain conflicts have emerged, particularly between producers and their suppliers and buyers, as well as between the state and various links of the chain. What distinguishes the period under analysis is the central

J. O'Farrell, *Business Power in Agriculture Value Chains*, Latin American Political Economy, https://doi.org/10.1007/978-3-032-06589-6_4

economic role assumed by a limited number of multinational corporations in organizing both production and commercialization of agricultural commodities.

Compared to the sector's traditional structure, the influence of the landowning producer has diminished, while input and service providers have become increasingly prominent. As a result, producers have become more dependent on input suppliers and have seen their bargaining power *vis-à-vis* exporters decline.

Most of the data, charts, and figures will cover the period 2003–2015, in line with the analysis of policy episodes of Chapters 4 to 6. However, this section extends the economic characterization through 2018, in order to incorporate data from the agricultural census conducted closer to the end of the period.[1]

4.1 Dependence on Agricultural Commodity Exports

Latin American economies are characterized by a strong reliance on the production and export of commodities (De La Torre et al., 2010). These products account for more than 50% of the region's exports, with significant variation between the more industrialized countries—such as Brazil and Mexico—and the less industrialized ones—such as Venezuela and Peru. Although the share of natural resources in total exports has declined over time, this reduction has been considerably less pronounced than in other emerging regions.

In Argentina, export-oriented agriculture plays a crucial role in the functioning of the domestic economy (Fig. 4.1). As noted in the introduction to this book, the agricultural sector contributes 15.3% to the country's gross value added and accounts for 11% of total employment. However, its most significant contribution is in terms of exports: the agricultural sector is responsible for nearly 60% of Argentina's total exports, divided between primary agricultural products (22.1%) and agro-industrial manufacturing (37.2%). The latter mainly consist of soybean, corn, and wheat derivatives, such as oils, flours, and pellets.

One distinctive feature of Argentina's exports is their high concentration in terms of products. The oilseed complex—including both primary

[1] The previous agricultural census dates from 2002.

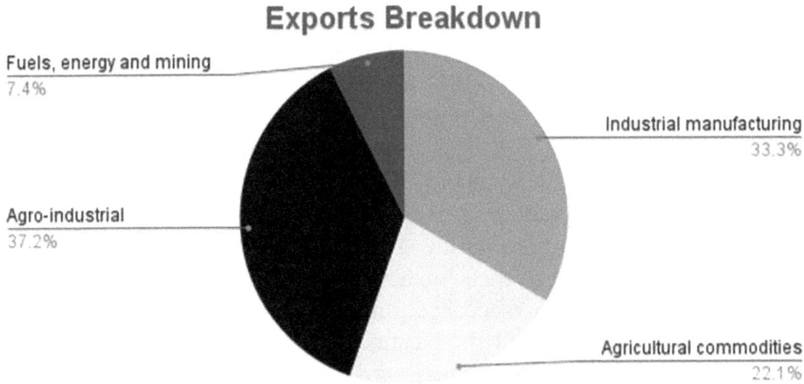

Fig. 4.1 Share of total exports (stated in %)—Argentina, 2018. *Source* Prepared by the author based on data elaborated by Argentina's Bureau of Statistics (INDEC)

and processed products—accounts for 45.2% of agricultural exports, followed by the grain complex with 22.1%, and the beef sector with 10.7%. Combined, the oilseed and grain complexes represent approximately 40% of Argentina's total exports (FADA, 2019). During the period under analysis, the oilseed complex emerged as the leading export sector, accounting for 28% of total exports, 5.5% of GDP, and 2.6% of domestic jobs. Between 2002 and 2012, export duties on soy and its derivatives represented at least 8% of total tax revenues (UNCTAD/FAO, 2017).

Argentina is one of the world's leading producers and exporters of agricultural products (UNCTAD/FAO, 2017). It is the third-largest producer of genetically modified soybeans, following the United States and Brazil. Together with Brazil, it accounts for roughly half of the global production and export of soybeans, two-thirds of soybean pellets exports, and 60% of soybean oil exports.

In comparative terms, Argentina belongs to the group of countries whose main export sector is agriculture. Indeed, UNCTAD categorizes Argentina as "highly dependent" on agricultural products.[2]

[2] Along with Paraguay, Uruguay, Ecuador, Guatemala, New Zealand, Afghanistan, Syria, Tanzania, Kenya, Ethiopia, Uganda, and Côte d'Ivoire.

Argentina's dependence on agricultural exports has increased over the past decades: while they accounted for 54% of total exports in 1995, this figure rose to 61% by 2017 (Fig. 4.2). This level of reliance places the country alongside other agricultural economies in the region, such as Uruguay and Paraguay, but well above Brazil (40%), and even further ahead of countries like Australia (17%) and Canada (16%).

This economic structure makes Argentina particularly vulnerable, both economically and politically, to the fluctuations in international commodity prices. Due to their impact on the terms of trade, these prices play a decisive role in key macroeconomic aspects such as public finances, economic activity levels, and the balance of payments.

In the early 2000s, there was a sustained increase in international commodity prices, which propelled Argentine agricultural products to levels not seen since the 1970s (De La Torre et al., 2010). For Latin American and Caribbean countries, this boom was the longest-lasting and involved the greatest number of primary goods and beneficiary nations. Prices for Argentina's main export products—soybean, wheat, and corn—began rising exponentially from late 2006, reaching their peak by mid-2012, before starting to decline (Fig. 4.3).

Finally, Argentine food exports are highly concentrated not only in terms of products but also by destination. In 2018 the oilseed complex (soybean, peanut, and sunflower) and the grain complex (corn, wheat, barley, and rice) together accounted for 40% of the country's total exports. Regarding buyers, China purchased 96% of soybeans; Brazil imported 44% of wheat exports; 54% of corn exports were distributed among four countries—Vietnam, Algeria, Egypt, and Malaysia—; and 43% of oil exports go to India. Vegetable meals (soybean and sunflower) were somewhat more fragmented, distributed among Vietnam (10%), Indonesia (9%), the United Kingdom (6%), Poland (6%), and Spain (5%).[3] The most significant change in recent decades has been the rise of China as the main buyer of all agro-industrial products.

[3] Rosario Stock Exchange (2018).

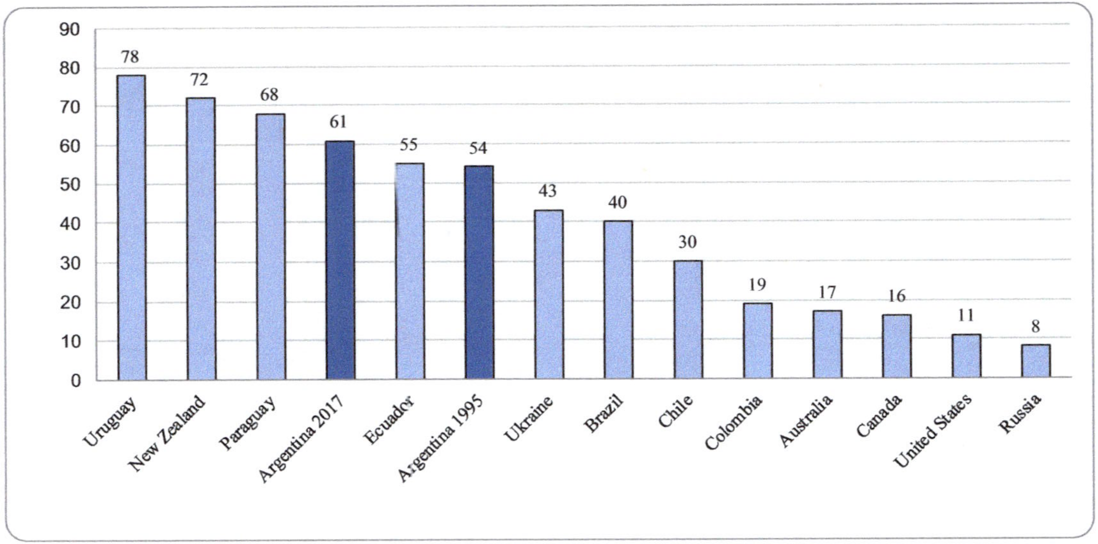

Fig. 4.2 Agricultural exports as a percentage of total exports. Selected countries (It differs from the previous classification in that it includes the lumber complex). *Source* UNCTAD Commodity Dependence Report 2019

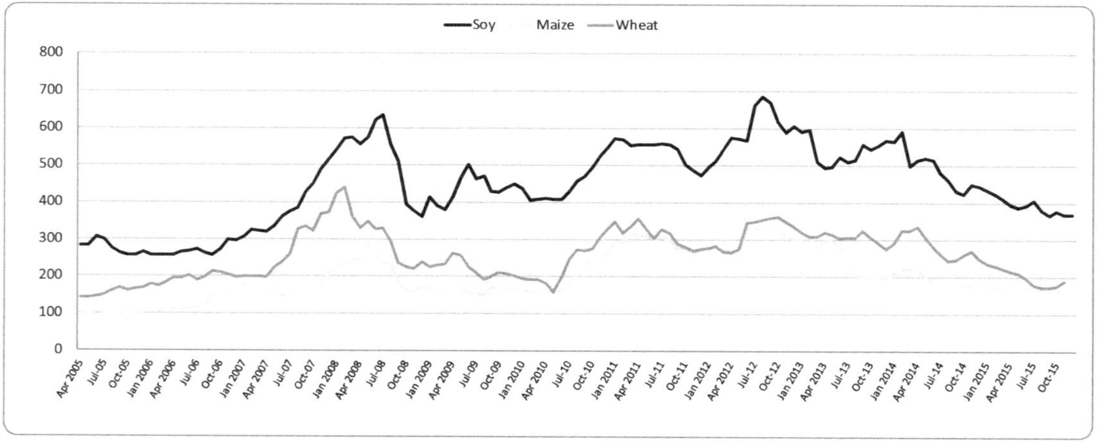

Fig. 4.3 Evolution of international prices of soybean, corn, and wheat (in US$) 2005–2015. *Source* Prepared by the author based on World Bank data

4.2 Recent Transformations in the Organization of Agricultural Production

This cycle of boom and subsequent decline in international prices coincided with the consolidation of profound transformations in the organization of agricultural production and commercialization, characterized mainly by the growing prominence of a limited number of multinational input and trading companies, to the detriment of agricultural producers (Bisang, 2008; Turzi 2010; Gras and Hernández 2016). Since the 1980s, economic liberalization began to fuel foreign direct investment and vertical integration of these multinationals, expanding across all links in the agribusiness value chain, from input supply to production, financing, and trading. The strategic position and high concentration of these companies grant them substantial control over the value chain, decisively influencing agricultural production methods and the distribution of profitability (UNCTAD, 2006; Sell, 2009; Turzi, 2010).

It is essential to place this transformation in historical perspective. As Hora (2012) points out, the dominance of multinational companies is a defining feature of the period that began in the 1990s with the adoption of no-till farming.

This new production and commercial structure, together with technological developments such as agricultural biotechnology, drove unprecedented increases in agricultural production and productivity (Bisang et al., 2008). However, as noted by various international organizations, these processes also generated adverse social, distributive, and environmental impacts. These include the decline in value added captured by commodity producers in developing countries (UNCTAD, 2006),[4] health damage due to agrochemical use (Arancibia, 2013), displacement of populations

[4] In 2004, the São Paulo Consensus, signed by the United Nations Conference on Trade and Development (UNCTAD), warned that "the added value retained by many developing countries' producers of commodities is decreasing in some sectors, and their participation in domestic and international value chains is a major challenge. This situation may be further complicated by concentrated market structures at the international and national level." In response to this call, UNCTAD published a report in 2005 to assess the level of concentration in the commodities market. It concluded that there was clear evidence of a consolidation process in global agribusiness, resulting in a few companies controlling the ownership of agrochemicals, seeds, and genetic traits: three companies controlled half of the agrochemical market; agrochemical companies entering the seed business created an unprecedented convergence across key segments of agricultural markets (seeds, agrochemicals, and agricultural biotechnology). The report also

and deterioration in the living conditions of small farmers due to the gap between consumer prices and farmers' revenues (Lapegna, 2017, World Bank, 2016), as well as environmental problems such as deforestation, soil fertility loss, and biodiversity loss (World Bank, 2016).

In sum, the international price boom of the 2000s occurred on top of a production structure and web of interests, and within the framework of distributive conflicts, that were significantly different from those characterizing agriculture just a few decades earlier.

4.3 Input Provision

4.3.1 Transformations in the Seed Industry toward the End of the Twentieth Century

The provision of agricultural inputs has expanded and undergone profound transformations since the 1960s, driven by a combination of technological factors (development of hybrid and transgenic seeds), economic factors (processes of mergers and acquisitions), legal factors (strengthening of intellectual property rights), and policymaking factors (deregulation and reduction of public investment in R&D).

The first major leap in the seed industry occurred during the 1960s, in the context of the so-called "Green Revolution." During this period, the adoption of new practices and technologies enabled a significant increase in agricultural productivity. Business interest in the seed industry intensified with the introduction of new genetic improvement techniques, particularly the development of hybrid seeds (Sztulwark, 2012). These seeds, which lose some of their properties after harvest, increased producers' need to purchase new seeds rather than reuse them, thus making the seed business more profitable.

Business opportunities—and the need to attract capital—received a further boost in the 1980s with the so-called "genetic revolution." In 1973, the development of recombinant DNA technology enabled the insertion of genes into microorganisms, marking the beginning of commercial biotechnology (Sell, 2009).[5] With the introduction of

highlighted the increasing "coordination" referring to contractual arrangements, alliances, and tacit collusive practices.

[5] Biotechnology is based on the manipulation of genetic information to obtain new outcomes that are commercialized. The OECD defines it as the application of scientific and

biotechnology and new molecular biology-based methods, part of the breeding process shifted from seeds to genes, and from the field to laboratories (Sztulwark, 2012).

Consequently, this externally developed technology became a key factor underpinning the competitiveness of export agriculture in Argentina and worldwide (Anlló et al., 2013; Bisang et al., 2008; Marín and Stubrin, 2017), which some historians consider the most profound transformation in the history of Argentine agriculture in the twentieth century (Barsky & Gelman, 2009). Biotechnology primarily impacts agriculture through plant breeding. Genetically improved seeds can lead to: i) increases in crop yields and more efficient use of resources such as land and climate; ii) cost reductions[6]; and iii) improvements in seed attributes as raw materials for food and industrial products (Bisang et al., 2011).

During the 1980s and 1990s, investment in the sector gained new momentum following a series of U.S. judicial rulings that extended patent protection to genetically modified microorganisms, seeds, and plants derived from these technologies. In 1980, the landmark *Diamond v. Chakrabarty* case established that an artificially created bacterium could be patented. This ruling set a precedent for subsequent decisions, expanding intellectual property rights over living organisms, providing greater legal certainty for the development of commercial biotechnology, and helping startups attract venture capital investments (Sell, 2009).

A third key factor shaping the development and consolidation of the agricultural input sector was the successive waves of mergers and acquisitions among seed and chemical companies. The first wave occurred in the 1970s,[7] followed by a second wave in the late 1990s and early 2000s.[8]

engineering principles to the processing of materials by biological agents to provide goods and services. There are different forms of biotechnology, among which transgenesis is the best known: (i) conventional genetic improvement or plant breeding, (ii) mutagenesis, (iii) tissue culture, the use of molecular markers, or bioinformatics, and (iv) transgenesis or genetic engineering (Pellegrini, 2013).

[6] This can be achieved in various ways, such as generating resistance to diseases caused by bacteria, fungi, or viruses; improving tolerance to unfavorable environmental conditions; increasing resistance to pests caused by insects or other organisms, among others.

[7] In the 1970s, 50 seed companies were acquired by multinational corporations (Fernando-Cornejo et al. 2002 cited in Marín and Stubrin 2017).

[8] In 1999, DuPont acquired Pioneer, which had previously bought several small seed companies in the 1970s and 1980s. In 2000, AstraZeneca and Novartis (chemical and

As a result, by 2009 six companies controlled 75% of the agricultural input market (Clapp, 2018). Finally, from 2015 onward, a third wave took place: Dow and DuPont merged to form DowDuPont; ChemChina acquired Syngenta in February 2016; and Bayer acquired Monsanto in September 2016. Consequently, by 2019 only four companies (ChemChina, Bayer, DowDuPont, and BASF) controlled nearly 75% of the global agricultural input market.

Lastly, another notable trend is the increasing privatization of research and development (R&D) in seed improvement (Amin Filomeno, 2013; Pellegrini, 2013; Sztulwark, 2012; UNCTAD, 2006). Until the 1970s, these processes were mostly publicly funded and directed by the state through research and experimental institutes. However, in the new context, R&D became dominated by a small number of multinational companies, most of which come from the chemical industry (Sztulwark, 2012).[9]

Thus, following these technological, legal, economic, and political transformations, agro-input companies assumed a central role in the global restructuring of agriculture, increasingly influencing the modes of production—that is, the definition of what and how to produce. In this regard, various studies highlight a significant loss of autonomy among producers, understood as the shift of part of the decision-making related to the production process to input suppliers, as well as the expansion of asymmetric relationships and subordination of producers to suppliers (Anlló et al., 2013; Gras and Hernández, 2016; Turzi, 2010). Moreover, market concentration has led to a decline in the value added obtained by commodity producers in developing countries. International organizations have warned that the proliferation of patents—especially those on

pharmaceutical companies) formed Syngenta. Monsanto acquired several seed companies in the 1990s and merged with Pharmacia and Upjohn in 2000. Dow Chemical acquired Mycogen in the mid-1990s and subsequently purchased several seed, chemical, and biotechnology companies to form Dow AgroSciences in 2000. In 2001, Bayer acquired Aventis CropScience (Clapp, 2018).

[9] A case illustrating this transition in the Argentine context is the experimentation with transgenic potato seeds. The first advances in transgenics in Argentina were developed in the 1980s by two scientists with public funding. They created a transgenic potato resistant to droughts typical of the northern region of the country. As will be discussed later, this model (socially oriented, publicly funded, and designed to address specific local producers' problems) gradually gave way in the 1990s to the model of transgenic soy, in which a private company develops a transgenic event (RR soybean) resistant to a herbicide it also commercializes (glyphosate), replicating this model worldwide (Pellegrini, 2013).

research tools—and the control of technology by a few companies may discourage innovation by creating barriers for innovative startups and inhibiting public research and development, as well as posing a risk of appropriation of knowledge developed in the public domain (UNCTAD, 2006).

The economic significance of these companies and their influence on agricultural production are further strengthened by the fact that they provide producers not only with the technological package—seeds and agrochemicals—but also financing and technical advisory services. Consequently, service centers, key institutions in technology diffusion, expanded nationwide, transforming the dissemination of the new technical package into a business that tends to foster producer loyalty through financing (Anlló et al., 2013; Bisang et al., 2008). These centers, together with technical associations such as AACREA and AAPRESID, have gradually replaced the public outreach services formerly provided by INTA (Regúnaga, 2009).

The prominence of these companies is also political, as they wield significant influence in setting rules and negotiating forums internationally, particularly in the United States. Their structural power is based on their position within the seed industry, marked by two key factors: the strengthening of intellectual property rights (IPR) and market concentration. This increases their profitability and market power, making their decisions significantly impact seed access and entangling farmers in a complex web of licensing and royalty obligations (Sell, 2009).

Beyond these structural and legal sources of power, these companies possess greater resources to finance the participation of their representatives in international meetings compared to NGOs and consumer associations. Furthermore, the complexity and lengthy timelines of negotiations favor companies over developing countries (Sell, 2009) and other less-resourced social actors (Smythe, 2009). The complexity of the regulatory environment, coupled with forum shifting—that is, the shifting of negotiation venues among bilateral, regional, and multilateral arenas—increases the vulnerability of developing countries vis-à-vis biotech companies and public agencies from supporting countries such as the United States Trade Representative (USTR) (Sell, 2009). These companies maintain close ties particularly with the U.S. Department of Agriculture, which early on supported biotechnology as a frontier technology where the United States had comparative advantages (Smythe, 2009). It is estimated that biotech companies contributed US$ $3.5 million to U.S. election campaigns between 1995 and 2002, and the leading industry association (Biotechnology Industry Organization) spent US$ $143 million on lobbying activities between 1998 and 2002 (Smythe, 2009). Another key source of instrumental power is these companies' membership in policy committees of U.S. trade institutions (Sell, 2009). These committees assist negotiators in policy design for bilateral, regional, and multilateral agreements; in agriculture, the most important is the Agricultural Trade Advisory Committee (USTR).[10] Many also participate in the USTR's Industry Trade Advisory Committee on Intellectual Property Rights, which also includes pharmaceutical companies.

The influence of these companies is often moderated or challenged when public scandals related to health, environment, or food resonate with the public agenda. Such episodes have enabled critics to demand greater participation in regulatory processes and transparency regarding genetically modified foods, spurring mobilization among consumers and environmental organizations, fostering divisions between powerful state actors such as the United States and the European Union (Smythe, 2009), and especially bringing visibility to conflicts among different business sectors in the agri-food chain (Falkner, 2009). Intra-industry conflict reduces the power of companies promoting GMOs, while opening political space for non-business actors to influence the development of agricultural biotechnology. These conflicts often occur between multinational corporations and local companies—the latter naturally less inclined to harmonize rules internationally—between leading and lagging companies—the former generally more competitive under new international regulations—and between biotech firms and agricultural producers (over royalties) or retailers (over labeling policies) (Falkner, 2009).[11] In sum, a notable feature of the supply chain structure is the presence of diverse actors with heterogeneous interests, creating multiple entry points for social and political actors seeking to influence food production and to form alliances with business interests not aligned with biotech firms.

[10] It includes the following companies: Altria, Archer Daniels Midland, Blue Diamond Growers, Burger King, Campbell Soup, Cargill, ConAgra, CropLife America, General Mills, Hershey Foods, HJ Heinz, Land O'Lakes, Louis Dreyfus, McDonald's, Monsanto, Sunkist Growers, Sun Maid Growers, Wal-Mart, and Yum! Restaurants.

[11] It was the food retail sector that first put a brake on genetically modified foods in Europe and East Asia, amplifying consumer concerns and imposing restrictions on food content, and it was the supermarkets that led the "pro-GM labelling" movement (Falkner, 2009).

4.3.2 *Current Structure of Seed Supply*

Following the transformations discussed in the previous section, the seed sector is broadly composed of two main types of companies: those that develop patentable transgenic events which are later introduced in seeds, and those that focus on conventional improvement of germplasm—that is, the set of genes or genetic resources of the seeds. Unlike transgenic events, the seeds themselves are not patentable. Many of these companies also engage in seed multiplication and commercialization (Fig. 4.4).

Transgenic seeds consist of a complex "assemblage" of several components: a transgenic event and several other traits—such as resistance to emerging diseases, indeterminacy, or a short maturation cycle—introduced through technologies like marker-assisted breeding or mutagenesis, as well as all the other characteristics embedded into seeds resulting

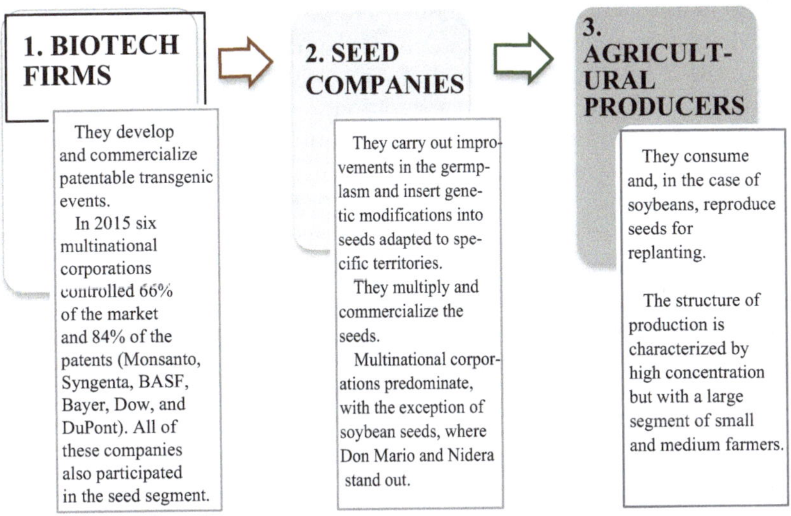

Fig. 4.4 Seed Value Chain Structure. *Note* Strictly speaking, some "seed companies" (technically called breeders or plant breeders) are also biotechnology firms due to the type of seed improvement they perform. For simplicity, I maintain the commonly used distinction between biotechnology companies and seed companies

from years of germplasm improvement by farmers, private companies, and public institutions (Marín & Stubrin, 2017).

The transformation of seeds begins at the research laboratory, where so-called "transgenic events" are developed. These are genes with specific traits, such as resistance to certain chemicals, drought, or insects. Prior to the 2015–2016 wave of mergers, during the period of interest for this study, the global market for transgenic events was dominated by six firms—Monsanto, Syngenta, BASF, Bayer, Dow, and Dupont—which accounted for 66% of the global market and 84% of patents (82% of seeds are patented) (Marín & Stubrin, 2017).

The most widely commercialized transgenic seeds are soybean, maize, cotton, and canola. Between 1998 and 2013, 29 transgenic events were approved in Argentina—all developed by multinational corporations (Marín & Stubrin, 2017).

In the soybean seed market, Monsanto—now owned by Bayer—is the undisputed leader, both in Argentina and globally. It holds the patent for the "RR" transgenic soybean event, a glyphosate-resistant gene, as well as for "RR2 Intacta." Argentina, as the world's third-largest producer of transgenic soybean, represents a significant share of Monsanto's market. In 2016, the company's net sales in Argentina reached US$ 856 million, equivalent to 6.3% of its global sales, according to its 2016 annual report.

Although some public institutions hold patents—for example, Brazil's agricultural research agency EMBRAPA—they are a minority. The extent of the privatization of agricultural biotechnology research and development is stark: just two companies, Monsanto and Syngenta, hold more plant biotechnology patents than all public and academic institutions worldwide combined (Pellegrini, 2013).

In Argentina, until the 1990s, the state remained a central actor in providing technological advances in genetics, and domestic companies maintained a strong presence in the market (Marín & Stubrin, 2017; Gras & Hernández, 2016). Since then, disinvestment and institutional decline at the INTA (National Agricultural Technology Institute)—a deterioration that began with reforms in 1975—and broader reductions in science and technology funding have deepened the privatization of technological development in the country (Amin Filomeno, 2013; Gras & Hernández, 2016; Regúnaga, 2009). One of the key blows to INTA under the Menem administration was the elimination of export taxes, a portion of which had been legally earmarked for INTA. With this source of revenue cut off in 1995, INTA lost its financial autonomy, leading to a sharp decline in institutional capacity and significant losses in technical staff (Amin Filomeno, 2013).

Competing in the development of transgenic events is no easy task to domestic firms: R&D costs are extremely high, and substantial technical and administrative capacity is required to navigate the costly regulatory approval processes and defend intellectual property in international courts (Sztulwark, 2012). In fact, it is estimated that patenting and deregulation costs are 10 times greater than the cost of developing the transgenic event itself (Marín & Stubrin, 2017).

Given these dynamics, many analysts argue that it is multinational corporations that have led the seed innovation process (Bisang, 2003; Trigo, 2011). However, the gains in yield and productivity are largely attributable to the work of traditional seed companies—also known as breeders or plant-improving firms—which purchase transgenic events through licensing agreements and integrate them into seeds to which they add further improvements (Marín & Stubrin, 2017). This improvement process is essential for local adaptation, diversification, and market competition. Today, this segment is also internationally dominated by a few multinationals, many of which—originally biotech or chemical firms—expanded into the seed business by acquiring local seed companies in different countries.

In Argentina, local companies were responsible for approximately 65% of the new seed varieties registered and approved for commercialization during the study period (Lowenstein, 2014; Marín & Stubrin, 2017). Looking at the National Cultivar Registry (RNC) between 1997 and 2013 for major crops (soybean, maize, wheat, and sunflower), the top two firms registering varieties were Argentine: Nidera,[12] a company with Argentine and Dutch capital (30.7% of all registrations), and Don Mario (16.3%), with wholly domestic capital. Five of the top ten firms were Argentine: Nidera, Don Mario, ACA, Klein, and Bioceres.

Unlike maize seed, which loses yield potential in second-generation plantings, soybean yield remains unchanged across successive generations, allowing farmers to either sell the harvested grain or reuse it as seed. As a result, producers are not required to purchase new seed each season.

This characteristic, combined with lax state oversight, has given rise to an extensive market for uncertified or illegal seed, commonly known as

[12] Including Nidera, back then of Argentine and Dutch capital. In 2017, the company was acquired by Syngenta, controlled by ChemChina.

the "*bolsa blanca*." It is estimated that only 36% of the soybean area is planted with certified seed[13]—either directly purchased or reused with proper royalty payments. The remainder consists of farmer-saved seed and seed from the illegal market. The Argentine state's passive approach to enforcing certified seed use has effectively transferred significant value from biotech and seed companies to producers, offsetting the export taxes they are required to pay to the government.

This has hence reduced the profitability and appeal of the soybean seed business, which helps explain the relatively limited presence of multinational corporations in this segment in Argentina compared to other crops. In 2013, the certified soybean seed market included 22 companies, but only two—Don Mario (50%) and Nidera (40%)—accounted for nearly 90% of sales. Both companies are also market leaders in Brazil (Marín & Stubrin, 2017).[14]

Industry actors argue that the low profitability caused by the prevalence of illegal seed negatively impacts the entire sector, especially small and medium-sized domestic breeders. These firms consistently call for a stronger regulatory role and expanded powers for the INASE (National Seed Institute), which oversees seed certification and enforcement. The companies that survived did so by internationalizing and diversifying their income streams—Don Mario, for instance, became a leading player in Brazil.[15]

In addition to calling for restrictions on illegal seed, breeders generally favor strong intellectual property rights. Unlike many agricultural producers who oppose royalty payments, breeders prefer to pay royalties to ensure access to new technologies. They defend their right to free access to genetic events for research purposes (known under Argentine law as the "breeder's exception"), while advocating for stricter controls on the white bag market and farmers' seed reuse.

It is important to note, however, that breeders' alignment with multinationals often stems more from technological dependence than shared preferences. Multinational corporations tend to treat their portfolios of

[13] ASA-UBATEC (2017)

[14] Just as a reference, the maize seed chain biotech industry is dominated by five multinational corporations (Monsanto, Syngenta, Bayer, Dow, and Dupont) that also control the traditional seed sector (breeders) for maize. This is because of maize agronomic conditions, which increase the profitability of innovation (Sztulwark, 2012).

[15] Interview with a representative from the seed firm Don Mario.

licenses and patents as strategic assets, often refusing to license technologies, imposing unreasonable terms, or blocking competitors from using them (Sell, 2009). In this new context, breeders face intellectual property restrictions not just on genes, but also on techniques, varieties, and technologies. This fragmentation of technological rights means that denial of access to a single component can block the development of an entire variety. This is one reason traditional seed firms have not challenged the dominance of multinationals or pushed for regulatory frameworks aligned with their interests.

Both the leading biotech firms and breeders are represented in the *Asociación de Semilleros Argentinos* (ASA), founded in 1949, which includes 84 member companies. These range from multinational corporations like BASF, Bayer, Dow Agro, Monsanto, Nidera, Pioneer, and Syngenta to domestic firms like Don Mario, Bioceres, Relmó SA, and Satus Ager SA. The influence of multinational firms is evident in ASA's operations. According to its executive director, one of the association's challenges is its perceived alignment with Monsanto.[16] This contrasts with other sectors, such as pharmaceuticals, where leading domestic firms hold a larger market share and are politically organized in associations separate from their multinational counterparts (Shadlen, 2017).

The shift in the production model also entailed an intensification in the use of agrochemicals to combat weeds, pests, and diseases. Since the 1990s, the agrochemical market in Argentina and globally has become increasingly concentrated (Regúnaga, 2009). The main companies operating in the Argentine herbicide and insecticide market during the study period included Monsanto, Syngenta, BASF, Dow Agrosciences, Advanta, Atanor, Bayer Cropscience, Nidera, Dupont, Nufarm, Merck, and Repsol-YPF. However, unlike the fertilizer market, the agrochemical sector still includes small and medium-sized firms. Fertilizers are produced or imported by the same major exporters and processors—primarily Cargill, Bunge, Nidera, Dreyfus, AGD, and the local cooperative ACA (Regúnaga, 2010). Agrochemical firms are grouped into the *Cámara de Sanidad Agropecuaria y Fertilizantes* (CASAFE) and the *Cámara de la Industria Argentina de Fertilizantes y Agroquímicos* (CIAFA). Despite overlapping corporate actors, seed and agrochemical companies maintain

[16] Interview with a representative of ASA.

separate trade associations due to their distinct branding and communication strategies. As one industry representative put it: one group "defends life" (seeds), the other "defends death" (chemicals).[17]

Agrochemical use in Argentina increased by 1000% over the past two decades, from 26,000 tons in 1992 to 256,000 tons in 2011 (FAOSTAT, 2015, cited in World Bank 2016). This rise was driven not only by expanded cultivation but also by more intensive application per hectare. Agrochemicals usage rose from approximately 0.5 kg/ha in 1990 to 2.5 kg/ha in 2011. This fivefold increase contrasts with the reduction in pesticide use in other parts of Latin America. The shift to glyphosate-resistant genetically modified soybeans spurred herbicide use (AGN, 2015; World Bank, 2016).

Among agrochemicals, glyphosate saw the largest rise, in line with the increased adoption of RR soybeans: its use grew from 50.1% to 75% of total applications by 2006 (World Bank, 2016). Glyphosate consumption rose exponentially: from 28 million liters in the 1997–98 season, to 100 million in 2003–2004 (Pengue), and 200 million in 2012 (Arancibia, 2013; Lapegna, 2019). Some studies report that Argentina applies more glyphosate per hectare than the United States: Argentine producers apply it an average of 2.3 times per year, compared to 1.3 times in the United States (Benbrook, 2003, cited in Lapegna 2019).

Fertilizer use also multiplied. By 2014, Argentina was using nearly eight times more fertilizer than in 1991. Fertilizer use per hectare increased by 408% between 1991 and 2014, although it has declined slightly during the 2010s (CIAFA 2015), largely in response to rising prices rather than any self-imposed restraint (i.e., if prices fall, usage could rise again). While the average was 13 kg per sown hectare in 1993, by the 2006–07 season it had risen to 81 kg/ha (Bisang et al., 2008).

4.4 Production

The second link in the export-oriented agriculture value chain also underwent profound transformations. Among the most significant changes were the steady growth in output, driven by both improvements in productivity and the expansion of the agricultural frontier (Hora, 2012); an increase

[17] Interview with a representative of the agricultural supply sector.

in sectoral concentration (Regúnaga, 2009); a shift from a vertically integrated model to a network-based structure; the proliferation of so-called "service contractors" as key agents in the dissemination of new technologies; and the emergence of new financing mechanisms (Anlló et al., 2013).

Between 1995 and 2010, the production of grains and oilseeds rose from 42 to 102.5 million tons, with an average annual growth rate of 6.5%. Soybean cultivation, which in 1980 covered just over one million hectares, had grown 18 times larger by 2010. Between 2005 and 2010, soybeans accounted for over 50% of the total volume of agricultural exports and an even higher share of their value (Hora, 2012: 169). This expansion was accompanied by the extension of the agricultural frontier beyond the traditional Pampas region into northern provinces historically focused on domestic markets—particularly Salta, Chaco, and Santiago del Estero—thus broadening the social and regional base supporting export-oriented interests (Hora, 2012: 172).

As noted in the previous section, these developments occurred in a context marked by the declining autonomy of the production segment relative to other actors in the chain—especially input suppliers and traders—and by a shift in the roles played by the public and private sectors in the development of agricultural technologies (Gras & Hernández 2016; Sztulwark, 2012).

These processes were accompanied by—and in some cases directly caused—a marked increase in output (especially soybeans) and in productivity (Regúnaga, 2009), as well as a proliferation of socio-environmental conflicts linked to the new agricultural model (Lapegna, 2019; Svampa, 2013).

The trend toward concentration has been unfolding for more than five decades and is reflected in the steady decline in the number of production units and the concurrent increase in their average size. Between 1988 and 2018, the number of agricultural production units fell by 41%, from 421,000 to 250,000, while the average size grew from 421 to 627 hectares. One possible explanation for this concentration lies in the increasing importance of economies of scale under the new technological paradigm, which led many small landowners to lease their land to agribusiness companies, trusts, or investment funds (Regúnaga, 2009) (Fig. 4.5.).

Land concentration is also evident in the unequal distribution of agricultural area among *Explotaciones Agropecuarias* (EAP), the unit of

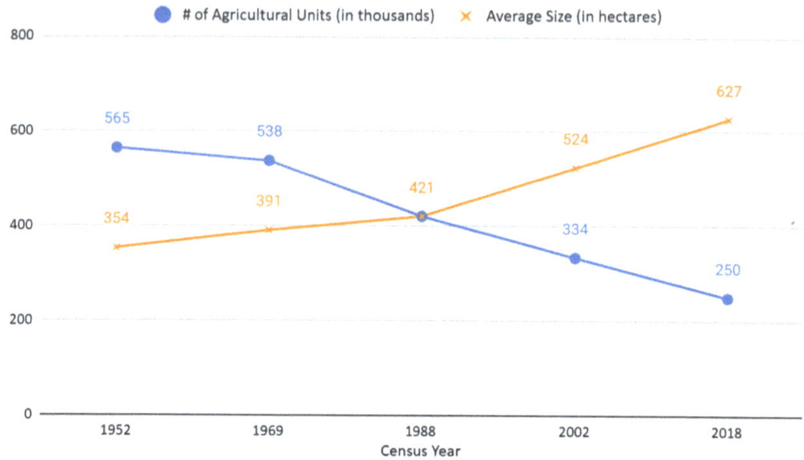

Fig. 4.5 Number and Average Size of Agricultural Units. *Source* Prepared by author based on the National Agricultural Census, Indec

production used by the agricultural census. In 2018, only 12% of EAPs—approximately 27,000 units larger than 1000 hectares—controlled 80% of the country's agricultural land (Fig. 4.6.). This level of concentration is similar to that observed in 2002, when 10% of EAPs held 78% of the land. In contrast, the vast majority of producers—comprising the remaining 88%—operated units smaller than 1000 hectares and had access to only 20% of the total area.

Among the largest EAPs, 863 of them control 0.4% of the total, harnessing 21.8% of the total agricultural land (Fig. 4.7. and Table 4.1.).

Source Prepared by author based on National Agricultural Census, Indec.

In comparative terms, Argentine agriculture differs from that of other countries in the region due to the predominance of medium and large-scale farms. According to OECD data, while the average agricultural unit in Argentina spans 627 hectares, the figures for other countries are notably lower: 361 hectares in Uruguay, 121 in Chile, 107 in Paraguay, 64 in Brazil, 20 in Mexico, and an average of 51 hectares across Latin America.

From an organizational perspective, the traditional model of agricultural production is being replaced by a network-based production model

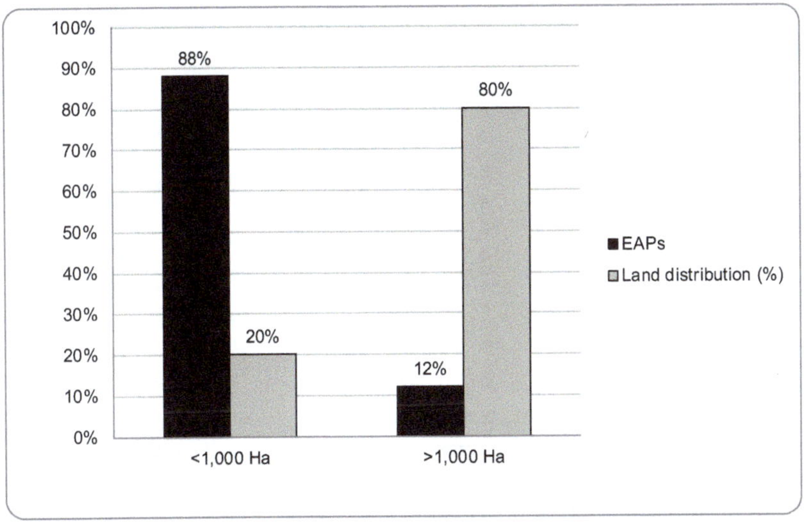

Fig. 4.6 Distribution of Agricultural Units by Size (2018 Census). *Source* Prepared by author based on the 2018 National Agricultural Census, Indec

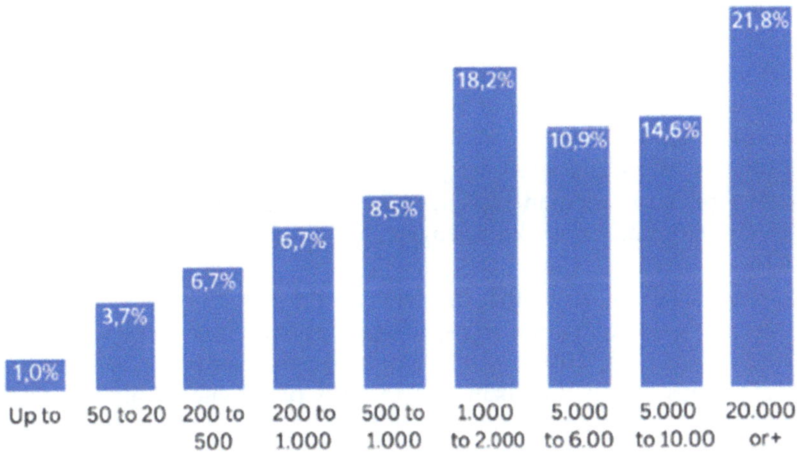

Fig. 4.7 Distribution of agricultural area per unit size in hectares (in %) 2018 Census. *Source* Prepared by author based on National Agricultural Census, Indec

Table 4.1 Number of agricultural units, unit percentage, and distribution of agricultural land per unit size

Size of EAP (range in hect.)	*Number of EAPs*	*% of EAPs*	*% Agricultural Area*
+ 20,000	863	0.4%	22%
+ 10,000	2473	1.1%	36%
+ 5000	5678	2.5%	51%
+ 2000	14,870	6.5%	70%
+ 1000	27,107	11.9%	80%

(Anlló et al., 2013). Traditional agriculture was characterized by land ownership and direct management by the producer, who independently determined production strategies, carried out most processes internally, and acquired as much equipment as possible. Regúnaga (2009) portrays the traditional farmer as an isolated economic agent with few relationships along the value chain or with other producers. In this model, public R&D agencies played a key role in transferring technology to farmers.

In the emerging network model (Anlló et al., 2013), the agrarian actor becomes more complex. The traditional farmer is replaced by a variety of players: landowners who are not always involved in production, agricultural companies, and service contractors. As noted earlier, part of the capital comes from input suppliers, exporters, or oilseed companies, intensifying producers' ties with other actors along the chain (Regúnaga, 2009). From a sociological perspective, land has ceased to be the fundamental pillar of agrarian class identity, becoming secondary to a new defining element: expert knowledge and innovation (Gras & Hernández, 2016).

While some will argue that the new network-based organization entails a process of differentiation and specialization that boosts production efficiency (Regúnaga, 2009), others emphasize the asymmetrical nature of relationships within the chain and the loss of producers' autonomy to decide what and how to produce (Campi, 2013; Turzi, 2010; Gras & Hernández, 2016).

This technological and productive transformation has created winners—such as agricultural investment funds, trusts, large agribusiness, capitalized medium producers, and input suppliers—and losers, notably small-scale farmers, peasants, and wage laborers (Gras & Hernández,

2016). Among the most significant emerging sociopolitical reconfigurations is the rise of the transnational "mega-enterprise" (Gras & Hernández, 2016): economic actors operating across multiple segments of the agri-food chain and in several countries. Companies such as El Tejar, MSU, Los Grobo, and Adecoagro not only expanded internationally but also moved upstream and downstream in the value chain, forming joint ventures with global financial, chemical, and biotech actors, or directly acquiring foreign companies within the chain.

This new scenario has heightened tensions between transnationalized sectors and those more dependent on the domestic economy. Nationally oriented firms, more exposed to local political conditions, tend to lead demands such as reducing tax pressure (Gras & Hernández, 2016).

Regarding intellectual property rights (IPR), producers tend to prefer flexible systems that allow them to reuse seeds without paying royalties. Traditional sectoral organizations (SRA, CRA, FAA, and Coninagro) mobilized to halt legislative proposals aimed at modifying the Seed Law in favor of seed companies, with the exception of some CRA members also involved in the seed business.

Peasant and small-scale farming organizations, such as Mocase and Vía Campesina, also reject the use of patents. These actors, openly antagonistic to agro-biotech companies, advocate for strict biosafety regulations and even moratoriums or bans on genetically modified seeds. Beyond ideological opposition to the large-scale, corporate farming model, small-scale farmers and producers face significant structural and financial barriers to adapting to it due to their size and production methods. The royalty system disrupts traditional practices like seed saving, and transgenic seeds are also perceived as a threat to biodiversity.

Unlike small and family owned-farms, larger producers—primarily focused on yield maximization—do not usually prioritize biodiversity. Instead, they advocate for more flexible biosafety regulations that facilitate the approval of new transgenic events. NGOs such as Greenpeace run awareness campaigns on the environmental risks of GMOs and agrochemicals. Due to rising health issues in towns near soybean fields, new grassroots actors have emerged, including neighborhood organizations that oppose agrochemical use or call for tighter regulation.

The expansion of the agricultural frontier discussed above, largely enabled by GM seeds adapted to previously unsuitable regions, has led to increased conflict. On one hand, disputes over land ownership have intensified, particularly in areas traditionally inhabited by indigenous peoples; on the other hand, deforestation has escalated. As a result, indigenous groups and human rights organizations, often in alliance with environmental groups, resist the expansion of GMO-based agriculture.

Nevertheless, the Argentine Seed Association (ASA) has found allies among producers as well. One notable partner is AAPRESID. Founded in 1989 by a group of producers inspired by Eduardo López Mondo, then CEO of Monsanto, AAPRESID promoted no-till farming, which became widespread with the approval of transgenic soy. Given Monsanto's early support, AAPRESID's image is sometimes linked to the company.[18] Despite having only 1650 members, it is one of the sector's key players, and its annual conference is the main gathering of soybean producers. ASA also counts on support from large-scale producers grouped in crop-specific associations such as ACSOJA (soy), Maizar (corn), and ASAGIR (sunflower). These new "product-centric" associations, which emerged between the late 1990s and early 2000s, aim to offer integrated solutions from initial genetic development to industrial processing, based on the premise that each link in the chain must perform efficiently for the whole to perform optimally (Anlló et al., 2013).

In sum, since the new production model favors economies of scale, recent decades have seen increasing concentration. Many small-scale producers have struggled to maintain profitability, as reflected in the declining number of agricultural units. Larger producers, able to buy inputs and sell outputs in greater volumes, are in a better position to negotiate with suppliers and traders. Consequently, associations representing smaller producers tend to adopt more confrontational stances toward companies controlling both ends of the agriculture value chain.

4.5 Commercialization

4.5.1 Deregulation and Vertical Integration of Export Companies

A small number of multinational companies dominate the commercialization of agricultural commodities. These firms, in turn, control a significant share of global trade and port infrastructure. Indeed, just four corporations—ADM, Bunge, Cargill, and Dreyfus, collectively known as

[18] Interview with AAPRESID representatives.

the "big four" or "ABCD" firms—account for 70% of global agricultural commodity trade (Heinrich Böll, 2017). In Argentina, the top five companies—Cargill, ADM, Bunge, COFCO, and AGD—control 54.4% of the agricultural commodities export market, while the top ten hold a combined 90% share (see Table 4.2.). Despite their long-standing presence in the sector—some dating back to the late nineteenth century as family-run trading companies with regional specialties (Morgan, 1979)—these firms have gained increased prominence in recent decades through vertical and horizontal integration across the value chain.

Source Prepared by author based on data of the Rosario Stock Exchange (2019).

From the 1930s to the 1980s, agricultural export countries implemented various forms of regulation, among which marketing boards stood out. These boards held a legal monopoly on grain purchases and the power to stabilize markets through buying and selling transactions. Among other objectives, such regulations aimed to mitigate the impact of international price volatility on domestic food prices, transfer resources from the agricultural sector to the industrial sector, ensure product quality, and prevent collusive behavior among major grain traders (Ahmed et al., 2014; López, 2010; Morgan, 1979; Pierri, 2014; Turzi, 2010).

The 1980s saw the beginning of a global deregulation process within the framework of the Uruguay and Doha Rounds of the World Trade

Table 4.2 Main Traders of agricultural commodities in Argentina (as % of total) 2018

	Company	*Market share*
1	Cargill	14%
2	ADM	11%
3	Bunge	10%
4	COFCO (including Nidera)	10%
5	AGD	10%
6	Vicentin	9%
7	Dreyfus	9%
8	Oleaginosa Moreno	7%
9	Molinos agro	6%
10	ACA	5%
	Top 5	54.4%
	Top 10	90.3%
	Top 15	96.1%

Organization (WTO), with the objective of liberalizing food markets. In Argentina, the dissolution of the National Grain Board in 1991 marked the end of state intervention in the foreign trade of these products. The approval of Law 24.093 on port activities and Decree 769/93, which authorized the creation of private ports, accelerated the privatization of grain trade infrastructure and the installation of soybean and corn oil production plants (Pierri, 2014).

Argentina's case stands out for its high degree of privatization and foreign control of grain foreign trade. Unlike Argentina, most exporting countries maintained some form of state involvement, either through grain boards or through state trading enterprises that compete internationally and perform similar functions (O'Keefe, 2018; Zeolla, 2014). In countries such as Canada, the functions of state traders were transferred to agricultural cooperatives, while Australia privatized its National Wheat Board in 2008, driven by rising transportation costs and the financial crisis of that year, which deepened the trend toward deregulating state monopolies.

It is important to contextualize that state or mixed agricultural trading enterprises are not an exception but rather the norm (Zeolla, 2014). The United States, Canada, New Zealand, Russia, Ukraine, Kazakhstan, China, India, Thailand, and Vietnam, among others, have state entities involved in food exports. These companies, known as STEs (State Trading Enterprises), are key tools of agricultural policy, both for ensuring stable prices for producers and consumers in domestic markets and for promoting exports and strengthening competitiveness in international markets.

In Argentina, beyond the loss of state involvement and the displacement of domestic companies, sector concentration increased significantly from the late 1980s, in line with global trends. In 1994, 90% of the foreign trade in agricultural commodities and their derivatives was controlled by 15 companies; by 2008, that number had dropped to eight dominant firms (Sbatella & Barrera, 2011).

In this context of growing global demand and driven by fiscal incentives such as differential export taxes, Argentina's soybean crushing industry significantly expanded its processing capacity, consolidating its position among the most modern and competitive in the world (Regúnaga, 2009). Soybean crushing is largely controlled by the same exporting companies and has remained significant despite the decline in the share of domestic firms. Notable multinational players include Cargill, Dreyfus,

Bunge, Glencore, and Cofco (Nidera); while the major domestic firms include Molinos Río de la Plata, Aceitera General Deheza (AGD), and Vicentin. The top six (Cargill, Bunge, Vicentin, Molinos, Dreyfus, and AGD) account for 93% of the country's processing capacity. The sector's boom was driven by the expansion of soybean crushing by multinationals, which increased processing capacity from 49,000 tons per day in 1990 to 94,000 in 2000.

Market liberalization was followed by a vertical integration of traders (expanding their presence throughout the value chain) and their horizontal integration (through mergers and acquisitions), evolving into more complex business structures. These now encompass processing, logistics, financing, consulting, food production, and input supply. This has also transformed their relationships with producers, who no longer just sell grains, but also engage in contracts for the provision of inputs, financing, and other services (Regúnaga, 2009).

Alongside the diversification of services offered by exporters, a growing share of producers began selling directly to exporters and processors (Regúnaga, 2009). In earlier decades, most production was delivered to storage facilities, and only large producers with their own storage capacity sold directly to traders and processors. Traditionally, it was the storage companies and cooperatives that mediated relationships with exporters and processing firms, often resulting in higher transaction costs. More recently—especially in the soybean value chain—producers have established direct relationships with exporters and processors through the regional networks developed by these firms. These networks not only purchase grain but also offer financing and sell inputs, often under arrangements where payment is made with the harvested crop.[19]

In Argentina, there are approximately 1200 companies and 500 cooperatives that account for over 50% of the country's total grain storage capacity. These entities not only provide storage services but also sell agricultural inputs, which are often partially financed and paid for with the delivery of the harvest (Regúnaga, 2009). Unlike countries such as the United States and Canada, where producers typically have extensive storage infrastructure, Argentine producers only hold 22% of total storage

[19] Although there are no official statistics on these transactions, some private estimates suggest that approximately 50% of grain is marketed through grain handlers, 25% via cooperatives, 18% directly through brokers, and 7% directly without intermediaries (Pierri 2014).

capacity, 11% of processing plants, 7% of ports infrastructure, and 4% of the total number of mills. One of the most significant changes during this period was the introduction of "*silobolsas*," a low cost grain storage technology that began to be used in 1995 and, within a decade, was storing approximately 20 million tons of grain. This innovation reduced reliance on silos owned by cooperatives or grain handlers, allowed for more efficient use of transport, and increased producers' bargaining power by enabling them to store their harvests while waiting for more favorable price conditions (Pierri, 2014).

Another major structural change has been the rise of intra-firm trade, whereby international buyers are often subsidiaries of the same companies that export from Argentina. For example, Cargill Argentina exports grain to Cargill Netherlands (Pierri, 2014).

Traders' strategic decisions are largely driven by the goal of reducing risks. These risks include those posed by government regulation as well as by competition in deregulated markets (O'Keefe, 2018). In fact, the vertical integration strategies previously discussed respond to the need to control such risks. In the Argentine context, an especially relevant aspect of traders' preferences concerns export duties. These taxes do not directly affect traders, as they are passed on to producers through lower prices paid for their grains. For this reason, exporting companies rarely mobilize against export duties, while they do typically resist other forms of regulation that affect their operations, such as port controls, inspections, shipment deadlines, foreign exchange settlement periods, and broader state oversight of foreign trade.

Financialization is another defining feature of the current organization of the commodity trade and has become one of the main sources of profitability for major trading companies (Ahmed et al., 2014). Until the 1990s, regulations limited the ability of these firms to invest in financial markets. However, the approval of the Commodity Futures Trading Act in 2000 opened the door to greater speculation in agricultural derivatives markets. This trend intensified after the 2008 financial crisis, contributing to the global rise in commodity prices and exacerbating food crises in importing countries.

Another important development is what some authors refer to as the globalization of the agri-food system (Ahmed et al., 2014), meaning that these companies began operating in hundreds of countries. For instance, Cargill—the largest trader and the biggest food company in South America (Heinrich Boll, 2017)—operated in over 160 countries by

2013, reporting revenues of US$ 136 billion and employing more than 142,000 people. In the international wheat market—the most important among traded agricultural commodities—companies like ADM and Cargill can manage significant stocks, invest in futures markets, and thus manipulate global prices to maximize profitability (Ahmed et al., 2014).

4.5.2 *Impacts of the 1990s Trade Liberalization Reforms*

One of the positive aspects attributed to Argentina's 1990s reforms, according to some specialists, was the streamlining and increased efficiency of foreign trade. This is reflected, for example, in the reduction of costs associated with preparing goods for export (fobbing). This was coupled with the elimination of export duties, which led to a substantial decrease in the differentials between international market quotations and the prices actually paid in local markets (López, 2010). However, this interpretation has been criticized: some authors argue that deregulation and trade liberalization failed to eliminate unfavorable price differentials in national ports, traditionally attributed to the so-called "Argentine cost" due to excessive state intervention, which persisted even in deregulated market (Pierri, 2014a, 2014b).

In the international arena, criticisms of liberalization's outcomes point out that it failed to achieve the goal of generating competitive markets, instead favoring large traders at the expense of farmers (Ahmed et al., 2014; Sexton, 2013; Turzi, 2010; UNCTAD, 2006).[20] Furthermore, there is no conclusive evidence that sector consolidation has resulted in improved food access for consumers (Ahmed et al., 2014). Critical approaches emphasize that liberalization structurally transformed market organization and the relationships between actors within agricultural value chains. They also highlight that the state's withdrawal led to increasing concentration and control of trade by a small number of actors, facilitating collusion and asymmetrical relationships between multinationals and producers (Ahmed et al. 2014; Pierri 2014; Sexton 2013). According to this perspective, the main winners of this process were multinational corporations, due to their greater capacity to dominate liberalized markets, supported by financial, informational, and market

[20] For analyses along these lines regarding South America, see Turzi (2010) and Pierri (2014); for the case of Australia, see O'Keefe (2018). For an economic analysis of market power in agricultural trade in the United States, see Sexton (2013).

access advantages (Turzi, 2010). References to the power of these companies emphasize the structural weight afforded to them by vertical and horizontal integration processes, which allow them to control large segments of agri-food value chains (Ahmed et al., 2014; Clapp, 2015; Turzi, 2010). This strategic role, in addition to translating into market power, grants them significant leverage in negotiations with national governments and in international forums (Clapp, 2015). The companies themselves often present their activity as "supply chain management," and in their strategic communication, they emphasize that government decisions hindering their ability to link producers with consumers represent a threat to food security (O'Keefe, 2018). Furthermore, they constitute a politically powerful actor in the United States, both due to their lobbying power and their structural weight in key sectors such as grains, milling, and maritime transport: Cargill and ADM alone concentrate 40% of U.S. grain exports (Murphy, 2006; Clapp, 2009).

CHAPTER 5

Intellectual Property Rights over Seeds

5.1 Actors and Power Resources

Seeds are the primary input in Argentina's most important export activity. The definition of the intellectual property rights (IPR) regime for seeds generates a distributive conflict between agricultural producers—the end users of seeds—and seed and biotechnology companies—the developers and owners of the technology. This conflict is especially pronounced in the case of self-pollinating crops such as soybeans, for which farmers can reproduce and reuse seeds without purchasing new ones each season. This also enables the illegal commercialization of a portion of the reproduced seeds.

As analyzed in Chapter 4, advances in biotechnology and genetically modified organisms (GMOs) have introduced new actors and reshaped the landscape of conflict. One of the most significant developments has been the growing interest of multinational corporations in controlling the agricultural input market. Broadly speaking, the seed sector came to be composed of two types of firms: those that develop patentable transgenic events subsequently inserted into seeds, and those engaged in conventional breeding of germplasm. In the soybean seed market, Monsanto—now owned by Bayer—emerged as the dominant player in the field of patentable events, both in Argentina and globally. The company holds the patent for the Roundup Ready (RR) transgenic trait, which

J. O'Farrell, *Business Power in Agriculture Value Chains*, Latin American Political Economy, https://doi.org/10.1007/978-3-032-06589-6_5

confers resistance to glyphosate (the most widely used herbicide in agriculture), as well as for the RR2 Intacta trait. Monsanto licenses its technology to seed companies. During the period analyzed in this book, two companies accounted for nearly 90% of certified soybean seed sales: the Argentine-owned Don Mario (50%) and the mixed-capital firm Nidera (40%).[1] Monsanto, along with other multinational corporations and the majority of domestic seed companies, is represented by the *Asociación de Semilleros Argentinos* (ASA). The interests of biotechnology and seed companies—which favor stricter intellectual property regimes—are in tension with those of agricultural producers, represented by various trade associations. These producers range from large agribusinesses to small farmers and tend to prefer more flexible regulatory frameworks. At the heart of the dispute lies the struggle over the price paid for technology.

This conflict may be mediated through both public and private arenas: by way of ministerial resolutions, congressional legislation, judicial rulings, as well as through market-based negotiations and private agreements.

The overall outcome does not reveal a clear winner. As discussed in the following section (5.2), neither party has succeeded in securing legal reforms fully aligned with its interests. Nonetheless, both biotechnology companies and agricultural producers have found mechanisms to increase their appropriation of innovation rents. The former succeeded in blocking regulatory initiatives contrary to their interests—such as the technology compensation fund proposed by the government in 2005—but yet failed to influence legislative reform in their favor. For their part, producers managed to block congressional approval of a new Seed Law, but were ultimately compelled to pay higher royalties through a private royalty collection system implemented by Monsanto, which neither producers nor the state were able to dismantle.

The episodes analyzed in this chapter provide valuable insight into the factors that shape the balance of power among the actors engaged in this distributive conflict. In particular, they highlight the strategic importance of technology and market access as sources of structural power for biotechnology firms. They also demonstrate how these companies deploy technology as a resource of power not only in their interactions with the state, but also in negotiations with other private actors (Table 5.1).

[1] Data as of 2013.

Table 5.1 Actors and power resources

Actors	*Biotech firms*	*Traditional seed firms*	*Agricultural producers*
Power resources	Structural power based on ownership of patentable technologies (transgenic events) Power depends on the ability to legally protect their technologies Use of technology licensing to discipline the value chain and to block local actors' access to international markets	Structural weakness: Non-patentable technologies and dependence on transgenic event licenses held by multinational corporations	Structural weakness but advantage in legislative arenas *vis-à-vis* multinational corporations: (i) Electoral incentives for legislators and the territorial anchoring of production strengthen their legislative representation; (ii) Social legitimacy and support from public opinion

Argentina's domestic seed companies are critically dependent on licensing agreements with multinational corporations (MNCs), which control nearly all transgenic events in the country's primary export crops: soy and corn. As will be discussed, Monsanto successfully blocked proposed legislation and resolutions due to its strategic position as a technology licensor for traditional seed companies. This enabled the company to exert significant discipline over the value chain. Unlike seeds, protected by the Seed Law, transgenic events are protected under the Patent Law. This regulatory framework grants companies like Monsanto greater leverage to restrict access to their technology for seed companies compared to agricultural producers. Consequently, they possess greater political leverage over the former. We will explore how Monsanto has managed to halt the advance of certain regulations by aligning the rest of the seed sector with its stance against the government.

In this regard, the power of biotechnology companies stems not exclusively from the technology itself, but from how laws, patents, and licensing agreements structure the technology market. Litigation, whether against private actors or the state—or even the mere threat of legal action—constitutes a primary mechanism through which these companies assert their intellectual property as a power resource. Such lawsuits are often protracted and costly, demanding significant financial resources that only a few actors in the chain can afford. Moreover, the mere threat of litigation heightens perceived levels of uncertainty and risk for government officials and other sector stakeholders.

At its most extreme, and owing to the substantial market influence these companies wield in the global input market, this form of private authority can even obstruct local actors' access to export markets. When local regulations are unfavorable, companies may attempt to shift the conflict to another jurisdiction to which Argentina exports. During the period analyzed, Monsanto made at least two attempts to leverage its legal and market power abroad to pressure the Argentine government by threatening its exports. The first one, unsuccessfully, in the European Union, and the second, successfully, in China. Argentina's reliance on soy exports elevates this conflict from a sectoral dispute to a matter of national importance.

Another pertinent aspect is the recurring use of explicit disinvestment threats by biotechnology companies, though their effectiveness has varied. As will be examined, Monsanto threatened to suspend research and development programs in Argentina, withdraw its soybean seed from the Argentine market, and even cease introducing new technologies, specifically the RR2 Intacta seed. However, the credibility of these threats was relatively low, given that Argentina represents a significant share of the company's global market. As the world's third-largest producer of transgenic soy—following only the United States and Brazil—Argentina's bargaining position is strengthened, while the potential costs for the company in case of conflict increase. Against this backdrop, it is also illustrative how multinational corporations utilize their instrumental power—for instance, by funding advertising campaigns, research centers, and conferences, or through the intervention of U.S. government officials—to sensitize officials and producers to the strategic importance of their investments and technologies.

The power of biotechnology companies is constrained in Congress when their interests conflict with those of agricultural producers. Producers often possess comparative advantages in the legislative arena because the territorial grounding of agricultural production aligns with legislators' electoral incentives (Freytes, 2015). Furthermore, producers have effectively framed their demands as coinciding with national development interests (Amin Filomeno, 2013b). In such cases, social legitimacy and electoral incentives tend to outweigh the structural or instrumental power of multinational corporations. In other words, these companies see their power diminished when other actors—such as agricultural producers or environmental organizations—possess the legal and political capacity to defend themselves, either through pre-established norms or direct political influence. Social legitimacy also plays a crucial role: Monsanto's power is limited in matters of public visibility, as a significant portion of public opinion associates the company with environmental contamination and health risks.

These findings challenge the perspective of previous studies that emphasize the ability of biotechnology companies to influence regulations on genetically modified organisms (GMOs) in Argentina and other countries. The most frequently cited of these works posits the existence of a "biohegemony," sustained by an alliance between biotechnology companies and large grain traders, which successfully promoted the use of transgenics in the country through a combination of institutional, discursive, and, critically, material power derived from control over production and technologies (Newell, 2009). However, that approach focuses on biosafety regulations—i.e., the requirements for GMO approval—and does not analyze why this same material power proves ineffective in strengthening intellectual property rights. Comparing the outcomes in both regulatory areas (biosafety and intellectual property) provides a more comprehensive understanding of the effectiveness of the various power strategies deployed by these companies.

5.2 Policies and Distributive Outcomes

The regulation of intellectual property rights over seeds has a direct impact on technological innovation and modes of production in the agricultural sector. These regulations also influence who develops innovations and with what goals, while determining who captures the profits generated by such innovation. The main distributive cleavage lies between users of the technology (agricultural producers) and its developers (seed and biotechnology companies).

Law 20,247 on Seeds and Plant Breeding, in force since 1973[2] and unreformed despite persistent pressure from seed and biotech firms,

[2] This law guarantees plant breeders the exclusive right to commercially exploit a newly registered seed for a certain period, but allows farmers to reuse seeds (farmer's privilege) and breeders the right to use those seeds as a source of information for future improvements (breeder's exemption).

grants farmers the right to reuse seeds without paying royalties to the supplier. In the absence of private contracts stating otherwise, this regulation allows Argentine producers to access transgenic seeds at a much lower cost than in other countries, effectively transferring profitability from biotechnology companies to producers.

One of the central arguments for reforming this law is the coexistence of the Patent Law. While the Seed Law applies to plant varieties—i.e., improvements in germplasm through conventional breeding—the Patent Law applies to genes or transgenic events introduced via genetic engineering.[3] Tensions arise because the Patent Law permits bypassing both the farmer's privilege and the breeder's exemption. However, these regulatory inconsistencies have not resulted in dual protection under both legal frameworks. [4] (See Box 5.1 for a summary of the international regulatory framework.)

During the period analyzed, the most significant conflict revolved around Monsanto's efforts to increase royalty collection, whether through proposed changes to the Seed Law or through private agreements. During these years, the Argentine government successfully resisted the pressure from the multinational company.

Prior to Monsanto's implementation of a private royalty collection system, the main winners in this conflict were farmers. Sztulwark (2012) estimated the appropriation of innovation rents across the three main segments of Argentina's soybean value chain. The concept of "innovation rent" refers to the "differential gain" (compared to competitors) earned by an economic actor adopting a given innovation.[5] According to the estimates, between 1996 and 2006, only 1% of the innovation rent was captured by the segment developing transgenic events

[3] The Patent Act does not consider "plants, animals and inherently biological reproduction processes" eligible for patents, but does provide for patenting of organisms whose natural status has been genetically modified.

[4] For an analysis of the regulatory framework, see Perelmuter (2018) and Chapter 6 of Pellegrini (2013).

[5] There will be an innovation rent if adopting an innovation generates differential income relative to a non-adopting competitor, and if the differential income exceeds the differential cost (also relative to a non-adopter) arising from that adoption. Thus, innovation rent (IR) equals differential income (DI) minus differential cost (DC) (Sztulwark, 2012).

(termed the "biotechnology" link),[6] 11% by traditional seed companies (the "industrial" link), and 88% by farmers (the "agricultural" link) (see Fig. 5.1).

The author highlights the striking nature of the case: "Monsanto, the world's leading agricultural biotechnology company, was able to capture only an insignificant portion (1%) of the total innovation rent derived from the diffusion in Argentina of a technological event it owned." As a point of comparison, the case of corn proves illustrative: since certain traits are lost in subsequent generations, producers are incentivized to purchase new seeds for each planting cycle. In this case, the biotechnology segment captured 46% of the innovation rent, while the agricultural segment appropriated 35%, and the industrial segment 19%.

At the same time, multinational biotechnology firms managed to block government initiatives aimed at collecting royalties from large-scale agricultural producers to establish a biotechnology development fund designed to promote domestic companies. This resistance adversely

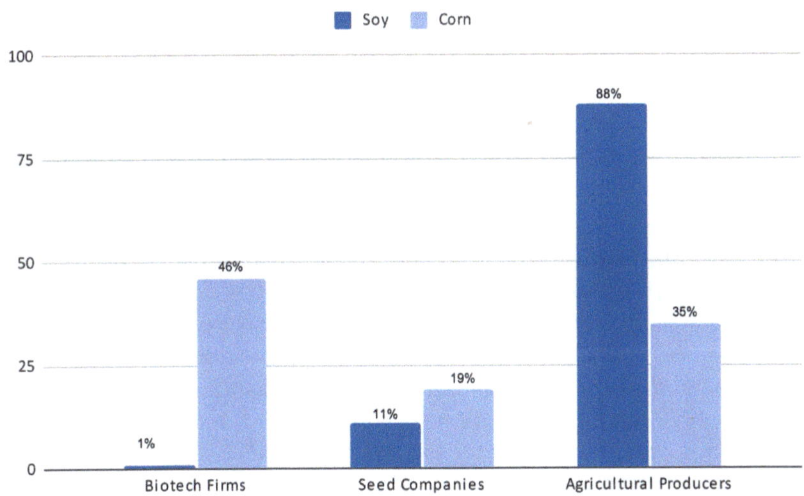

Fig. 5.1 Distribution of Innovation Rents in Soybean Production (1996–2006) (*Source* Prepared by author based on Sztulwark [2012])

[6] As noted in Chapter 4, this label is not entirely accurate, since some traditional seed companies also develop biotechnology, although they do not perform transgenesis.

affected the domestic seed sector, which, due to low profitability during the period, experienced a decline in investment and a reduction in the number of active firms.

The rents appropriated by major soybean producers[7] and the companies developing transgenic events for this crop could have financed a national biotechnology development strategy. The US$ 15 per ton that Monsanto claimed would amount to an estimated US$100 to US$150 million annually—figures that exceed, for instance, the annual budget of Argentina's National Institute of Agricultural Technology (INTA) (Schvarzer & Tavosnaska, 2007). This scenario limits the potential to enhance national economic competitiveness and to strengthen the innovation capabilities of local actors.

In 2014, biotechnology and seed companies—led by Monsanto—succeeded in implementing a private royalty collection system for its Intacta technology, known as "Bolsatech," thereby partially reversing, at least with respect to that technology, the previously unfavorable outcomes in terms of innovation rent appropriation.[8]

This arrangement disproportionately benefited Monsanto, the owner of Intacta technology, over traditional seed companies, which continued to capture only a marginal share of sectoral profits. The private system is considered to have been effective in monitoring and collecting royalties for the use of Intacta technology. However, its adoption reached only around 15% of total soybean production, thus limiting the distributive impact in favor of Monsanto (most production continued to rely on RR technology, which is off-patent and not subject to the Bolsatech system).[9]

Indeed, the distributive outcome shows that until 2014, soybean producers were the primary beneficiaries in terms of rent appropriation, and from that year onward, Monsanto—the developer of the RR and RR2 Intacta genes—was able to partially reverse that outcome in its favor.

The biggest losers in that period—beyond agricultural actors excluded from export-oriented agriculture—were seed and biotechnology firms that do not engage in transgenesis. This outcome also signifies a missed

[7] As noted in Chapter 4, export-oriented agriculture in Argentina is highly concentrated: 2.5% of agricultural units account for 51% of the total cultivated area, while 12% of establishments control 80% of that area.

[8] This system remained in place until 2022, when it was replaced by a similar one called "Sembra Evolución."

[9] *Bichos de Campo*, September 30, 2018. https://bichosdecampo.com/gustavo-idigoras-el-94-de-la-cosecha-de-soja-paso-por-el-sistema-bolsatech/

opportunity to leverage sectoral rents to strengthen local technological capabilities, a critical prerequisite for fostering a sustainable economic development trajectory.

Box 5.1: International Regulatory Framework on Seeds Intellectual Property

International laws on intellectual property (IP) rights on seeds closely follow the regulatory framework established in the United States. From 1930, when plant breeders' rights (PBRs) were first introduced, until 1980, these rights allowed seed companies to commercialize newly developed varieties. However, they did not prevent farmers from saving and replanting seeds—a practice known as the "farmer's privilege"—nor did they restrict plant breeders from using existing varieties to develop new ones, known as the "breeder's exception." A major turning point was marked by the 1980 U.S. Supreme Court's decision in *Diamond v. Chakrabarty*, allowing for the patenting of living organisms in the United States. This ruling enabled patent holders to legally circumvent both the farmer's privilege and the breeder's exception (Marín & Stubrin, 2017)

These changes significantly influenced the conventions established by the International Union for the Protection of New Varieties of Plants (UPOV), an intergovernmental organization created in 1961. The UPOV Convention has undergone several revisions—in 1972, 1978, and 1991. Argentina is a signatory to UPOV 1978, which retains both the farmer's privilege and the breeder's exception. In contrast, the 1991 revision of the UPOV Convention substantially restricts these exemptions and extends the duration of plant variety protection from 15 to 20 years.

Both the United States government and leading agricultural biotechnology firms actively lobbied for stronger intellectual property protections to be incorporated into multilateral trade negotiations under the General Agreement on Tariffs and Trade (GATT) and, later, the World Trade Organization (WTO). As part of the GATT negotiations, the United States spearheaded the development of the Agreement on Trade-Related Aspects of Intellectual

Property Rights (TRIPS). Article 27 of the TRIPS Agreement mandates that all signatory countries implement a system of intellectual property protection for plant varieties—whether through patents, a sui generis system, or a combination of both. (Both UPOV 1978 and UPOV 1991 are examples of sui generis systems.) Argentina played an active role in the coalition of countries opposing the inclusion of patent-related issues in WTO negotiations. Nonetheless, like all WTO member states, Argentina eventually signed the TRIPS Agreement during the 1994 Uruguay Round. This marked a significant turning point: with the incorporation of TRIPS into the WTO framework, enforcement mechanisms for intellectual property rights were introduced for the first time. Countries that fail to comply with TRIPS obligations may face sanctions through the WTO's dispute settlement mechanism (Van Zwanenberg et al., 2011)

System	*UPOV 1978*	*UPOV 1991*	*Patents—TRIPS Agreement*
Subject matter	Plant or seed	Plant or seed	Plant, seed, or specific characteristics (e.g., genes)
Granted rights	Breeder's right: grants the holder of a new plant variety the ability to establish conditions for third parties to reproduce or commercialize the protected material	Same as UPOV 1978, but with more restrictive provisions	The patent holder has the right to prevent third parties from manufacturing, using, or selling the patented product
Duration (years)	15	20 (from the date the title is granted)	20 (from the date of the patent application filing)
Farmer's privilege	Yes	No*	No
Breeder's exemption	Yes	No*	No

Source Prepared by author based on Marín and Stubrin (2017) and Pellegrini (2013).

*Although UPOV 1991 does not explicitly eliminate these exceptions, in practice it significantly limits their application. For this reason, many analyses equate its provisions to those established under the TRIPS Agreement.

Table 5.2 Summary of IPR: policies, distributive outcome, and relevant power resources

Policy episode	*Distributive outcome*	*Power resources*
Technological compensation fund is blocked by Monsanto and ASA (2005)	Limit to the government's developmental capacities and its attempt to strengthen local companies and public organizations	Strong structural power of biotechnology companies: use of technology licenses to discipline the value chain and achieve their support in negotiation with the government
Seed law project promoted by Monsanto and ASA does not enter Congress (2012)	Absence of reform implies a transfer from biotechnology and seed companies to agricultural producers	Weak power of biotechnology companies in Congress: visibility and electoral incentives moderate influence and strengthen agricultural producers
Implementation of private royalty collection system driven by Monsanto (Bolsatech) (2014)	Transfer from agricultural producers to Monsanto (low appropriation of profitability by local seed companies)	Strong structural power of Monsanto: ability to discipline the chain thanks to the ownership of the technology. Ability to affect Argentine exports to China

5.3 Episodes

Despite the absence of formal legislative reform, the period was marked by an intense process of negotiation and conflict surrounding various proposals to amend the Seed Law, which were debated across multiple institutional arenas. Concurrently, the period was characterized by heightened conflict not only between corporations and the state, but also within the agricultural value chain itself. The Table 5.2 summarizes the three most significant milestones for understanding the outcomes of these distributive conflicts and the role of power dynamics in shaping them.

5.3.1 *"Maradona Soybean": Argentina as the Gateway to the Southern Cone*

The first episode we will examine illustrates that Monsanto did not patent Roundup Ready (RR) soybeans in Argentina because its priority was to access the South American agricultural market through the rapid spread of RR seeds, which in turn boosted glyphosate sales. This is relevant because the lack of a patent prevented the company from implementing a private royalty collection system. As will be analyzed later, this suggests that what gives transgenic event holders power is not always the technology itself, but rather the ability to control access to it through patent enforcement. In this sense, corporate power is shaped by how laws and patent regimes structure technology markets.

Monsanto's top priority in the 1990s was to expand the market for its soybean seeds in order to increase sales of its flagship herbicide, Roundup. RR soybeans are genetically engineered to tolerate glyphosate, the active ingredient in Roundup; thus, the more seeds sold, the greater the market for glyphosate. However, Monsanto's patent on glyphosate expired in 2000, and over the following years it began losing market share to the local company Atanor and to Chinese imports offering more competitive prices. Monsanto protested, claiming that Chinese imports were being dumped at unfair prices, and pressured the Argentine government to adopt trade defense measures. In February 2004, however, the government sided with China and rejected Monsanto's anti-dumping request. This decision reflected China's strategic importance as a key export partner and was welcomed by Argentine producers, who opposed any conflict with the country's main trading partner (Newell, 2009: 42).

Faced with declining glyphosate revenues, Monsanto shifted its business strategy and began lobbying for increased royalties from RR soybean seeds. In October 2003, the company warned the Argentine government that, due to the lack of a clear intellectual property rights (IPR) protection policy, it would suspend a planned US$ 40 million investment in the country. Although the threat received some media attention, it did not alter the government's course of action (Delvenne et al., 2013).

In parallel, Monsanto sought to establish a private royalty collection system at export ports—charging US$ 15 per ton of soybeans—through an agreement with grain traders. However, the Secretariat of Agriculture rejected the initiative, arguing that Argentine law did not permit such a system and that Monsanto did not hold a patent for the RR gene in the country. The government also justified its decision by stating that it could not intervene in private contractual relationships or mandate royalty payments by decree. The only apparent alternative was to amend the law.[10]

The fact that Monsanto had not patented RR soybeans in Argentina therefore warrants closer examination, as it represents one of the most salient features of the Argentine case. It limited the company's ability to restrict access to the technology, resulting in a low appropriation of technological rents. Moreover, as noted by Argentine officials involved in negotiations with the company, the absence of a patent strengthened the government's bargaining position.[11]

Monsanto had secured a patent for "glyphosate-resistant plants" in the United States in 1990 but did not apply for patent validation in Argentina until 1995. This unusual delay resulted in the patent being denied in Argentina because the gene had already been released to the market by the company Nidera, thereby failing the "novelty" requirement necessary for patentability (Newell, 2009).

This oversight, along with other passive stances by the company regarding seed licensing and enforcement, has been cited by intellectual property experts as evidence that Monsanto deliberately chose not to file a timely patent application in order to promote rapid adoption of the technology in Argentina. The hypothesis that this was a calculated decision—not a mistake—aimed at gaining a foothold in the Southern Cone market through Argentina was originally proposed by intellectual property scholar Carlos Correa (Correa, 2006). It has also been suggested by Argentine officials[12] and supported by various studies on sectoral policy (Newell, 2009; Delvenne et al., 2013; Pellegrini, 2013).

A key point in assessing the balance of power lies in the strategic importance of the Argentine market within Monsanto's global business portfolio—not only as a significant market for seeds and agrochemicals but also as a gateway to Brazil and Paraguay, the second- and fourth-largest producers of transgenic soybeans in the world, respectively. The early and rapid adoption of transgenic crops in Argentina provided Monsanto with exponential growth in glyphosate sales and,

[10] Interview with Miguel Campos, Secretary of Agriculture (2003–2006).

[11] Interview with Miguel Campos, Secretary of Agriculture (2003–2006); and interview with an official from the Ministry of Science, Technology and Productive Innovation.

[12] Statements made by Argentine officials to the chairman of the U.S. Congress Finance Committee during meetings held at the Argentine Ministry of Foreign Affairs in 2006, as revealed in cables leaked by Wikileaks (Arza & Van Zwanenberg, 2014).

more importantly, access to other major soybean-producing countries in South America. Unlike Brazil, Argentina's biosafety regulatory framework was far more permissive toward genetically modified crops. In Brazil, RR soybeans faced years of delay due to court rulings and were only approved in 2005, after the government was forced to admit to European Union importers that much of the soybean production in the southern part of the country originated from RR seeds smuggled in from Argentina. Brazilian producers dubbed these seeds "Maradona soybeans" (Correa, 2006). In other words, Brazil was compelled to legalize transgenic crops only after they had already entered the country illegally via Argentina. As a result, while Monsanto could enforce its patent on the RR gene in Brazil—preventing seed companies from multiplying and selling it without authorization—it was unable to do so in Argentina, where RR soybeans were distributed to nearly all producers without contracts requiring royalty payments.

5.3.2 *Why Does the* Exit *Threat Fail?*

The second episode demonstrates why Monsanto's disinvestment threats had little effect. On one hand, the company's threats to halt R&D investments and ceasing seed commercialization did not alarm government officials, who did not believe such actions would harm the agricultural sector. On the other hand, more extreme forms of exit—such as leaving the country altogether—would have entailed significant costs for the company, given the volume and quality of Argentina's agricultural biotechnology market.

In early 2004, Monsanto announced that it would cease commercializing its own soybean seeds in Argentina and suspend its research and development (R&D) activities related to soybean varieties in the country.

These warnings received substantial media coverage. Between 1998 and 2011, *La Nación* published 287 articles in its rural section related to Monsanto, 23% of which mentioned intellectual property rights (IPR). "While since 2004 a large share of the articles have referred to IPR-related issues (31%), prior to that date only 5% had done so. Since 2004, and especially in recent years, the implementation and enforcement of a stronger IPR regime have been explicitly mentioned in media statements as a necessary condition to ensure that Argentine farmers can continue accessing the latest technologies in the future" (Arza & Van Zwanenberg, 2014).

Nonetheless, these threats failed to alter the government's stance. Interviews with the Secretary of Agriculture at the time, Miguel Campos—who led negotiations with the company—reveal that officials did not perceive any of the threats as detrimental to sectoral performance. Among other points, Campos noted that Monsanto's contribution to R&D investment in Argentina was negligible in terms of its impact on production. Likewise, the withdrawal of the company's soybean seeds would not jeopardize agricultural activity, since other companies held licenses to commercialize seeds containing the RR gene. Because Monsanto did not hold the RR soybean patent in Argentina, it had no right to exclude competitors. As such, its exit threats were not credible, as clearly reflected in officials' remarks:

> It was a threat, an extortion. What did I tell them? Leave, if you don't know what you're saying—it's a lie. You're bluffing.[13] RR is already here.[14]

Subsequent developments confirmed the government's position. Monsanto followed through on its threats: it suspended its R&D program in the country and did not sell its own soybean seeds between 2004 and 2012. However, because other companies held licenses to market RR soybeans, this had no effect on farmers' access to technology.

From 2008 onward, the company's main threat became delaying the introduction of a new soybean variety, RR2 Intacta, which combined the original RR technology with a Bt trait that conferred insect resistance. Monsanto, supported by major media outlets and technical associations, framed the lack of reform in the Seed Law as a factor that would leave Argentina behind in the "biotechnology race" and severely impact agricultural yields. But government officials were unconvinced: they believed that Intacta would not deliver substantial productivity gains, and that yields could be maintained using the "old" RR seed, which was still commercially available through other companies. From their perspective, Monsanto's push to introduce the new technology was not about

[13] The expression used by the official in Spanish was "Correr con la vaina," a typical lunfardo expression from the Rio de la Plata. It means threatening, causing fear, using appearances to impose one's position, as in a bluff or simulated threat.

[14] Interview with Miguel Campos.

innovation or efficiency. The Bt trait did not represent a meaningful technological leap, but was inserted to create a patentable novelty and increase royalty revenues. This product strategy—also common in the pharmaceutical sector—is known as "evergreening," a tactic whereby functionally similar technologies are repackaged and patented to extend periods of exclusivity.[15] Many officials, several of whom had previously worked in biotechnology firms, understood that this was precisely Monsanto's objective:

> Producers don't need Intacta; they can keep using RR. Does Argentina need the Bt Intacta? No. Why is Intacta being launched? Because Monsanto doesn't have the RR patent. They add Bt because that one is patented—because it's the only way to claim any rights.[16]

Despite public statements made during technical conferences, expos, and media advertising emphasizing Intacta's superiority, behind closed doors and among experts, few believed that the sector was missing out on essential technology. The perception that Intacta would not enhance yields was also shared by experts from the AACREA technical farming association. They described how Monsanto had tried to overstate the perceived value of its technology by taking credit for productivity gains that were actually due to improvements made by local seed companies:

> RR2 can't generate better yields. What Monsanto did well was tell Don Mario [Argentina's leading seed germplasm company] to insert the gene into its top-performing varieties (the top 15% in yield). What improved from RR to Intacta was what Don Mario improved in the original variety. No one will ever admit it other than off the record, but it's the absolute truth. There's not a single scientific paper that proves otherwise. Monsanto's was not a lie—it was a fallacy.[17]

Interestingly, this case contrasts with academic literature suggesting that public officials with private sector experience are more likely to side with corporate interests. Here, it was precisely their experience in the private

[15] See, for example, Lowenstein (2014).

[16] Interview with the Ministry of Agriculture from 2009 to 2015, and former manager of a multinational biotech firm.

[17] Interview with a member of AACREA.

sector that allowed them to reject disinvestment threats. Having previously negotiated from the corporate side, they understood that product development strategies are often driven less by innovation than by efforts to boost royalty collection.

Government pressure also came from some producers demanding access to the latest technologies. Underlying this was a broader debate: are yield improvements driven by transgenic traits inserted into seeds, or by advances in germplasm? As one leader from CRA put it: "It depends on producers' mindset and where they think yield comes from. Many believe it comes from the trait, not the germplasm—which is a mistaken view." At the time, perceptions of Intacta's usefulness and producer demand also varied regionally, with higher interest in the north than in the country's central agricultural belt: "RR2 technology has a bigger impact in marginal regions—those are the areas demanding Monsanto's technology. [...] In the core region, it doesn't make much difference. It works better in the northern part of the country; south of Route 5, it makes no sense."[18]

Given the limited impact of these threats, one might imagine that a more drastic disinvestment strategy—such as shutting down all business units in the country—could have caused serious harm to Argentina. However, as previously noted, this option would have been even more costly for Monsanto, given Argentina's significance in the global agricultural market. In 2016, Monsanto's net sales in Argentina amounted to US$ 856 million, or 6.3% of its global revenues (Monsanto Annual Report, 2016). Argentina is the world's third-largest producer of transgenic soybeans, after the United States and Brazil, which strengthened the government's bargaining position and raised the potential costs to Monsanto of withdrawing from the country. As a former Minister of Agriculture put it: "Given the kind of market we are, we're in a position to set the terms. They need Argentina and Brazil."[19]

Former Secretary of Agriculture Miguel Campos offered further justification along these lines, recounting that he made this point explicitly in meetings with then–U.S. Secretary of Agriculture Mike Johanns and several U.S. senators, who on multiple occasions questioned him about royalties:

[18] Interview with a representative of the *Federación de Centros de Acopiadores de Cereales*, 30/05/2019.

[19] Interview with an FPV Minister of Agriculture, 8/11/2016.

> Argentina is the United States' most important biotechnology partner. We have the second-largest transgenic planting area in the world, and we've increased off-season planting from 300 to 10,000 hectares. [...] If you push Argentina out of this business—the most important transgenic-producing country after the U.S.—someone else will step in. DuPont has the technology.[20]

Officials involved in negotiations with Monsanto also emphasized the importance of Argentina's soil fertility and genetic resources, which position the country as a key player in the global seed industry. This was underscored by the Director of International Agri-Food Relations at the Ministry of Agriculture between 2004 and 2012, an expert in seed intellectual property:

> It's a win-win. Argentina holds a major advantage due to its climate and its genetic resources—its land, its expertise. Argentina is a pioneer in the development and adaptability of [seed] varieties. It has great potential. For the company, it's not the same as Algeria. If you look at the world map, there are only a few fertile zones left, and this is one of them. It benefits the company to have production here using its event.[21]

Faced with the ineffectiveness of disinvestment threats, the company shifted strategies and sought to leverage its global patent rights and legal capacity to pressure the Argentine government by targeting the country's exports.

5.3.3 *"See you in Rotterdam": Strategic Litigation to Halt Exports*

In response to the Argentine government's continued resistance to its demands, Monsanto adopted a more aggressive negotiating stance. "See you in Rotterdam" was the remark made by Alfonso Alba, then CEO of Monsanto Argentina, to Secretary of Agriculture Miguel Campos in March 2005, after Campos once again refused to authorize royalty collections beyond what was allowed under Argentina's Seed Law.[22] Rotterdam, Europe's largest port, is a major entry point for Argentine

[20] Interview with Miguel Campos, Secretary of Agriculture 2003–2006, 11/07/2017.

[21] Interview not for attribution, 05/07/2019.

[22] Interview with an official of the Ministry of Agriculture.

exports. This phrase encapsulated the company's political strategy: to exert pressure through legal and market power in foreign jurisdictions by putting Argentina's exports at risk.

The threat had been on the table since at least September 2004, when Monsanto published an open letter warning that, if it failed to reach an agreement to collect higher royalties in Argentina, it would instead do so forcibly at the destination ports where it held valid patents (Sztulwark, 2012). This strategy materialized in March 2005, when the company detained shipments in the Netherlands and Denmark, conducting tests to detect the presence of the RR1 gene and initiating lawsuits in those countries' courts for alleged patent infringement regarding its Roundup Ready technology.[23]

As a result, European importers began replacing Argentine soy imports with shipments from Canada and the United States, given the logistical costs and financial risks of facing litigation against a company with the legal and economic resources to sustain protracted trials. Pressure on the Argentine government intensified from domestic exporting firms that were losing market share. It is worth noting that soybean meal is Argentina's main export product, accounting for 16% of total exports, with 30% of that directed to EU markets. A Secretariat of Agriculture official responsible for the matter explained that this pressure occurred in a particularly sensitive macroeconomic context, just a few years after Argentina's 2001–2002 financial crisis:

> The exporting companies were asking Campos to settle [with Monsanto], because due to the threat of ship detentions, no one was buying from them. Importers, just at the thought of their ships being detained, and the storage costs... the business just didn't work for them anymore. It was a very logical perspective—settle. We were just coming out of 2001, we didn't have a penny. Everything was being financed through export taxes. Blocking shipments and suspending purchases of Argentine production was a direct attack on the sustainability of a democratic government. This wasn't just any product—we depended on it. Importers turning to other countries instead of Argentina was devastating. It wasn't just another measure—it had a profound impact back then.

[23] Science (2010) European Ruling Curbs Monsanto's Claims on GM Crops https://www.science.org/content/article/european-ruling-curbs-monsantos-claims-gm-crops.

In response, the Argentine state took an active role in the dispute, presenting itself as a third party at interest in the proceedings before the European Commission on Trade and the Internal Market. While the Ministry of Foreign Affairs favored reaching a settlement with Monsanto, the Secretariat of Agriculture convinced then-President Néstor Kirchner to pursue litigation. Within the government, Monsanto's strategy was widely interpreted as one of attrition, relying on its superior legal resources and the likelihood that each case would last at least five years, including appeals.

Several officials argued that the outcome of the conflict within the EU was significantly influenced by Campos's personal resolve and technical expertise, which were instrumental in resisting the pressure to capitulate exerted in ports of destination.[24] Finally, in July 2010, the European Court of Justice ruled against Monsanto in a decision binding across all 27 EU member states.[25] The court held that patent protection did not extend to derivative products—specifically, soybean meal. In other words, the patent did not cover the gene itself, but rather the function it conferred—glyphosate resistance—which is present in the soybean seed but not in its processed derivatives. Had the exports involved whole soybeans, Monsanto's legal strategy might have succeeded, since the grain can be used for planting and would thereby express the patented trait.[26]

The favorable outcome for Argentina can be attributed not only to the technical knowledge and political will of government officials,[27] but also to their personal and professional commitment to confronting a powerful multinational. The EU court's ruling had implications that went beyond the Argentine case, establishing a broader precedent that patents could not, under any circumstances, be applied to derivative products: "[It was a] landmark ruling that goes beyond the case itself. The private sector hates it because of that case... In the public sector, we often lack that kind of expert. For [Miguel] Campos, it cost him everything—lawsuits,

[24] Interview with an officer of the Ministry of Science and Technology, 7/7/2014, and interview with an officer of the Ministry of Agriculture, 05/07/2019.

[25] Science (2010) European Ruling Curbs Monsanto's Claims on GM Crops https://www.science.org/content/article/european-ruling-curbs-monsantos-claims-gm-crops.

[26] Interview with a Director of International Agri-food Affairs of MAGYP, 05/07/2019.

[27] Miguel Campos, Secretary of Agriculture at the time of fiercest confrontation with the company, is an agricultural engineer with a PhD in Genetics by Florida University.

prosecution…We don't have personnel trained in intellectual property. Monsanto ran into a somewhat 'crazy' secretary and a legal team it didn't expect… it's rare. Our governments are usually weak."[28,29]

The pressure proved effective in prompting the Argentine government to move forward with a reform that had been under consideration at the Secretariat of Agriculture since early 2004. As Campos explains: "We pushed for the global royalty scheme because we didn't know what else to do to stop the pressure—they had started threatening to stop the ships."[30]

5.3.4 *A Limit to Developmentalist Policies: Monsanto's Ability to Discipline the Value Chain*

Although, as previously discussed, Monsanto did not succeed in getting the government to fully accommodate its preferences, the company was nonetheless able to block a policy initiative that went against its interests. As noted in the section on regulatory outcomes, the approval of the global royalties scheme would have significantly contributed to the development of local biotechnology capabilities. This initiative was ultimately thwarted by Monsanto, which exercised its capacity to discipline the value chain due to its strategic role as a provider of technological licenses to seed companies.

The global royalties scheme proposed by the Secretariat of Agriculture on January 25, 2005—intended to defuse the conflict with Monsanto and avoid lawsuits in the European Union—consisted of the creation of a technological compensation fund (Fiduciary Fund for Technological Compensation and Seed Production Incentives). This fund would be financed through royalties paid by agricultural producers—ranging from 0.35% to 0.95%—at the time of crop sale to exporters or processors. The proposal preserved the right to save seeds free of charge for producers

[28] Interview with an officer of the Ministry of Agriculture.

[29] Between 2006 and 2016, Campos was prosecuted for alleged irregularities in the allocation of beef export quotas (the so-called Hilton quota). He suspects the charges were driven by Monsanto and the meat-exporting consortium ABC as retribution for his decision to oppose the company. Miguel Campos, personal interview, 11/07/2017 and La Nación 20/04/2006 https://www.lanacion.com.ar/politica/procesaron-a-miguel-campos-secretario-de-agricultura-nid799060.

[30] Miguel Campos, personal interview, 11/07/2017.

with holdings under 65 hectares and established penalties for the illegal use of seeds. The fund would be used to compensate seed companies and breeders. However, for Monsanto, the proposal meant lower royalties than it demanded and a lack of the control afforded by patent ownership. Moreover, royalties would be paid for a maximum of seven years, thereby excluding RR soybean, which had been approved in 1996 (Vara, 2005: 28–29).

For these reasons, Monsanto refused to support the project and pressured the rest of the input supply chain to do the same. Miguel Campos claims that both producers' associations and a large segment of seed companies were initially willing to support the government's proposal but changed their position due to Monsanto's pressure. Beyond its influence within the *Asociación de Semilleros Argentinos* (ASA) (Newell, 2009), Monsanto's control over transgenic event licenses granted it substantial power over seed companies. Unlike public officials, companies in the sector are highly responsive to such pressure, as the contracts governing their operations depend on those licenses. Notably, of the 35 transgenic events approved between 1996 and 2015, 11 were owned by Monsanto, most of them for corn and cotton. Through ownership of these events, the company enters into licensing agreements with seed companies, which then incorporate the events into different seed varieties. Maintaining access to these licenses is vital to their business strategy (Vara, 2005; Sell, 2009; Delvenne et al., 2013; Arza, 2014). Monsanto's influence over other actors to oppose the project rested on the threat to suspend gene licenses to seed companies and to halt seed commercialization to producers.[31]

The power imbalance between the owners of transgenic events and local seed companies—rooted in licensing dependencies—was central to the outcome of this conflict and has been highlighted by some actors and studies on the sector's policy dynamics.[32] As previously mentioned, the fact that transgenic events in Argentina are protected under patent law (via the Patent Act), while seeds are protected under plant breeders'

[31] Miguel Campos, personal interview, 11/07/2017.

[32] Gabriel Delgado, personal interview, 11/11/2016.

rights (via the Seed Law), clearly favors those who develop transgenes over those who develop the seed varieties.[33]

As analyzed in Sect. 4.3, due to the high entry and approval costs associated with transgenics, national companies prevail in conventional breeding—the weakest link—while multinationals dominate in transgenic events—the strongest link. According to INASE, the national seed registration and oversight body, around 62% of registered plant varieties are held by national companies, while 38% belong to foreign firms. In contrast, only about 2% of plant biotechnology patents registered in Argentina are owned by national companies, compared to 98% by foreign companies (Lowenstein, 2014).

5.3.5 *The "Monsanto Law" Moves Forward in the Executive but Stalls in the Legislature*

From 2007 onward, the conflict between Monsanto and the Argentine government began to subside, giving way to increased cooperation. This shift was reflected in the government's decision to promote a reform of the Seed Law and to expedite the approval process for transgenic events. The cooperative nature of this new phase in the relationship was acknowledged by sector representatives,[34] government officials,[35] and statements from the U.S. embassy.[36]

[33] According to Arza (2014: 20), "thus, biotechnology companies that insert modified genes into the germplasm developed by other national seed companies or by INTA can register the new transgenic seeds as a novel variety in the National Institute of Seeds (INASE) and then market it without asking for any type of authorization from whoever developed the original germplasm. This cannot be done, however, if the variety contains a patented gene. For this, the approval of the patent holder of the transgene would be required since otherwise, that patent would be infringed because the protection extends to all the matter that contains the protected material (in this case, the transgene). In this way, the breeder's exemption, which contemplates the law of plant varieties, is impracticable in the cases that it is about transgenic varieties. So, even though seeds cannot be patented, with a patented transgene, the intellectual property of the transgenic varieties is, in practice, regulated by the Patent Law."

[34] Interview with two representatives of ASA and a former Minister of Agriculture.

[35] Since 2008, Monsanto became the "pet child" of the Ministry of Science and Technology, according to an officer of that Ministry (interview).

[36] A 2008 wire leaked in Wikileaks highlights this new position as to royalties: "On the positive side, there are some signs of progress on the longstanding dispute between

The reform bill was drafted at the Intellectual Property Center of Universidad Austral and coordinated by Miguel Rapela, Executive Director of ASA. Among its proposed amendments were restrictions on the breeder's exemption and on the "farmer's privilege," which would lead to higher royalty payments to companies holding patents on transgenic events (Perelmuter, 2018).

However, the 2008 conflict with agricultural producers halted the project, as the government did not want to open another front with the farming sector. The project was also shelved in 2009 and 2011, both election years.[37]

Throughout these years, multiple negotiation and debate forums were held between producers and seed suppliers. In 2012, a consensus was reached on a new draft bill with the support of the main associations in the Mesa de Enlace, except for the Federación Agraria and part of CRA.[38] In June 2012, President Cristina Fernández announced her commitment to submitting the bill to Congress before year's end. On the same day, along with Agriculture Minister Norberto Yahuar and Monsanto Argentina President Pablo Vaquero, she announced the company's investment in a new transgenic corn processing plant in Córdoba—the largest in Latin America—and the approval and launch of the new RR2 Intacta soybean, owned by Monsanto.

Despite these intentions from the Executive Branch—particularly from Agriculture Ministry officials involved in the project—the bill was never submitted to Congress.

Why did the new administration change its position and propose a bill aligned with Monsanto's and ASA's preferences? And why, despite the president's public commitment, was the bill never formally introduced in Congress?

Regarding the first question, one possible explanation is that some government officials, particularly within the Ministry of Agriculture, believed that beyond favoring Monsanto, the project would also benefit

the government and Monsanto on the collection of royalties for Monsanto's seed varieties. Monsanto is now in discussions with the government on the introduction of new seed varieties and payment for the technology, a significant departure from the previous government policy of refusing to negotiate over the issue."

37 Interview with Miguel Rapela, executive director of ASA.

38 Interview with a representative of CRA and interview with a representative of Federación Agraria.

national seed and biotechnology firms.[39] It is also likely that pressure from the United States government—which expressed concerns about seed IP in meetings with Argentine officials—played an important role. It was evident that promoting this bill would allow the Argentine government to defuse a major conflict with a company that, supported by the U.S. embassy, had demonstrated—albeit with limited success—its willingness and capacity to sustain a prolonged and costly dispute. The European lawsuits had set a precedent for possible future attempts to block Argentine exports, and the negotiations had also revealed Monsanto's power over the local seed sector through licensing agreements. In terms of corporate influence, some testimonies even suggest Monsanto attempted to "buy" off officials.[40]

However, the project's progress within the Executive sharply contrasts with the roadblock it encountered in Congress once it gained public visibility. On one hand, consistent with the limited effectiveness of disinvestment threats discussed earlier, there is no evidence that officials involved in drafting the bill did so out of concern for potential economic harm if the bill was not approved.[41] On the other, it was clear from their statements that supporting a company with a negative public image would impose significant political costs on the government, without any potential economic benefits. The Secretary of Agriculture involved in the initiative noted that the association with Monsanto was a decisive factor:

> There was a maneuver by the opposition and the *Federación Agraria* to muddy the waters—they started calling it the 'Monsanto law.' If people start hearing that the bill is being promoted by Monsanto, then it's likely that some lawmakers or even the president herself said, 'Better not move forward with this right now because it'll just generate more conflict.'[42]

This view aligns with that of another official, who argued that Monsanto's poor reputation outweighed even U.S. pressure in legislators' calculations:

[39] Interview with a former Secretary of Agriculture.

[40] Interview with an officer of the Ministry of Agriculture.

[41] Interview with a former minister, a former secretary and a former Undersecretary of Agriculture.

[42] Interview with a former secretary of Agriculture.

> The government resisted changing the Seed Law not to protect producers, but because politically it pays to be against Monsanto. The company is a symbol of environmental harm and everything negative associated with corporations. In politics, what matters is '*Who does this benefit? And what kind of political badge does it give me?*' If there's no badge, it doesn't move forward. No matter if Trump, Hillary or Obama try to push it, nobody wants to carry that burden.[43]

Despite Monsanto's visible efforts to improve its public image—through media campaigns and sponsoring scientific and technological events—the Secretary of Agriculture who attempted to revive the bill in 2014 offered a similar assessment as to why it was never debated in committee:

> GMOs are linked with glyphosate and with poisoning people. When that gets to Congress, the parties are naturally going to try to make political capital out of it—at the expense of Argentina's seed industry.[44]

Several industry representatives acknowledged Monsanto's reputational problem when it came to lobbying. Some even remarked that the situation had become so dire that the company had "lost its social license" and needed a name change.[45]

These observations are consistent with other studies of the period, which found that producers—especially those associated with *Federación Agraria*—succeeded in framing their opposition to the reform as a matter of national sovereignty, while Monsanto's demands were seen as narrow sectoral interests (Amin Filomeno, 2013). Added to this was the reputational issue tied to environmental and public health concerns.

In this case, the legitimacy of the interests at stake was not only relevant to the general public—mobilized by environmental and health issues—but especially to voters in rural areas, concerned about the distributive conflict between producers and Monsanto. As the literature has pointed out, one of the political advantages producers hold is their territorial rootedness, which—combined with Argentina's federal institutions—grants them an institutional lever to influence national politics through Congress

[43] Interview with a former Undersecretary of Agriculture.

[44] Interview with a former Undersecretary of Agriculture.

[45] Interview with an institutional representative of the input sector.

(Freytes, 2015). As the next section shows, however, this leverage was not sufficient to ensure debate on a reform favorable to producers.

For a deeper understanding of the clash between producers and biotechnology companies, it is necessary to consider both offensive and defensive interests. Just as the Executive's bill—supported by Monsanto and ASA—was never submitted to Congress, opposition-led bills favoring producers over biotech companies also failed to advance beyond the Agriculture Committee in the Chamber of Deputies. This is significant in terms of distributive conflict outcomes, as these alternative proposals would have blocked the royalty collection system Monsanto implemented in 2014.

In 2012, amid discussions about the potential submission of the Executive's bill, two bills were introduced in the Agriculture Committee of the Chamber of Deputies by lawmakers aligned with agricultural producers. Neither obtained committee approval. In addition to defending farmers' seed-saving rights, these bills declared the Seed Law to be a matter of public interest in order to prevent biotech companies from enforcing private royalty collection systems or from shifting seed regulation into the purview of patent law, which would further restrict access to technology.[46]

This episode reveals that the fragmentation of the "agro-deputies" and their inability to coordinate common positions prevented their proposals from obtaining committee approval and reaching the congressional floor. As the then-president of the Agriculture Committee noted: "The agro-deputies ran the committee and had a majority in the House [in fact, the opposition] between 2009 and 2011, and they couldn't agree on a single bill." [47] This suggests that producers in Congress do not wield as much influence as some studies claim (Amin Filomeno, 2013b), but neither are they as weak as others suggest (Freytes, 2015).

[46] The project signed by the members of the Frente Amplio Progresista, including Barchetta (Partido Socialista) and Orsolini (UCR), both members of FAA, established that the law should be of public policy. Chamber of Deputies. File: 8236-D-2012 Date: 21/11/2012.

[47] Personal interview with FPV representative.

5.3.6 *Capacity to Influence Access to International Markets and Impose "Private Export Duties"*

As will be shown in this final section, the distributive conflict over seed royalties took a turn in favor of Monsanto, which succeeded in partially offsetting the loss of profitability caused by the lack of reform to the Seed Law and the existence of an illegal seed market.

In the second half of 2014, Monsanto began requiring traders and grain handlers[48] to test soybeans at the time of purchase, requiring that royalties be withheld if the presence of Intacta technology (owned by Monsanto) was detected (without the producer having previously declared it). Both traders and grain handlers resisted acting as withholding agents, concerned about sparking conflict with producers, who accused them of collaborating with the multinational in collecting "private export duties."[49]

In response to this resistance, Monsanto threatened traders with withholding the "biosafety certificate" required to export soybeans to China. Chinese customs authorities require that imports of grains or by-products containing biotech events be accompanied by a biosafety certificate issued by the company that developed the technology.[50] Monsanto then began to condition the issuance of this certificate—which until then had been a mere formality—on traders agreeing to include the so-called "Monsanto clause" in their sales contracts. This clause obligated them to inspect the

[48] Known in Argentina as "*acopiadores*" (commercial intermediaries between farmers and traders).

[49] Grain handlers concentrate between 40 and 50% of producers' purchases, so this system triggered a significant problem in their relationship with the producers (interview with a representative of the Federación de Acopiadores).

[50] This is a particular feature of the Chinese case. In other countries, customs authorities directly verify which events are approved for import, so the importer is not required to present any biosafety certificate.

product and collect royalties.[51] The risk of noncompliance was that shipments could be rejected upon arrival at Chinese port terminals.[52] Without these contracts, the chain was blocked: producers could not sell to grain handlers, and exporters could not sell to importers.

In this way, Monsanto's ability to influence market access forced other actors in the chain to sign contracts they had previously resisted. The key question then begs: why does a company hold authority over a biosafety certification process in China? Interviews conducted for this research suggest that Monsanto's lobbying power over mid-level Chinese customs officials played a decisive role. [53] The certification process is bureaucratically inefficient, given that the product in question is already approved in China; customs authorities could simply verify that Intacta technology is authorized in the country. In this case, the high-ranking Chinese political officials were not involved in the initial agreement, but once the administrative requirement was established, they recognized the incentives to maintain it, as it could be arbitrarily used as a non-tariff barrier to punish a country by blocking its exports.[54]

Several forms of power are at play in this case. On one hand, power derives from structural factors: first, Monsanto's monopoly over the Intacta transgene; second, Argentina's dependency on China's soybean

[51] The purchase agreement stated: "The producer/collector acknowledges and accepts that the soybean grain delivered, sold, or consigned as described in this document may contain technology patented by third parties, the use of which by the producer/collector gives rise to the payment of royalties in favor of the owner of the patented technology, according to the terms of use established by said owner. Therefore, the producer/collector accepts that the grain delivered, sold, or consigned may be analyzed to identify the presence of third-party patented technologies and, if detected, agrees that the corresponding royalty and/or substitute payment—to be specified periodically by the owner of the technology—be deducted. Said amount will be deducted on behalf of and by order of the technology owner or its designated agent."

[52] Interviews with a representative of the Federación de Acopiadores, the Director of International Agri-Food Relations, and an official from the Biotechnology Directorate of the Ministry of Agriculture, Livestock, and Fisheries (MAGYP), and http://www.valorsoja.com/2015/09/29/argentina-esta-a-un-paso-de-implementar-una-retencion-privada-para-el-cobro-de-regalias-en-semilla-acopiadores-piden-el-gobierno-que-intervenga-para-evitar-el-avasallamient/#.XlEQyhMzY6h.

[53] Interviews with the Director of International Agri-Food Relations, an official from the Biotechnology Directorate of the Ministry of Agriculture, and a representative from the *Federación Agraria Argentinan* (FAA).

[54] Interview with an official from the Biotechnology Directorate.

purchases—soybean exports account for 7% of Argentina's total exports, with 96% destined for China. Moreover, this structural power is reinforced by the authority granted by the Chinese government to the technology-developing company to issue import certificates.

Despite complaints filed by agricultural producers to the National Commission for the Defense of Competition (CNDC) for abuse of dominant position, the royalty collection system was ultimately endorsed by the administration that took office in December 2015. At the beginning of 2014, while royalty payment contracts were being extended, the Ministry of Economy maintained that, since Monsanto did not hold a patent for Intacta, it could not legally compel producers to pay royalties.[55] The *National and Popular Agrarian Movement* (CANPO)—a sectoral organization close to the government—together with a group of cooperatives and seed multipliers,[56] filed a complaint with the CNDC[57] accusing Monsanto of abuse of dominant position. In February 2016, the FAA and the SRA expanded the complaint, after confirming that Monsanto did not possess a valid patent.[58]

Although this issue had been settled by 2016, it still remained a contested matter in 2014 and 2015, even among legal and technical experts advising sectoral organizations. The disagreement arose from the fact that Argentine patent law does not allow for the patenting of living organisms, as permitted by U.S. law, since these are considered naturally occurring entities that may be discovered but not regarded as inventions. Therefore, biotechnology companies in Argentina do not hold patents

[55] Interview with an official of the Ministry of Agriculture.

[56] *Federación de Cooperativas Federadas* (FECOFE), *Cámara Argentina de Semilleros Multiplicadores* (CASEM) and *Federación Argentina de Ingeniería Agronómica*.

[57] Página/12 (09/03/2014) https://www.pagina12.com.ar/diario/economia/2-254411-2014-09-03.html.

[58] In a statement from February 2016, the Argentine Rural Society (SRA) reported that the National Institute of Industrial Property (INPI) confirmed Monsanto did not hold the patent for this technology. "Monsanto is forcing producers to waive the rights granted under Seed Law 20.247 and is attempting to collect royalties for alleged intellectual property rights that the law and national authorities do not recognize (as confirmed by the National Institute of Industrial Property in response to an inquiry from the SRA in June 2015)." Sources: AgrofyNews: https://news.agrofy.com.ar/noticia/152873/monsanto-no-tiene-patente-soja-intacta-rr2-pro /. Clarín https://www.clarin.com/economia/Rural-denuncio-Monsanto-Defensa-Competencia_0_S1PKO6dw7l.html and Telam https://www.telam.com.ar/notas/201602/135702-federacion-agraria-dara-detalles-denuncia-monsanto-abuso-posicion-dominante.html.

on genes themselves, but on the processes used to develop the transgenic seeds. In the case of Intacta, this involves a series of patents on the mechanisms by which the gene is inserted into the seed.[59] Concurrently, another challenge to the patent's validity argued that Intacta was not a genuine innovation, but rather a stack of two prior innovations (RR and Bt), and could not thus be considered an invention, and only inventions are eligible for patent protection under international law.[60]

Nonetheless, even in the absence of a valid patent, the CNDC stated that the royalty contract could only be challenged if the Seed Law were classified as a matter of public policy, meaning that private contracts cannot be above the law.[61] For this reason, Monsanto's success in blocking legislative reform efforts that sought to introduce such a change—such as the one promoted by the government in 2014—becomes even more significant. The most salient elements of that proposed reform included collecting royalties solely at the point of seed purchase, strengthening the enforcement authority of INASE to regulate the informal seed market ("bolsa blanca"), and establishing the public policy nature of the Seed Law. These changes would have disabled the private royalty collection system and fostered the development of domestic seed companies and multipliers.[62]

The outcome remained unchanged with the new administration beginning in 2016: at the legislative level, none of the initiatives advanced, despite several reform proposals being introduced in 2016 and 2018. Meanwhile, the government ultimately endorsed Monsanto's royalty

[59] "Monsanto's defense then consists of requiring the other party to prove how they obtained the product if not through the patented procedures. Theoretically, to cover 100% of the gene, five patents are needed for different parts of the method. Some claim to have two or three out of five, and Monsanto says it holds all of them." (Interview with a representative of a farmer organization in charge of the intellectual property agenda).

[60] Interview with a manager from an agricultural input company and a representative from FAA. See also: https://www.lanacion.com.ar/economia/campo/juan-iglesias-perez-hoy-el-sistema-global-es-un-obstaculo-no-estimula-la-investigacion-nid1998383.

[61] Interview with a director of International Agri-Food Relations at the Ministry of Agriculture.

[62] "We believe that the seed sector's major development potential lies in fostering not only biotechnology companies but also germplasm firms and seed multipliers. This compensation system (charging at the port) rewards only biotechnology firms. Then there's the question of how much of that Monsanto passes on to Don Mario. We opposed that." (Interview with a former Secretary of Agriculture).

collection system, although it assigned the role of contract data oversight to INASE. Initially, Agriculture Ministry officials—most of them with backgrounds in farmer organizations—took a confrontational stance toward Monsanto, in line with allegations of abuse of dominant position. However, they eventually accepted the system, concerned about jeopardizing soybean exports to China: "Faced with the possibility of compromising soybean exports to Argentina's main trading partner, the State ultimately had to authorize the control system."[63]

Both the debate over patents and the issue of the biosafety certificate—two highly technical domains with significant implications for sectoral development and distributive conflicts—demonstrate that technical expertise and state capabilities in biosafety and intellectual property are crucial not only for the legal design of regulatory frameworks, but also for governments' political assessments and strategies. These evaluations require knowledge of both the intellectual property legal framework and biotechnology itself, as well as institutional capacities—from agencies such as the CNDC and the INPI—that shape the government's political leverage, its power vis-à-vis biotechnology firms, and the distributive outcomes along the agricultural value chain. This is evident in the testimonies of officials involved in the 2005 EU legal proceedings as well as in the 2014 conflict with China. However, it is equally clear that even in a hypothetical scenario in which the government possesses qualified personnel and effective institutions, and firms are transparent in disclosing information about their technologies, the ultimate determinant of distributive outcomes is the capacity to block access to international markets—something Monsanto can achieve even without holding patents for its products in Argentina.

[63] Interview with an Undersecretary of Agriculture.

CHAPTER 6

Taxes and Regulations on Foreign Trade

> We are the flour in your bread, the wheat in your noodles, the salt on your fries. We are the corn in your tortillas, the chocolate in your dessert, the sweetener in your soft drink. We are the oil in your salad dressing and the beef, pork or chicken you eat for dinner. We are the cotton in your clothing, the backing on your carpet and the fertilizer in your field.
> (Cargill ad, 2001)

6.1 Actors and Power Resources

Agricultural commodities exporting countries employ a variety of foreign trade regulations, including taxes, quotas, permits, reference prices, and state-owned or mixed enterprises, among others. These measures pursue objectives ranging from securing domestic food supply and prices, determining the quantities of different goods produced, to the collection of public revenue. In countries highly dependent on agricultural exports, such as Argentina, these regulations extend to foreign exchange flows and can therefore impact exchange rate stability.

The main actors affected by these measures are agricultural producers, exporting companies or traders, and the domestic population—particularly lower-income sectors, more vulnerable to food price increases.

J. O'Farrell, *Business Power in Agriculture Value Chains*, Latin American Political Economy, https://doi.org/10.1007/978-3-032-06589-6_6

As analyzed in Chapter 4, the trader link in Argentina is composed of a small number of firms, most of them multinationals. During the period under study, the five leading companies—Cargill, ADM, Bunge, COFCO (which acquired Nidera), and AGD—accounted for over 50% of the grain and grain derivative (oils and flours) export market, while the top ten companies controlled 90% (see Table 4.2). The level of concentration is even higher at the international level: only four companies (ADM, Bunge, Cargill, and Dreyfus—known as the "big four" or "ABCD") controlled 70% of global agricultural commodity trade during the study period (Heinrich Böll, 2017). In Argentina, these firms also control a significant portion of the infrastructure, including ports, and play an important role in financing the agricultural sector.

Alongside agricultural producers, this chapter highlights the role of consumer interests—particularly those of low-income or working-class sectors—since trade regulation affects their purchasing power due to its impact on domestic food prices. This was one of the priorities of the Peronist government during the period under analysis when managing trade policy.

The *Frente para la Victoria* (2003–2015) administrations succeeded in implementing regulations—such as export duties and permits—that transferred resources to consumers, albeit to the detriment of agricultural producers and to the benefit of traders' profit margins. However, it failed to advance its initiatives aimed at increasing direct state control over grain trade. As argued here, this outcome can be explained by the relative power of each of the involved actors.

Table 6.1 Actors and power resources

Actors	*Agricultural producers*	*Traders*	*Consumers/popular sectors*
Power Resources	Instrumental and structural weakness	Strong structural power: control of domestic and international trade and infrastructure. Ability to interrupt foreign currency flows	Core constituency of the FPV government

The fragmentation of the value chain and the diverging economic and political interests of its segments allow the government to impose costs—such as export duties—on the weakest link in the chain: agricultural producers. This weakness is evident both in relation to the government and to other actors in the chain not affected by export taxes, and is both instrumental and structural in nature.

The structural power of traders stems from their dominant position in international grain trade, which allows them, among other things, to affect Argentine exports at destination ports, that is, in importing countries. This has been a consistent feature of the sector's relationship with all governments and is the underlying reason why no initiative aimed at increasing direct state control over grain marketing advanced during this period. This power grew as a result of the deregulation and privatization of grain trade beginning in the 1980s, when most trade began to take place between companies—or even between subsidiaries of the same company—rather than between states (see Chapter 4).

At the national level, traders can obstruct the flow of foreign currency by delaying its settlement or by temporarily suspending or postponing exports. This power increases with the degree of concentration in the segment: as noted in Chapter 4, during the period under analysis, ten companies controlled 90% of the foreign currency produced by the agricultural sector, which in turn accounted for nearly 60% of the country's total foreign exchange earnings. These levels remain consistent today.[1]

The structural power derived from the generation of foreign currency is sometimes expressed through market-based decisions—such as stockpiling exports in anticipation of a devaluation—but also through political means, via coordination among firms and deliberate action aimed at extracting concessions from the government. This resource was key during the 2008 agrarian conflict in sustaining the producers' commercialization strike. The disruption of the foreign exchange flow was a central concern for the government during the protest, as it exerted pressure on the exchange rate in an international context marked by the global financial crisis and devaluations among Argentina's main trading partners. Although traders exercise their power on issues confined to the interests of their own segment and are not directly affected by export duties, in

[1] This includes primary agricultural products (22.1% of the total) and agro-industrial manufactures (AIM) (37.2% of the total). AIMs are mostly derivatives of soy, corn and wheat (oils, flours, pellets) (*See* Chapter 3.1 for more information).

the years preceding 2008 they had viewed with concern the government's growing interventionism in the sector. In this context, the government's political defeat in the conflict with rural associations over export duties ultimately favored the interests of the traders.

The structural power associated with foreign exchange control is contingent on the macroeconomic context and diminishes when the economy runs a trade surplus, or when the government holds high levels of reserves or sound borrowing capacity. An economy with greater ability to generate foreign currency places the government in a stronger bargaining position. As long as the Central Bank holds sufficient reserves, it can intervene in the market by selling dollars to alleviate exchange rate pressures. Under such conditions, the government's capacity to impose costs on this segment through regulatory threats and selective incentives increases, while the credibility of corporate threats diminishes. These instruments raise the costs faced by companies when entering into conflict with the government, thereby reducing their structural power. However, the government also incurs costs when applying some of these threats—such as export bans—in terms of economic activity and efficiency. Moreover, such threats become less credible in contexts where the economy is under acute foreign exchange stress.[2]

These findings align with the observations made by Fairfield (2015) regarding the structural power of traders in the aftermath of the 2001 crisis. The author presents export strikes and foreign exchange withholding as credible, at times materialized, disinvestment threats, strengthened by a context of sovereign default and capital flight, which contributed to macroeconomic instability. She also underlines the distinction between market decisions and coordination: while foreign exchange withholding generally stems from market-based decisions ("largely market coordinated withholding threats that jeopardized state solvency and macroeconomic stabilization"), during the period she analyzes there is also evidence of coordinated inaction and deliberate discussions among

[2] A paradoxical outcome in this regard is that, while a significant portion of the literature associates external debt with diminished national sovereignty, during the period under analysis, the ability to borrow—constrained by the country's exclusion from international credit markets—could have partially alleviated the shortage of foreign currency. This, in turn, would have granted the government greater decision-making autonomy.

firms about suspending exports to strengthen their bargaining position.[3] One of the key challenges in analyzing this form of power is empirically attributing traders' motivations when delaying the liquidation of foreign currency and distinguishing market-based speculation on exchange rates from politically motivated actions intended to secure concessions or undermine the government.

The structural power of traders does not lie in the possibility of exit but rather in their ability to block the access of local public and private actors to markets and foreign currency. This represents a significant departure from the literature on structural power and multinational corporate politics reviewed in Chapter 2, which tends to focus on disinvestment or exit strategies. In this case, as with input suppliers, I show that the power of traders does not lie in the threat of disinvestment—a threat constrained both by their substantial sunk costs in ports, elevators, and processing facilities, and by Argentina's status as a leading global producer of agricultural commodities. Instead, the structural power allowing traders to capture greater profit margins and safeguard their dominant market position stems from their ability to influence exports at destination ports.

In the same vein, whereas the literature asserts that globalization has strengthened corporate power by facilitating capital mobility and exit strategies, this work shows that globalization has increased the power of MNCs by expanding their capacity to shape countries' participation in international markets.

Two features of the Argentine economy make this form of power particularly relevant: its recurrent balance-of-payments crises and the high share of agricultural commodities on total exports. Both factors heighten the impact of any business action threatening foreign currency inflows, to a far greater extent than in countries with economies less vulnerable to this type of crisis.

6.2 Policies and Distributive Outcomes

As previously noted, during the period under analysis, traders were the primary beneficiaries in terms of profitability appropriation within the value chain, and the actors who demonstrated the greatest capacity to

[3] The difference is that she argues that power is instrumental rather than structural in cases where there is coordination (Fairfield, 2015:201).

reject or resist government initiatives. The two most significant policies contributing to this outcome were export duties and export permits.

6.2.1 *Export Duties*

One of the most important instruments during this period was the imposition of export duties on agricultural commodities. These duties have a long-standing history within Argentine tax policy, with records dating back to the late nineteenth century. Throughout the twentieth century, they were widely used by governments across the political spectrum, especially following currency devaluations or in the context of high international prices (Allan et al., 2024). They are customs tariffs levied on the export of various goods, such as wheat, corn, soybeans, and their derivatives.

As previously mentioned, from a distributive standpoint, export duties represent a transfer of resources from producers to the state and consumers. However, they do not affect exporters' profit margins, as exporters function merely as withholding agents and pass the tax burden onto producers.[4] The transfer from producers to the state via export duties between 2005 and 2014 is estimated at US$ 66.2 billion (see Table 6.2).

At the same time, consumers benefited from the fall in domestic prices of basic food basket items such as cooking oil and bread. The transfer to consumers is estimated at US$ 13.6 billion during the same period, largely due to export duties on soybeans (used for edible oil), corn, wheat, and sunflower. Consumers also benefited from the creation of an "oil trust fund" aimed at subsidizing vegetable oils sold in the domestic market. This fund was initially financed by the state and later by the traders, who were required to pay a 1% fee on the FOB value[5] of soybean and soybean meal exports.[6]

[4] For a comprehensive analysis of the distributive effects and the political economy of export duties, *see* Allan et al. (2024).

[5] FOB stands for "free on board" free of shipboard expenses. FOB prices are indicators of the price that external customers are willing to pay.

[6] The goal was to supply the domestic market with 40 million liters per month at a price set by the Secretariat of Commerce, which varied but was around 50% lower than the market price. (Interview with an executive from the Chamber of the Oil Industry in Argentina (Cámara de la Industria Aceitera en la Argentina (CIARA)).

6.2.2 *State Control over Foreign Trade*

In addition to this fiscal tool, from the 1930s through the 1980s, Argentina, like many Latin American countries, implemented various forms of regulation on agricultural foreign trade. Among the most notable were commercialization boards, which held legal monopolies over grain purchases and had the capacity to stabilize markets through buying and selling operations. These regulations pursued multiple objectives: to buffer the impact of international price volatility on domestic food prices; to transfer resources from the agricultural to the industrial sector; and to prevent collusive behavior among large grain traders (Turzi, 2010; Pierri, 2014). Following the debt crisis of the 1980s and amidst the wave of market-oriented reforms, regional governments liberalized agricultural product markets. In Argentina, the dissolution of the National Grain Board in 1991 effectively put an end to state intervention in the foreign trade of these products.

The administration of the *Frente para la Victoria* (FPV) sought to implement reforms aligned with this interventionist approach, aiming to increase state control over foreign trade. However, as shown in the episodes analyzed, these initiatives failed to advance, as government officials and legislators understood that traders could retaliate against the country by ceasing to buy Argentine products at destination ports.

6.2.3 *Export Permits (ROE)*

In addition to export duties, the most significant policy measure in terms of its effects on the structure and distribution of profits within the export segment was the system of export permits for wheat and corn, known as the "Green ROE," implemented as of May 2008.[7] The *Registro de Operaciones al Exterior* (ROE)[8] replaced the previous system of *Declaraciones Juradas de Ventas al Exterior* (DJVE). Like the DJVE, the ROE consisted of a system of quotas and export authorizations. The main difference was that permits now had to be approved by the Secretariat of

[7] Resolution No. 543 dated May 28, 2008 from the former National Office of Agricultural Commercial Control (Oficina Nacional de Control Comercial Agropecuario (Oncca)).

[8] Law N° 21.453.

Commerce based on criteria that—according to company complaints—were not always explicit or objective, and their approval was often subject to unjustified delays. The objective stated by the government for implementing the ROE was to ensure domestic supply (referred to as "food security"). Discretion in the granting of permits and government control over their distribution increased after 2011, when the administration sought to boost the participation of domestically owned companies and agricultural cooperatives in foreign trade.[9]

Although the ROEs partially achieved their intended goals of securing domestic supply and increasing the market share of national cooperatives, they also produced a significant and unintended effect: a substantial increase in the profit margins of traders at the expense of producers. This occurred because export controls reduced competition between the two major players competing to secure purchase volumes: processors (of flour and oils) and exporters. This decline in competition negatively impacted the prices received by producers. Under the system of quotas and permits, processors knew they were guaranteed the volume of wheat and corn they required for the domestic market (since the government set the portion of the harvest reserved for domestic consumption), and exporters knew that—except in the cases examined in the following section, where the government distributed permits based on political considerations—they would obtain export authorizations, which were allocated by the exporters' chamber according to the volume exported in previous years ("past performance").

The reduction in competition between processors and traders significantly widened the gap between the theoretical export price (known as the theoretical FAS) and the actual market price resulting from negotiations between buyer and seller (or market FAS). The price that traders use as a reference to pay producers for grain is the theoretical FAS.[10] This price is estimated daily by the Rosario Board of Trade by subtracting from the international price—or FOB price[11]—the export duties and the various costs associated with the export process (commissions, loading and unloading at ports, customs costs, etc.). Traders always attempt to

[9] Interviews with a former Minister of Agriculture and with two former Secretaries of Commerce.

[10] Or export parity price (FAS for its acronym in English—"free alongside ship" or free of expenses alongside the ship).

[11] The main reference market for international prices is the Chicago market.

offer a price slightly below the theoretical FAS, as their profit margin depends on this difference. Conversely, agricultural producers aim not to accept a price below the theoretical FAS in order to maximize their income. The result of this negotiation determines the actual market price (or market FAS).

The gap between the theoretical FAS and the market FAS widened because traders, during negotiations, informed producers that they could not guarantee the issuance of the export permit and therefore bore the risk of having to store the grain for an extended period until the permit was obtained. The cost associated with this risk was deducted from the price paid to the producer. In practice, this risk premium was almost never realized, as permits were nearly always granted. Each year, once domestic demand had been met and the government temporarily increased the export quota, exporters were allowed to sell at international prices products they had purchased at depressed domestic prices.[12]

The magnitude of this transfer from producers to traders is hard to estimate, as it varied with each transaction. However, sources in the production, storage, and trading sectors, as well as officials from the Ministry of Agriculture and interviewed experts, all agree that profit margins multiplied by at least a factor of five on average.[13] Without the ROE system, an exporter could typically obtain, at best, a margin of US$5 per ton (since the trading business relies more on volume than on high unit margins). Under the permit system, margins increased to at least US$ 20–25 per ton, and many claim they were at times even higher. Both the *Cámara de Exportadores* and the *Federación de Acopiadores* acknowledge that margins surged during this period. One estimation of the distributive impact of the permits indicates that between 2005 and 2014, they generated a transfer of US$ 9 billion from producers to consumers, traders, and processors (see Table 6.2).

The table below summarizes estimations of transfers from producers to the state, consumers, and traders between 2005 and 2014—first, for exported grains and by-products, and second, for those consumed domestically. Export duties generated a transfer of US$ 66.2 billion from producers to the state, and US$ 13.6 billion to consumers (Table 6.2).

[12] Interviews with: a national representative and rural leader, an economist from the SRA and an export manager from AFA.

[13] Interviews with a member of AACREA, and with a representative of the *Federación de Acopiadores*.

The second column shows the distributive effects of the export permits. As previously noted, by reducing competition between processors (of flour and oils) and exporters, the permits depressed the prices received by producers and expanded the profit margins of traders and processors. This difference amounts to a total of US$ 5.8 billion for products purchased by traders for export and US$ 3.7 billion for those sold on the domestic market (Table 6.2).

Export permits also contributed to a deconcentration of the export market, marked by the loss of market share among multinational firms and the growth of domestic actors, particularly export cooperatives associated with agricultural producers. The Fig. 6.1 shows that exports declared by multinational companies (such as Cargill, Bunge, and Dreyfus, for illustrative purposes) declined significantly, while those by national cooperatives ACA and AFA increased. However, this data tends to overstate both the extent of deconcentration and the "nationalization" of foreign trade, and does not accurately reflect the actual proportions exported by each firm. In practice, it was often the case that some companies obtained export permits but, lacking export capacity, sold them to multinational traders, who ultimately carried out the export operations.[14] A crucial point to consider is that a policy of this nature, aimed at promoting national actors in foreign trade, sees a clear structural limitation in the foreign ownership of export infrastructure (ports and grain handlers) and, more importantly, in the concentration of international trade control in a few multinational firms. Beyond infrastructure, for the policy to be genuinely effective, domestic companies must also develop greater capacity to place their products in importing countries. Under the current structure of trade organization, the measure had a redistributive effect in favor of cooperatives, but not in terms of market power. Furthermore, export permits also played a political role, functioning as a tool for state negotiation—an aspect analyzed in detail in Section 6.3.

In sum, the ROEs negatively affected the profitability of agricultural producers. For traders, they entailed a reduction in market share but a significant increase in profitability—more than compensating for the loss of market presence.

[14] This is pointed out off the record by representatives of the public and private sector interviewed for this work.

Table 6.2 Distributive impact of export taxes and permits: estimated transfer from producers to the State, Traders and Consumers

Exported products	*Export duties*	*Export permits (3)*	*Export duties + Export permits*
	US$ billions	**US$ billions**	**US$ billions**
Soybean	11.4	−0.147	11.3
Industrial Soybean (1)	41.5	1.0	42.5
Sunflower	0.019	0	0.019
Industrial Sunflower (1)	1.9	0.457	2.3
Wheat	3.8	2.0	5.8
Corn	5.7	2.1	7.8
Sorghum	0.471	−0.017	0.454
Others (7)	1.2	0.313	1.5
Sub-Total	**66.2 (transfer to the State)**	**5.8 (transfer to traders)**	**72.1**
Products consumed domestically	***Implied export duties (2)***	***Implied permits (3)***	***Implied export duties + Implied permits***
	US$ billions	**US$ billions**	**US$ billions**
Industrial Soybean (1)	2.5	0.088	2.6
Industrial Sunflower (1)	2.5	0.570	3.1
Wheat	3.4	1.6	5.0
Corn	3.5	1.2	4.8
Sorghum	0.706	0.014	0.720
Others (4)	0.898	0.216	1.1
Sub-Total	**13.6 (transfer to consumers)**	**3.7 (transfer to traders and consumers)**	**17.3**
Total	**79.8**	**9.6**	**87.1**

Source Agritrend *Notes* (1) Soy/Sunflower industry includes oils and pellets weighted according to extraction percentage. (2) Implied export duties arise from applying the respective rates to consumed grains. (3) Calculation of the difference between market FAS prices and theoretical FAS prices due to permits and other restrictions. (4) Includes, in cereals: rice, oats, barley, rye, millet, and canary seed; in oilseeds: flax, rapeseed, safflower and derivatives; in regional: beans, cotton, and corn.

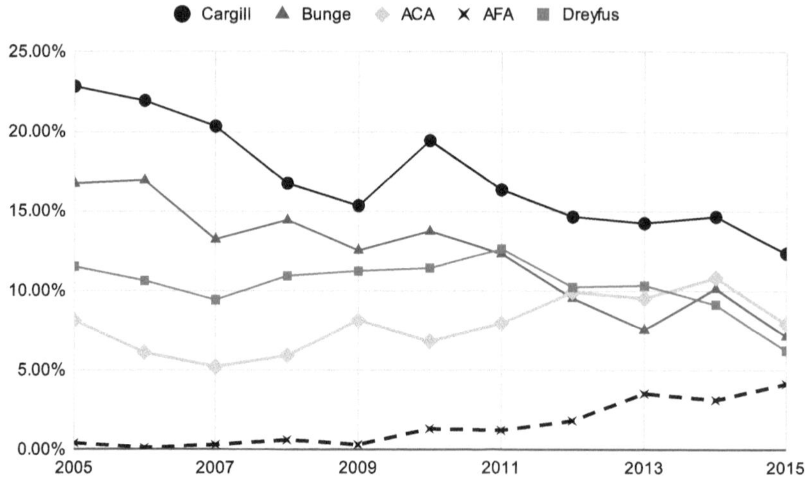

Fig. 6.1 Market share of grain exports by company (as a percentage of the total) (*Source* Prepared by author based on data provided by the Ministry of Agriculture) (*Note* The figure reflects the distribution of export permits which, due to the motives explained above on the secondary distribution of permits, does not accurately reflect the effective market share)

6.3 Episodes

This section analyzes the three most significant episodes of the period: the 2008 conflict following the increase in export duties; the failed attempts to expand state control over foreign trade; and the government's efforts to impose costs and regulatory threats on traders in order to redistribute benefits and compensate producers and consumers—measures whose effectiveness declined in line with the level of international reserves. The Table 6.3 summarizes the three most relevant milestones for understanding the distributive conflicts and the role of power in explaining their outcomes.

6.3.1 *Export Duties: The Role of Traders in the 2008 Conflict*

Argentina's power structure is not shaped by the 'Seven Sisters' [the nickname given to the seven largest export firms]. This is still an oligarchic

Table 6.3 Summary of foreign trade: Policies, distributive outcome, and relevant power resources

Policy episode	*Distributive outcome*	*Power resources*
High export duties	Redistribution from agricultural producers to the State and consumers (does not affect traders)	Weak structural and instrumental power of agricultural producers. Traders supported efforts to block increases in 2008
State control of foreign trade blocked by traders	The status quo favors traders over producers, the State, and consumers Traders win in both deregulated contexts and under the export permit system	Strong structural power of traders due to their control over trade and national and international infrastructure. Capacity to disrupt foreign exchange flows
Export permits (ROE)	Redistribution from producers to consumers and traders Traders lose market share, but increased profitability more than compensates for the loss Compensatory market share allocated to cooperatives linked to producers (ACA and AFA)	Weak structural and instrumental power of agricultural producers

country, dominated by large producers and the Sociedad Rural. It's not about the companies—that's a mistake rooted in an almost phyllo-Marxist conception.
Guillermo Moreno, Secretary of Commerce, 2006–2013 (personal interview)

The implementation of export duties was one of the most contentious and distributively significant measures in the period. In 2002, following a major currency devaluation, the administration of Eduardo Duhalde imposed export duties on the main agricultural commodities, with the dual aim of increasing fiscal revenues and cushioning the impact of international food prices on the domestic market. From 2003 onward, under the administration of the *Frente para la Victoria* (FPV), export duty rates were raised on several occasions between 2006 and 2008, in line with international price increases (Fig. 6.2). The substantial profitability generated by the 2002 devaluation and high global prices undermined the credibility of claims that increased export duties would discourage agricultural investment. Average per-hectare profitability between 2002 and 2004 doubled that of the 1991–2001 period. Furthermore, the steady increase in land prices served as a proxy for the government to verify that the sector remained profitable (Fairfield, 2015). In other words, the government perceived no credible threat of disinvestment, and producers held limited structural power. In such contexts, where the struggle centers on the appropriation of rents—understood as extraordinary returns relative to the opportunity cost of capital—producers face difficulties in conveying a credible disinvestment threat unless they manage to organize collectively (Freytes, 2015).

This finally occurred on March 11, 2008, when the government introduced Resolution 125, which established a new system of "sliding-scale export taxes" in which the rate varied in line with international prices. Agricultural producers, represented by the *Mesa de Enlace*, responded with a commercialization strike that would last four months and culminate upon rejection of Resolution 125 by Congress. The massiveness and persistence with which producers took to the roads can be explained

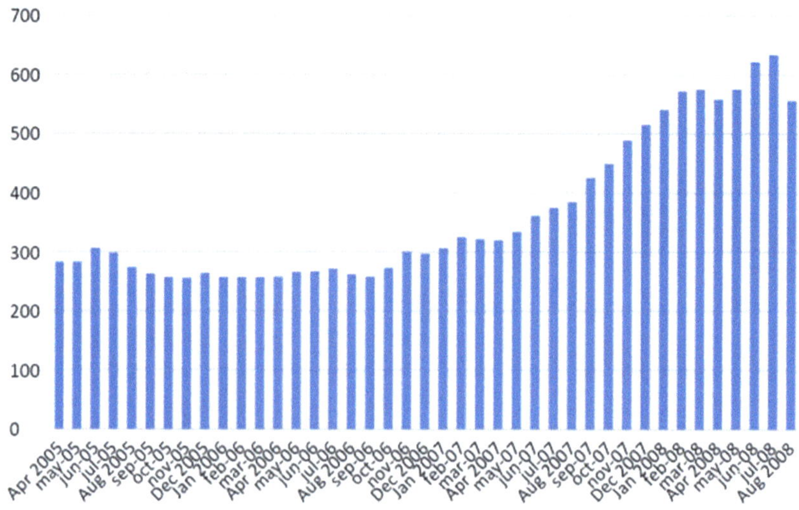

Fig. 6.2 International price of soybeans (2005–2008) (*Source* Prepared by author based on World Bank data)

by the design of Resolution 125, which established a variable rate that frustrated any expectation of future profits (with a rate of 95% if the international price of soybeans exceeded US$ 600) (Fairfield 2011).

The commercialization strike has long been a central component of the repertoire of protest tools employed by agricultural producers to voice opposition to government policies—an approach with varying degrees of success dating back at least to 1922, when the *Societal Rural Argentina (SRA)* called for a suspension of meat sales to major exporters (Hora 2010: 83). The absence of formal channels for policy influence helps explain producers' reliance on contentious strategies such as protest (Fairfield 2011; Freytes 2015; Mangonnet and Murillo 2017; Fernández Milmanda 2024). Yet the 2008 protests stood out from previous episodes in several important ways. In addition to their duration, they incorporated roadblocks alongside the traditional strike, a tactic that both amplified public visibility and generated food shortages in urban areas. Moreover, producers forged alliances with segments of the business elite, middle-class sectors, opposition political forces, and major media outlets (Basualdo 2008; Lapegna 2017). Several factors further bolstered the mobilization: effective coordination through local producer associations—most notably *Confederaciones Rurales Argentinas* (CRA) (Mangonnet and Murillo 2017); intense pressure on legislators from constituencies heavily dependent on agriculture (Basualdo 2008: 47–53; Freytes 2015; Fernández Milmanda 2019b: 27); the localized economic disruptions caused by the strike and their electoral consequences (Mangonnet et al. 2017); and the increasing legitimacy of the agricultural sector as a perceived "driver of national development" (Hora 2010: 104).

This section focuses on a factor less explored in the literature but essential to the success of the protest: the role of traders in the economic damage caused by the interruption of exports. Recent studies have focused on the political damage. The mechanisms through which the protests affected the economy, although prominently featured in the media,[15] remain scarcely systematized. Paradoxically, although the capacity to generate (or block) foreign currency is the structural variable most frequently mentioned in both contemporary and historical literature on the sector's power, it is the least analyzed. It is often cited as a given

[15] *See* for example the chronology of Teubal and Giarraca (2009), and Hora (2010).

and highlighted as the sector's power base, but the mechanisms through which it operated and generated influence have not been adequately dissected. Moreover, we know little about the role of other actors in the supply chain during the protest—a particularly relevant point when it comes to traders, as they exert the most control over foreign currency flows. What role did economic damage play in the protest's effectiveness and in the concerns of government officials? What financial or material capacity did producers have to sustain a commercial strike for so long? What role did exporting companies play during the protest? What was their relationship with the government and with producers?

Two issues stand out: first, that traders had incentives to cooperate with producers in the protest and to weaken the government. Second, that their capacity to block foreign currency flows was crucial to the sustainability of the commercialization strike.

Parallel to the roadblocks, tensions between the government and traders intensified during the conflict, as traders had already been on alert since the previous year due to unofficially circulating government projects aimed at increasing state control over the grain trade. Exporting firms' concern was reflected in the pressure exerted by the United States embassy on the Argentine government, prompted by protests from Cargill. In June 2008, in the midst of the conflict over Resolution 125, the president of Cargill Argentina, met with the ambassador and expressed the companies' discontent "about the growing flow of regulations aimed at increasing the Argentine government's control over agricultural exports." The ambassador conveyed the protest against these "unreasonable regulations" and "the frustration over the lack of access by his company and other major exporters to key government figures [...] who make decisions within a very small and closed group, [...] and issue major regulations without prior consultation."[16]

Among the mentioned regulations was the government's intention to charge retroactive export duties (referring to a tax debt the government had been claiming since 2007), arbitrariness in the use of export permits, and new regulations that shortened the time frame for shipments once a permit was approved. Notably, export duties were not mentioned. The ambassador agreed to raise these concerns with the appropriate officials,

[16] Cristian Sicardi, CEO of Cargill Argentina, Wikileaks https://wikileaks.org/plusd/cables/08BUENOSAIRES1288_a.html. *See also* O'Donnell, S. (2011).

without naming the company (which expressed "concern that the Argentine government would make the company a target"), and emphasized that arbitrary controls and attempts to collect retroactive taxes would seriously undermine future investments, with the associated risks for economic activity. He also pointed out that bilateral investment treaties provided certain guarantees to protect the company.

The statements made by Cargill's president at the embassy in 2008 also reflect the sector's concern that the government might take more extreme measures:

> It is unclear whether ONCCA's [National Agricultural Trade Control Office] insensitivity to the logistical efficiency of the commodity export sector, combined with efforts to collect retroactive taxes, is part of the president's 'divide and conquer' strategy—whereby the government punishes large exporters to gain the support of small farmers, who criticize the large exporters and believe they are colluding—or whether there is a larger plan to control the sector.[17]

At this point, it is worth highlighting, first, that export duties were not part of the exporters' agenda of demands because, as mentioned earlier, the burden of such duties fell on producers. However, exporting companies were extremely concerned—and perceived it as a worrisome possibility—that the government might move forward with other forms of state control over trade. This concern was compounded by the fact that, as they told the ambassador, they had no access to decision-making processes within the ministries.

This may be deemed to explain the deeply held belief of some government officials, analyzed below, that exporters were responsible for stockpiling grain exports during the 2008 protest. Even if Resolution 125 was not among their priorities, from this perspective, all signs indicate that traders saw the protest as an opportunity to weaken the government and discourage interventionism.

To analyze this, it is important to systematize how the 2008 protests and agricultural commercialization strikes more generally inflicted economic damage. Two different ways have been identified in which the protests affected the economy, both of which were present in

[17] Wikileaks https://wikileaks.org/plusd/cables/08BUENOSAIRES1288_a.html. *See also* O'Donnell, S. (2011).

officials' concerns: (i) food supply and prices, and (ii) the flow of exports and foreign currency.

From the outset of the protest, the government was concerned about the potential for food shortages and rising prices. Over time, however, farm leaders came to recognize that these effects were damaging their movement in the public eye. In response, they sought to limit the scope of the blockades, focusing primarily on grains and beef.[18]

Interviews with officials from various government areas reveal that the interruption of foreign currency flows was one of the main concerns in terms of the economic damage caused by the protest, as it put pressure on the foreign exchange market and raised expectations of devaluation.[19] Officials' concern about the ability to block foreign currency flows and its impact on the governability of the exchange market persisted throughout the entire period, beyond the conflict over Resolution 125.

Studies that analyzed the impact of the strike indicate that it significantly depressed export activity, something also noted by the media.[20] If we look at the months of the protest (March to June), which coincide with the soybean harvest season, we see that the average soybean price during that period was US$ 582—74% higher than the average for the same months the previous year, when it was US$ 334 (Fig. 6.2). For corn, the increase was 55%. However, during those months in 2008, only 23% more foreign currency was settled than in the previous year (US$ 7.7

[18] The pickets once again took over the road, although from then onwards rural leaders showed greater sensitivity to the need to avoid antagonizing urban society. To counter the accusations that portrayed them as responsible for shortages, from that moment until the end of the conflict, the *Mesa de Enlace* committed to periodically allowing the passage of commercial traffic and people, limiting their blockades to the transport of grains and livestock. However, the agrarian leaders did not always have sufficient authority to compel the more hardline, self-organized pickets to honor these commitments (Hora, 2010). *See also* Fairfield (2015:204–205).

[19] Interviews with Guillermo Moreno and with Mercedes Marcó del Pont, former president of Banco Nación and former president of the Central Bank (2010–2013).

[20] See for example Pagni (2008): "The other siege on the State is fiscal. In the provinces, the payment chain has been broken and provincial accounts are deteriorating. In addition, the ruralists speculate with delaying the sale of the crops to stop exports and prevent the national government from collecting export duties. They know that the Treasury needs an additional US$ 3 billion to import fuel and avoid a collapse in electric generation. Kirchner, reluctant to cool down the economy, is achieving it in the least sophisticated way." https://www.lanacion.com.ar/politica/dos-estilos-enfrentados-nid1010950.

billion versus US$ 6.2) (Table 6.4). In sum, although both dollar inflows and tax revenues increased compared to the previous year, considering the difference in international prices confirms that the protests represented a very significant loss in terms of foreign currency inflow.

Uncertainty and disagreement emerged over who bore responsibility for the delayed inflow of foreign currency: was it the producers or the traders? And if it was the latter, was the slowdown a response to market dynamics—such as anticipation of a devaluation—or part of a deliberate political strategy to support producers and undermine the government?

As I analyze below, divergent interpretations existed within the government itself regarding which actor along the export chain was to blame for the disruption in the flow of foreign exchange. A close examination of the political struggle over foreign currency inflows during the 2008 conflict not only clarifies how state officials perceived this particular structural power resource, but also sheds light on the growing tensions between the government and exporting firms from that point forward. Interruptions in the inflow of foreign currency can occur at three different stages of the grain commercialization process: (A) when producers choose not to sell and instead stockpile their harvest; (B) when producers sell, but

Table 6.4 Foreign currency settlement from grain and by-product exports (US$ billions)

Month	*2007*	*2008*	*2009*	*2010*	*2011*
January	1.05	1.64	1.55	0.99	1.43
February	0.70	1.61	1.11	1.02	1.19
March	1.06	1.35	1.01	1.31	1.82
April	1.50	2.31	1.83	2.26	2.61
May	1.88	2.40	2.18	2.29	3.20
June	1.81	1.65	1.92	2.69	2.95
July	1.74	2.81	1.36	2.56	2.25
August	1.73	2.16	1.12	1.88	2.57
September	1.63	2.01	1.10	2.03	2.24
October	1.55	1.48	1.12	1.93	1.96
November	1.41	1.13	1.08	1.65	1.33
December	1.51	1.36	0.80	1.61	1.47
Annual Total	17.58	21.92	16.20	22.23	25.03

Source Prepared by author based on data provided by CIARA

exporters decide to hold on to the grains; or (C) when exporters make the sale but fail to liquidate the foreign currency proceeds.

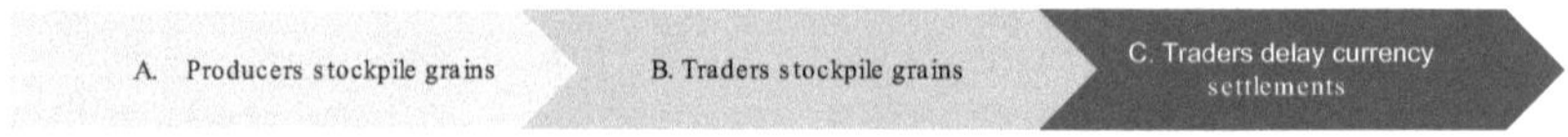

Decisions at these three stages may be driven by market logic or by political motivations; in other words, they constitute a form of structural power that can operate either automatically or deliberately and strategically. The preference of producers or exporters regarding when to sell grain or to liquidate foreign currency earnings varies according to international prices and devaluation expectations. For companies, bringing in dollars after a devaluation—and not before—is a rational decision aimed at maximizing the number of pesos obtained per dollar sold. Similarly, the decision to stockpile grain may be understood as an attempt to maximize income based on the evolution of international prices. However, these decisions may also respond to political criteria, taken in a coordinated manner, with the objective of pressuring the government to change a particular course of action.

Furthermore, the volume and financial resources held by the companies that control foreign trade grant them sufficient capacity to destabilize the foreign exchange market. Particularly in contexts where a devaluation is anticipated, speculative behavior can turn that expectation into a self-fulfilling prophecy. If actors believe there will be a devaluation, it is to be expected that they will purchase foreign currency either to safeguard its value or to sell it at a higher rate after the devaluation. This generates increased demand for foreign currency, which, if not counterbalanced by an increase in supply, ultimately forces a devaluation. This mechanism may operate automatically—through the individual actions of many agents—or intentionally, through the actions of a few actors with significant market power. Traders are among the actors with such destabilizing power. The impact of these behaviors is significant in relation to government objectives, as devaluation feeds into prices and erodes purchasing power.

In the case of the producers' commercialization strike—such as the one that took place in 2008—the blockage of foreign currency flows theoretically occurs at point A in the diagram, since it is the producers who stage the protest, not the exporters. However, the interviews conducted for this study indicate that, according to government officials, both producers (point A) and traders (points B and C) deliberately resorted to this mechanism during the period in question with the aim of pressuring the government to repeal Resolution 125. It also became clear that stockpiling continued even after the sliding export duties were rejected in Congress, in anticipation of a devaluation. In addition to the stockpiling and delayed currency liquidation—which affected the supply of dollars—demand for foreign currency increased exponentially in 2008, reaching the highest peak of external asset formation between 2003 and 2015: 5.7% of GDP (the second peak occurred in 2011, at 3.9%).[21]

At the time, Secretary of Commerce Guillermo Moreno—who, among many responsibilities, managed relations with traders and aimed to ensure a stable flow of foreign currency—believed it was the producers (in his view, "the oligarchy") who were stockpiling the crops. In fact, Moreno asserts that during his tenure (2006–2013), the relationship with traders "was correct and at times amicable," and that "there was no notable situation indicating a systematic obstruction of government policy."[22] He argues that "Argentina's power structure is not shaped by the 'Seven Sisters' [the nickname given to the seven largest export firms]. This is still an oligarchic country, dominated by large producers and the SRA. It's not about the companies—that's a mistake rooted in an almost phyllo-Marxist conception." For the former official, it is the landowners who have the power to destabilize the economy or the government, and they were the most critical actors to regulate in order to ensure domestic food prices and supply: "Food prices are directly tied to the landowners, who increase their wealth equation as the value of their land rises, and they pass that on to food prices. The success of our model is also its downfall, because food prices start rising—this is why we had to create the Secretariat of Commerce."

Beyond Moreno's particular view, the prevailing perspective within the Executive Branch was that in 2008, traders financed the producers' commercialization strike and were also behind the increase in demand

[21] Fundación de Investigaciones para el Desarrollo (FIDE) based on BCRA data.

[22] "With me, there was never a yes or a no. I'd walk into the meeting, everyone would stand up, and when I sat down, they'd sit down. 'Gentlemen, on your feet'—300 people would rise. I'd sit, and they'd sit. The president of Cargill, Bunge & Born included... I don't know if that tells you something." (Interview with Guillermo Moreno, 3/23/2017).

for foreign currency. In addition to these economic pressures, government officials were certain that traders provided logistical support for the protests, such as financing the most significant rally held on May 25, 2008, in Rosario (the latter is acknowledged by representatives of producer associations linked to the *Mesa de Enlace*).[23] Observing the effects of these actions on the exchange market, the Executive interpreted them as destabilizing speculation[24] and as a key financial pillar for sustaining the commercialization strike. In this regard, testimony from several former officials illustrates the position taken by both Néstor Kirchner and Cristina Fernández de Kirchner—one that did not respond to economic rationality, but rather to political logic: refusing to show weakness in negotiations with powerful actors—traders, in this case—who were challenging the government, even at the cost of potentially inefficient economic outcomes.

A key point here is that producers cannot stockpile indefinitely, as they lack the financial backing to do so and must sell in order to purchase inputs for the next harvest. Officials could confirm that producers had already sold to traders through cross-checking production, export, and grain liquidation data from the tax authority (AFIP) and the central bank (BCRA). This allowed them to verify when exporters had already purchased the harvest but had yet to export it (point B of the earlier diagram).[25] In this regard, the explanation of a former Central Bank president is particularly telling:

> Large exporters provide financing to producers by buying from them in advance. The agricultural export sector is concentrated in five or six companies—they are the ones that can push back, and they pushed back against the Kirchners every time it was necessary. You'd have situations where producers had already sold, but the large exporters were stockpiling it in their silo bags. They're the ones with the financial capacity to do that. We underestimated the strength of these actors. They are constantly arbitraging, and it was clear in 2008 how they operated to provoke a devaluation. From an economic point of view, it was madness that we

[23] Interview with an agricultural leader.

[24] Mercedes Marco del Pont, personal interview, 3/16/2017; and Augusto Costa, former Secretary of Commerce, personal interview, 4/3/2016.

[25] Mercedes Marco del Pont, personal interview, 3/16/2017.

> didn't devalue like Brazil and the rest of the world. But from a political standpoint, Néstor [Kirchner] and Cristina [Fernández de Kirchner], seeing these guys trying to steamroll you, made a political decision not to yield to the pressure of large exporters.

The same official adds that, despite the exporters' attempts to "steamroll" the government, in 2008 the macroeconomic situation provided enough resilience to negotiate from a position of strength—something that would diminish in subsequent years. As discussed in the third episode, those conditions began to shift after 2012:

> The thing is, we had the capacity—otherwise they would have steamrolled us. Capacity in terms of reserves, essentially; in terms of being free from debt (we didn't need dollars to pay off debt); and due to favorable trade balances until 2012. That's why we were able to withstand the 2008 strike, even despite the complex international context.

The "complex international context" refers to the consequences of the global financial crisis and the flight to quality,[26] which exerted pressure on emerging market currencies. As shown in Fig. 6.3, starting in March 2008 (the shaded area in the graph), the exchange rate began to appreciate significantly. In such a context—characterized by a sharp appreciation of the real multilateral exchange rate and following Brazil's devaluation—it is to be expected that traders would delay the entry of foreign currency and purchase dollars, speculating that their value would rise in the future. In this regard, the exercise of structural power may have stemmed either from market-based decisions or from a deliberate action aimed at forcing a devaluation, weakening the government, or extracting concessions from it. The evidence gathered here is insufficient to definitively establish which form of structural power was in operation.

In early 2009, noting that a significant portion of the 2008 harvest had not yet been exported, Secretary of Commerce Guillermo Moreno, head of the Federal Tax Authority (AFIP) Ricardo Echegaray, and Secretary of Industry Débora Giorgi held a meeting with representatives of the *Cámara Aceitera de la República Argentina* (CIARA) and the *Centro Exportador de Cereales* (*Grain Exporters Center* (CEC). According to

[26] Refers to the change in the flow of investments toward more stable and developed financial jurisdictions, typically in contexts of crisis in emerging markets.

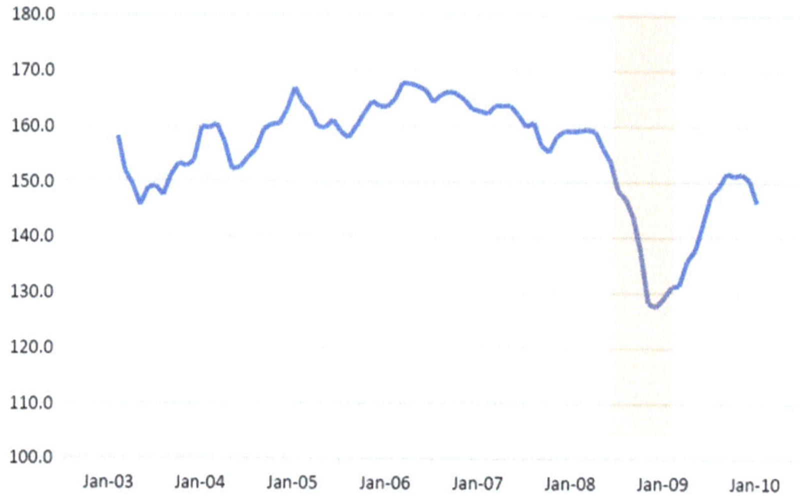

Fig. 6.3 Multilateral real exchange rate (2002–2009), base year 2015 = 100 (*Source* Prepared by author based on BCRA data)

representatives of these chambers, the officials accused them of financing producers to delay sales of their harvest:

> Their argument was: 'Eighty percent of production is in the hands of 5,000 or 6,000 producers; there are so few of them that you could invite them all to your children's weddings,' said Moreno [laughter]. 'So you go and tell them to sell, because if they don't, we'll revoke your temporary soybean import regime, which allows you to bring soybeans from Paraguay, process them, and export them without tariffs.' We replied, 'Look, we're not friends with the producers like you say—they sell if they want; we don't finance them.' And well... a week later they removed the regime because producers were still stockpiling their crops.[27]

Since 2004, exporters had benefited from a temporary import regime that allowed them to bring in soybeans from Paraguay for processing in Argentina and re-export without paying export duties. In April 2009, Echegaray announced the cancellation of that benefit, justifying it as

[27] Interview with representatives of CIARA.

an effort "to redirect exporters' purchasing power toward local production, which has millions of tons stored in silo bags," with the aim of "stimulating the economy and ensuring the inflow of foreign currency." According to private sources, around five million tons of the 2008 harvest were in storage; Echegaray also claimed that the soybean industry had evaded US$ 421 million in VAT and income tax in 2008 alone.[28] This episode represents a key precedent in the government's strategy to counter—albeit with varying degrees of success depending on the macroeconomic context—the structural power of traders and ensure the flow of foreign exchange through regulatory threats, a strategy analyzed in greater detail in the third episode of this chapter.

Taken as a whole, this episode reveals several features of power relations in Argentina's export agriculture sector. First, it underscores the fragmentation of the agro-export value chain and the frequent divergence of economic and political interests among its different segments. The government is able to impose export duties because these primarily affect the weakest link in the chain—agricultural producers—whose vulnerability is evident both in their relationship with the state and with other chain actors unaffected by such duties. This weakness is both structural and instrumental.

The 2008 conflict represented an exception to this long-standing weakness. Producers succeeded in inflicting significant political and economic damage on the government and in halting further increases in export duties. This was made possible by an unprecedented level of cohesion among producer associations, but also by the crucial role played by exporting firms, whose coordinated actions were key to the protest's effectiveness. Thanks to this cohesion, the sector's structural power as a supplier of foreign exchange translated into political leverage. However, this cohesion did not translate into institutional representation. As studies focused on instrumental power have pointed out, efforts to build a representative body encompassing the entire value chain faced considerable challenges due to heterogeneous interests and strategies. One of the most salient differences lies in the fact that, unlike the confrontational stance taken by producers, exporters tended to avoid direct conflict with the government.

[28] Crettaz, J. (2009) "*La soja. El yuyo que se volvió obsesión*" ("Soybeans. The weed that became an obsession"), *La Nación*, April 8, 2009.

Beyond blocking Resolution 125 in Congress, the 2008 protest politically weakened the government and constrained its approach to the sector between 2008 and 2015. In the aftermath of the conflict, the government sought to demobilize producers through selective compensation and by fragmenting the ruralist front, favoring producers in their disputes with other chain actors without altering the overall rate of fiscal extraction from the sector (Freytes and O'Farrell 2017).

Second, this episode sheds light on a dimension of the conflict that has received little attention in the literature: the critical role played by trader support in sustaining the producers' commercialization strike. The disruption of foreign exchange inflows became a central concern for the government, generating exchange rate pressures amid the 2008 global financial crisis, growing capital flight, and currency devaluations among key trading partners. While methodological challenges make it difficult to determine the extent to which the halt in foreign exchange inflows resulted from market-based decisions (driven by devaluation expectations) or from coordinated actions (aimed at pressuring and weakening the government), from the state's perspective the protest's economic impact was increasingly alarming. Evidence gathered through interviews suggests that trader support did not reflect an alignment with producers in opposing export taxes, but rather a strategic opportunity to weaken the government out of concern that further regulations might directly harm their interests. Since traders are not directly affected by export duties, they only ally with producers when it is strategically beneficial for their own narrow segment of the chain.

Finally, this episode marks a turning point in the government's relationship with the export segment. As a result of the conflict, proposals to expand state control over grain exports began to circulate within different factions of the ruling coalition. Government officials noted that tensions with this segment intensified due to traders' alleged financial support for producers during the commercialization strike.[29] Representatives from grain storage firms—a key intermediary between producers and exporters—suggested that, following the Resolution 125 conflict, "the center of gravity of agricultural policy shifted from producers to exporters." For their part, export firms stated that the government had become more hostile and deepened its interventionist stance. In the

[29] Interview with former President of the BCRA.

words of a representative of CIARA (a processors' association) and CEC (an exporters' association): "That whole period was a revolution for the sector—there were constant regulatory changes, much more bureaucracy, and increased scrutiny to obtain export permits."[30]

It is important to highlight that this adversarial relationship with the government coexisted with the high profit margins discussed in the regulatory outcomes section of this work. As in other sectors of the economy, business discontent with the Kirchner administrations stemmed less from profitability levels than from what firms perceived as excessive state interference in business decisions, the inefficiencies this created, and the fear of retaliation for criticizing or challenging government policies. An additional source of discomfort was the public exposure brought by the conflict. Historically committed to maintaining a low profile and presenting themselves as neutral, apolitical actors (Morgan 1979), traders were thrust into the public spotlight and forced to revise their communications strategy. They began professionalizing their institutional relations departments—previously managed directly by company presidents—and established more consistent contact with the media and government officials to mitigate reputational damage.[31]

As explained in connection with the next two policy episodes, the exporters' fears of increased state intervention proved well-founded. Within the administration, two positions emerged: some advocated for targeted controls to compensate producers and discipline traders, while others promoted more stable and ambitious mechanisms of state control over grain trade. In the following section, I analyze why the latter approach failed to gain traction in the government's agenda.

6.3.2 *Traders Exclude State-Control Projects from the Agenda*

From 2008 onward, various sectors within the ruling coalition intensified initiatives to increase state control over grain trade. Rising international food prices exerted upward pressure on domestic prices,[32] while capital

[30] Interviews with representatives of CIARA and with a manager of a multinational exporting firm (trader).

[31] Interviews with a manager of Institutional relations of a multinational exporting firm (trader).

[32] Inflation averaged 22% annually during the second term, between 2008 and 2011, and 28% in the third term, between 2012 and 2015 (Kulfas, 2019:48–49).

flight and exchange rate instability deepened. Several proposals were analyzed with a view to relieving these tensions through the establishment of an agency empowered to intervene directly in the market—from recreating the old *Junta National de Granos* (National Grain Board (JNG)) to expanding ONCCA's mandate—but failed to advance in either the Executive or the Legislature. This episode shows that this result is explained by the structural power of traders, given by their capacity to supply foreign currency and influence Argentine exports at destination ports.

During this period, multiple state-intervention proposals emerged, aimed at ensuring better prices for producers and a stable flow of foreign currency. Four were introduced in Congress by legislators from both *Frente para la Victoria* (FPV) and the opposition, while others were debated within the Ministry of Agriculture. Despite their varying institutional designs, all proposed a state entity with powers to intervene in markets: to buy and sell commodities, set price floors, sanction collusive or oligopolistic practices, enhance market transparency, and build public grain handlers and ports.[33]

One of these proposals was debated in the Agriculture Committee of the Chamber of Deputies and received a favorable report in May 2008, during the rural protests. The proposal, promoted by the ruling party, sought to create a state agency with the capacity to intervene in the grain market. It was spearheaded by the Committee's chair, Deputy Alberto Cantero Gutiérrez of the FPV, and was co-signed by several congressmen from the governing coalition. The initiative aimed to broaden ONCCA's powers to include storage, redistribution, commercialization, and the capacity to intervene in the market under specific circumstances, when distortions were deemed to exist. To this end, it proposed the creation of the *Ente Nacional de Promoción y Control Comercial Agropecuario y Agroalimentario* (National Agency for the Promotion and Control of Agricultural, Farming products and Agri-food Trade (ENPYCCAA)). This body would have the authority to sanction unfair, monopolistic, or oligopolistic practices; to monitor and control exports; and to implement measures (such as promotions, incentives, and tax benefits) to ensure food security. Its capacity for intervention went beyond the buying and selling of grain and encompassed the entire food chain. Key objectives included guaranteeing food availability for the domestic market and protecting

[33] For a detailed and technical analysis of these projects, *see* López (2010).

small producers. The proponents of the project argued, among other things, that the majority of the main wheat-exporting countries have either a state-owned enterprise (Russia, Ukraine, India, China, Turkey) or a farmer-controlled agency (Canada) that actively intervenes in foreign trade to protect farmers' incomes and ensure domestic food supply.[34] In this regard, Argentina was one of the countries that had advanced the most in deregulating the sector, with the dissolution of the JNG (Sbatella and Barrera 2011).

The ENPYCCAA bill was introduced in Congress in July 2007, but it was never debated, as it was deemed politically sensitive during an election year.[35] Opposition sectors expressed suspicion as to the government's intentions, interpreting its timing—coinciding with negotiations on Resolution 125 with the Mesa de Enlace—as a threat to producers.[36] Others saw it as a radical escalation in the government's anti-inflation approach.[37] Although it received a favorable opinion in the Agriculture Committee—backed by 20 of its 34 members—and preference motions on May 7 and 21 and June 11, the bill never reached the floor.

Producers' responses to the initiative were divided. According to Cantero Gutiérrez, it had the support of the *Federación Agraria Argentina* (FAA), Agricultores Federados Argentinos (AFA), and the Asociaciòn de Cooperativas Argentinas (ACA), since "it guaranteed producers a price and the country protection from depending on currency inflows from exporters." The SRA, however, was strongly opposed. Its president stated that "the new agency would have near-unlimited powers to control prices, buy, and sell. We oppose it with full force; it is yet another turn toward the interventionism that has harmed us."

[34] In the United States there are mechanisms of cross-subsidies between the Commodity Credit Corporation (CCC) and the state agency Farm Service Agency (FSA) that controls production quotas, sets reference prices and distributes subsidies. In Russia there is the state company United Grain Company, which since 2012 belongs 51% to the Russian state and 49% to the Russian capital group Ssuma, which owns the main ports. (Zeolla, 2014).

[35] Interview with Alberto Cantero Gutiérrez, congressman (FPV Córdoba), president of the Agriculture Commission of the Chamber of Deputies 2007–2009.

[36] La Nación 05/13/2008 https://www.lanacion.com.ar/politica/la-oposicion-rechazo-el-nuevo-ente-de-control-agrario-nid1012082 La Nación 04/25/2008 https://www.lanacion.com.ar/politica/se-moreniza-el-gabinete-nid1007276.

[37] La Nación 05/13/2008 https://www.lanacion.com.ar/politica/buscan-crear-un-poderoso-organismo-de-control-nid1012031.

Ernesto Ambrosetti,[38] chief economist at the SRA, echoed this, saying the ENPYCCAA "distorts prices and generates losses for producers. Even if it intends to defend small producers, its effect is to lower prices for everyone."[39] The proposal's timing—during a contentious conflict—sparked distrust even within the FAA, whose leaders threatened to "hit the roads" should it pass.[40]

One of the bill's sponsors claimed that major export firms blocked its treatment by offering the government to liquidate US$ 4–5 billion in foreign currency in exchange for its withdrawal: "Export companies met with a government official and offered to liquidate exports in a month when dollars were needed, but only if the attempt to create state-controlled agro-food trade was dropped."[41] As previously analyzed, at that time the Secretary of Commerce was negotiating with traders to pressure producers to sell their harvest—while exchange rate stability became one of the government's major concerns.

The bill also lacked the support of Secretary of Commerce Guillermo Moreno, the most influential official of the period. In addition to deeming it unnecessary, Moreno highlighted a structural limitation in the global food trade: transactions are no longer carried out between countries, but between multinational corporate subsidiaries. In his view, a state trading agency would lack commercial counterparts: "It was unnecessary and inefficient, because country-to-country trade no longer exists. Cargill Argentina's soybean client is Cargill China. Who would the JNG sell to?" Moreno maintained that the real dispute was over export taxes: "If the State wanted to capture oligarchic windfall profits, it would do so via export taxes. That was the real conflict… nothing else."[42]

[38] April 14, 2008 La Nación editorial https://www.lanacion.com.ar/politica/reflotan-un-proyecto-polemico-para-el-agro-nid1004171.

[39] Interview with Ernesto Ambrosetti (SRA).

[40] "If the rumors about a possible nationalization of foreign grain trade, or the creation of an agency to intervene by buying and selling cereals to set reference prices, are indeed confirmed, there will be an immediate reaction on the roads," warned Alfredo Bel, technical secretary of the organization and close ally of Alfredo De Angeli. La Nación, 03/01/2009. https://www.lanacion.com.ar/politica/el-campo-expectante-y-ansioso-por-el-mensaje-presidencial-nid1104384.

[41] Not for attribution interview with a sponsor of the bill and part of the governing coalition.

[42] Interview with Guillermo Moreno.

Traders' instrumental power was also decisive. Sources close to ENPYCCAA reported that the FPV senator for Córdoba (2003–2009), Roberto Urquía—owner of Aceitera General Deheza (AGD), one of the country's leading exporters—was instrumental in blocking the bill.[43] Besides their representation at the National Senate, these companies were also major donors to both leading political factions.[44]

Following that failed reform attempt, new proposals emerged. As inflationary and currency pressures deepened, the Executive revisited initiatives from factions within its coalition aimed at increasing state control over grain trade.[45] The proposal that advanced furthest was promoted by Corriente Agraria Nacional y Popular (CANPO),[46] an organization backed by Agriculture Minister Julián Domínguez to provide a counterweight to the *Mesa de Enlace*. CANPO comprised agrarian cooperatives, technical experts, rural workers, and family-farming organizations. Launched on April 20, 2011 at Luna Park arena with 10,000 attendees and President Cristina Fernández delivering the keynote address, CANPO's agenda included strengthening cooperativism, regulating land

[43] Interview with a representative of the organizations that promoted the ENPYCCAA.

[44] Ruiz (2020); https://www.lanacion.com.ar/politica/roberto-urquia-principal-aportante-campana-alberto-fernandez-nid2333812 InfoBase 23/10/2019 https://www.infobae.com/politica/2019/10/23/un-empresario-que-apuesta-publicamente-al-triunfo-de-alberto-fernandez-fue-el-mayor-aportante-de-la-campana-de-mauricio-macri/.

[45] "The multinationals of the sector were one of the main actors that forced the devaluation carried out in January 2014. … The already recurring situation of having to negotiate with the industry and grain companies the flow of foreign currency liquidation caused several sectors with heterodox economic views to refloat new mechanisms of intervention in the grain market and foreign trade, to avoid any scenario of speculation." Premici (2014) https://www.pagina12.com.ar/diario/economia/2-258163-2014-10-23.html.

[46] The project was triggered by a visit from Chinese authorities to Argentina in 2011, during which they presented their strategic economic plan to both government officials and representatives of the agricultural sector. As part of that plan, they emphasized their goal of building long-term business relationships, which, they argued, could only be achieved through State-to-State agreements. They explained that negotiating with private companies—such as closing a deal with Nidera in Argentina—posed legal risks, especially if political shifts in countries like the United States led to trade restrictions, as exemplified by the hypothetical scenario of Trump ordering a trade block with China. This created a challenge for Argentina, which at the time lacked a state agency or enterprise capable of engaging in such bilateral trade. In response, members of CANPO developed a proposal, which they brought directly to the Office of the President. Interview with the national coordinator of CANPO.

foreign ownership ("to protect jurisdiction over land and retain it in Argentine hands"), and approving a new legal framework for rural labor—legislation proposed the previous year and passed months later.[47] Just a few months earlier, the Minister of Agriculture had stated that he aimed for cooperatives such as ACA and AFA to command up to 30% of foreign grain trade.[48] He described them as the "main allies of his administration" and "strategic partners" for channeling rural finance, which justified advocating for a greater share of export quotas to be allocated to them.[49]

According to the authors, the initiative had technical backing within the Ministry of Economy, particularly from officials close to the then-Secretary of Economic Policy, Axel Kicillof. However, it was opposed by Moreno and officials within the Ministry of Agriculture. Ultimately, Moreno convinced the president that more modern mechanisms existed than traditional boards or agencies.[50] As analyzed in the next section, Moreno was confident he could control domestic prices and ensure foreign exchange inflows through one-on-one agreements with multinational corporations. An additional obstacle to these proposals was the confrontational relationship between the Kirchner administration and producers. Since such a state-owned grain-trading company requires trust-based relationships with producers to source its goods, there was a risk that producers would refuse to sell to the State.

In February 2014, amid negotiations with traders over foreign currency settlement in a sensitive macroeconomic environment, Chief of Cabinet Jorge Capitanich declared that the economic team was evaluating multiple initiatives aimed at strengthening state intervention in grain trade. He noted, "There are multiple initiatives, from a commercial association to the revitalization of the *Junta Nacional de Granos*." The main concern was currency inflows: "What we intend is to verify a methodology

[47] House of Government Press Release https://www.casarosada.gob.ar/informacion/archivo/6258-lanzamiento-de-canpo-en-el-luna-park-palabras-de-la-presidenta-cristina-fernandez.

[48] 04/21/2011 https://www.pagina12.com.ar/diario/economia/2-166686-2011-04-21.html.

[49] Interviews with a minister, a secretary, and an undersecretary from the Ministry of Agriculture.

[50] Interview with a representative of CANPO.

that allows us to guarantee a volume of liquidations compatible with the balance of payments."[51]

That same week, Senator Silvina García Larraburu (FPV-PJ, Río Negro) introduced a bill to establish a new national grain board intended to regulate trade in grains, oilseeds, and their by-products; ensure internal supply and price stability regardless of external market fluctuations; and discourage monocultures. In line with the 2007–2008 ENPYCCAA, the bill proposed setting minimum prices and export quotas and empowered Executive intervention in domestic and foreign trade "in defense of production or when market regulation necessitates it."[52] That same week various FPV deputies expressed support for increased state control of foreign trade. Congressman Carlos Kunkel, for example, stated: "the government must promote the creation of a National Grain Board, not to monopolize, but to guarantee that the producer has the option: either sell to private grain firms as now, or choose a route through Coninagro or cooperatives, partnering with the State." These initiatives also had backing from intellectuals close to the government, advocating progress in "mechanisms providing for state-managed foreign trade."[53]

Nevertheless, officials opposed to these proposals warned of multinational corporations' power to undermine Argentine exports in destination markets. The Ministry of Agriculture submitted a report to the Presidency explaining that, since trade was now primarily between multinationals and subsidiaries rather than between states, traders could penalize Argentina by halting purchases:

> There are global monopolies. You must transact worldwide where multinational corporations operate. You can propose something like a grain board, but if you want to sell to Uganda, the buyer there is Cargill. In Rotterdam, you need to beg ADM to unload, the same firm you challenged in Argentina. If they can't hurt you here, they will hurt you somewhere

[51] https://www.pagina12.com.ar/diario/economia/2-239605-2014-02-11.html.

[52] https://www.infocampo.com.ar/piden-la-creacion-de-una-junta-nacional-de-granos/.

[53] https://www.iprofesional.com/comex/180144-dolar-cerealeras-devaluacion-Por-el-momento-no-hay-proyecto-para-una-Junta-Nacional-de-Granos-afirmo-Capitanich.

else. We [the Ministry of Agriculture] stopped the grain board project and prepared a report explaining this to the president.[54]

An undersecretary of agriculture added that the Argentine State also depended on the infrastructure and logistics controlled by these traders, a decisive factor when evaluating any intervention project. This explained why, even when export permits (ROEs) reduced traders' market share, their operations remained largely unaffected: smaller exporters who received permits ended up selling to them at Argentine ports or to their subsidiary networks in Uruguay.

[Domestic cooperatives] ACA and AFA sell some domestically to big exporters and some abroad to Bunge or Dreyfus subsidiaries at the destination country. They always end up selling to the multinationals, who own the ships, transport, and insurance. Argentina doesn't own a single ship. That's why the multinationals didn't complain, because they still received the goods—themselves or their subsidiaries.[55]

Finally, the Chief of Cabinet ruled out the possibility of the government advancing any of the initiatives proposed by legislators, noting that one of the problems was that the State "does not have either the ports or the infrastructure that the agency once had."[56] Raúl Dente, president of the *Federación de Acopiadores* and former head of the *Junta Nacional de Granos*, denounced "the absurdity" of such projects, stating: "That's when several people started floating the idea of reviving the grain board. It's absurd, because back when the board existed, trade happened between countries. [Now] you depend on exporters because they have the infrastructure to export—almost all the ports are privatized. You can't 'kill off' your competitors, go up against Dreyfus or Bunge, because of the infrastructure."[57]

Javier Preciado Patiño, undersecretary of Agricultural Markets in the Ministry of Agriculture, Livestock and Fisheries in 2020 and coordinator

[54] Interview with a high-ranking official from the Ministry of Agriculture during the 2013–2015 period.

[55] Interview with an Undersecretary of Agriculture.

[56] https://www.infocampo.com.ar/piden-la-creacion-de-una-junta-nacional-de-granos/.

[57] Personal interview with Raúl Dente.

of agrarian policy for the PJ,[58] identified in 2014 the same structural constraint: the dominant role of multinational corporations (MNCs) in the Chinese market and in ocean logistics. He noted that while it could be possible to establish state-to-state agreements with countries like China, these could only play a complementary role in the current structure of global trade:

> There are structural factors in agricultural commodities trading that make it very difficult today to think about nationalizing grain trade. Cargill, a U.S. company in the business for more than 150 years, began operating in China in the 1970s and accelerated in the 1990s. It now operates four soybean processing plants—three in Guangdong and one in Jiangsu—and engages in animal nutrition, starches, and sweeteners. It employs more than 7,000 people there. But that's not all. Cargill plays a key role in ocean logistics, skillfully moving all types of bulk goods around the world. Alongside Cargill, ADM, Bunge, and Dreyfus also operate in China, where these companies control 80% of the country's soybean crushing capacity. In short, considering that these companies are now approaching 200 years of experience and have managed to survive all kinds of political, economic, and social upheavals, it is time to reflect — or rather, to rethink — Argentina's limitations when it comes to intervening in grain trading. It is conceivable that China may be interested in some kind of state-to-state agreement with Argentina, but such an arrangement would, in any case, be complementary to — not a replacement for — its existing supply system. At best, it might serve as a framework under which the rest of the operations would be arbitrated, but so far, this intention — expressed in more than one bilateral meeting — has yet to translate into concrete actions.

It is worth noting that, as mentioned earlier, most food-exporting countries have maintained some form of state board, agency, or company, proving that such experiences are feasible in today's international trade organization. However, the analysis presented here exposes the structural limits of re-nationalization projects. Once the sector was deregulated and control of trade transferred to multinationals, reversing that situation—as various testimonies indicate—entails risks that could seriously jeopardize the country's export flows.

[58] https://www.agrositio.com.ar/noticia/152936-granos-incluso-china-se-basa-en-el-aprovisionamiento-de-las-grandes-traders-globales-por-javier-preciado-patino.

Finally, even proponents of these initiatives acknowledged an additional obstacle: the open confrontation between the Kirchner administration and producers, the alleged beneficiaries of any such state entity. "No one would participate; it would be an absolutely coercive state agency... it is based on them selling to you [the State]... and people don't trust it. Those who support it represent only 15% of production—the smaller FAA members and family farmers."[59]

Following the failure of attempts to increase state control over grain trade, the strategy advanced by Guillermo Moreno prevailed, featuring a mix of regulatory threats and selective controls, particularly through export-permit allocation. As will be discussed next, these policies managed to redistribute resources in favor of producers and consumers, but their effectiveness diminished as the deterioration of the balance of payments weakened the government's negotiating position *vis-à-vis* the traders.

6.3.3 Export Permits: Structural Power as Conditioned by the Macroeconomic Context

As the government was unable to move forward with stricter state control over grain trade, it sought alternative mechanisms to impose costs on traders and to enhance its bargaining power—whether to induce foreign currency inflows or to facilitate redistribution toward producers and consumers. This subsection delves into the specific instruments deployed: export permits (ROEs), tax reimbursement mechanisms (such as VAT refunds), and various administrative procedures aimed at affecting firms' export operations.

Beyond the distributive effects discussed in previous sections, these tools proved effective in strengthening the government's power in particular circumstances, strengthening the government's power on occasion. However, such effectiveness was inherently limited: the very implementation of these tools could generate negative repercussions for the broader economy and jeopardize export flows. As a result, their utility was directly contingent on the availability of foreign exchange reserves at the Central Bank of Argentina (BCRA).

This analysis implies that the structural power of traders—based on their control over foreign exchange inflows—fluctuates over time,

[59] Interview with a representative of CANPO.

depending on the macroeconomic environment. In a context where the domestic economy is better positioned to generate foreign exchange, the state gains leverage in its negotiations with those who control such flows. Moreover, as long as the Central Bank maintains an adequate stock of reserves, it can intervene in currency markets to dampen exchange rate pressures. During such periods, the government's capacity to impose costs on grain traders—whether through regulatory threats or selective incentives—increases, while the credibility of traders' own retaliatory threats is simultaneously diminished. These instruments raise the cost firms face in the event of conflict with the government, thereby reducing their structural power.

One instrument employed to secure a steady inflow of foreign currency consisted in delaying the reimbursement of export-related VAT credits. The Secretary of Commerce, Guillermo Moreno, would ask exporters to advance their foreign currency liquidations. When companies replied that they lacked the necessary funds, he would suggest they request advances from their parent companies or commercial banks. Exporters in turn claimed they could not do so while the state was itself delaying VAT refunds. In practice, this dynamic resulted in Moreno summoning traders every six to eight months and demanding that they commit to liquidating a fixed amount of foreign exchange per month in exchange for the release of VAT reimbursements. For each dollar liquidated, the state would return a specific amount of pesos in VAT refunds—an amount that varied according to context and exchange rate fluctuations.[60]

The government's most significant bargaining instrument, however, was the system of export permits. As described above, the ROE (Registro de Operaciones de Exportación) system—introduced in 2008—replaced the previous system of export declarations (DJVE). The main difference was that permits now required approval by the Secretariat of Domestic Trade, based on criteria which, according to complaints from affected firms, were not always explicit or objective, and were often subject to arbitrary or unjustified delays. As with the VAT refund mechanism, the grain export chamber CIARA acknowledged that the need for state approval

60 Definitive exports are exempt from VAT payment. As exporters pay VAT when purchasing merchandise, the law establishes that the state must reimburse this payment. Fairfield analyzes the same dynamic of VAT negotiation for foreign currency at the exit of the 2002 crisis (Fairfield, 2015: 201).

of ROE requests placed companies in a structurally disadvantageous position. Chamber authorities noted: "The threat was always the closure of exports. [The Secretary of Commerce] would call you and say: 'You have to do such-and-such.' And if you didn't comply, you knew exactly what the threat was: halting exports. Eventually, he didn't even need to say it—you just knew he had the power. He simply wouldn't approve your ROE."[61]

As analyzed in the subsection on distributive outcomes, it is important to note that the ROE mechanism generated a transfer of resources from producers to traders. Traders' discomfort with the permit system was primarily political: depending on the arbitrary decisions of a state official in order to operate heightened their uncertainty and placed them in a more vulnerable position. The most vocal opponents of the export permit regime, however, were agricultural producers—particularly small- and medium-sized farmers—who were disadvantaged in price negotiations over their crops. Their protests targeted both the government and the traders. Illustratively, during a protest in 2011, Eduardo Buzzi of the Federación Agraria denounced what he framed as a modern-day equivalent of the Roca-Runciman Pact[62]: "Let's be clear: if there was ever a Roca–Runciman Pact in Argentina—which did so much harm to the country—today we are witnessing a Moreno–Cargill agreement," referring to the Secretary of Commerce and the U.S.-based trading firm.[63]

On other occasions, in order to induce exporters to comply with its demands, the government resorted to threats of shutting down exports—and found bureaucratic mechanisms to do so. These pressures were used, for instance, to push traders to subsidize a trust fund designed to maintain domestic prices for cooking oil—a program that until then had been financed by the state and managed by the ONCCA.[64] Initially, the

[61] Interview with a representative of CIARA.

[62] The Roca-Runciman Pact is a trade agreement signed in 1933 between Argentina and the then British Empire. It is remembered by a very important part of historiography and politics as an agreement that favored British interests over Argentine ones.

[63] https://www.lacapital.com.ar/economia/se-viene-un-tractorazo-productores-trigueros-frente-la-planta-cargill-rufino-n398219.html.

[64] Interviews with a representative of CIARA and managers of Institutional Relations from two traders.

traders refused to fund the trust.[65] To break the deadlock, the Secretary of Commerce threatened to block oil exports. When traders continued to resist, the Secretariat implemented a regulation requiring that all oil destined for export be certified as "genuine" by a test that could only be performed at the Customs laboratory—which, at that moment, happened to have a broken chromatograph. This effectively blocked oil exports for over twenty days. Since export halts impose significant costs on processing and exporting firms—forcing them to suspend operations as storage tanks fill up—the companies ultimately agreed to take over the subsidies for edible oil, one of the most essential goods in the national consumption basket.[66].

Another key policy area of conflict was taxation. The FPV administrations, characterized by increasing tax burdens (especially in the agricultural sector), clashed with companies frequently accused of tax evasion through profit-shifting schemes involving offshore jurisdictions. In addition to these allegations, these firms also had opportunities for speculative gains and could exploit the legal ambiguities that often emerge during changes in export tax rates (since, as previously noted, traders serve as withholding agents for these duties).[67]

The confrontation escalated with companies initially resisting AFIP regulations aimed at increasing transparency and state oversight of export operations. Tensions grew further when the government sought to collect

[65] The idea that export companies would cover the cost of domestic oil price subsidies first emerged in 2008. Economy Minister Martín Lousteau, the architect of Resolution 125, informed the president of CIARA that the Secretary of Commerce intended to raise export duties to 65%, and that he (Lousteau) was instead proposing a system of sliding-scale export taxes that would result in significantly lower rates. He told them that if they agreed to take responsibility for the oil trust fund, he could block the 65% increase pushed by Moreno and promote his own proposal for variable export duties. After several discussions at the Ministry of Economy, CIARA accepted the proposal, but it was never implemented. Following Lousteau's resignation in March 2008, Moreno revived the proposal and succeeded in getting the exporters to assume responsibility for the subsidies. Interview with CIARA representative.

[66] In the same way, the Secretary of Commerce obtained other contributions from the traders to the economy, such as donations of 50,000 tons of corn for cattle ranchers and pig farmers who had suffered a drought, and about 30 million pesos for those affected by a flood in the city of La Plata. "Everyone contributed because otherwise, they wouldn't give you the ROEs". Interview with a representative of CIARA.

[67] https://www.infobae.com/economia/2020/03/02/como-funciona-la-compleja-operatoria-con-la-que-muchas-grandes-agroexportadoras-evitan-el-pago-de-impuestos-en-el-pais/.

tax debts that traders had accrued due to rising export taxes between 2007 and 2008. In their role as withholding agents, exporters had been able to declare exports at the earlier, lower tax rates while charging producers the updated, higher rates. In November 2007, Congress passed a law—known as the Martínez Raymonda Law—designed to prevent traders from appropriating the difference. Armed with this legal tool, the government accused exporters of unlawfully pocketing US$ 1.7 billion between November 2007 and March 2008.

Between 2008 and 2012, the tax agency (AFIP) employed a wide range of coercive tactics to collect this debt, including fiscal inspections, export registration suspensions, and delays in VAT reimbursements. Between March and May 2011, AFIP suspended the export licenses of firms including Cargill, Bunge, ADM, Dreyfus, Toepfer, Nidera, and Oleaginosa Moreno. These companies were accused of engaging in illegal fiscal practices such as submitting falsified sales declarations, operating through shell companies to purchase grain, and artificially overstating domestic costs in order to reduce taxable income or claim undue tax credits. AFIP also warned that firms failing to regularize their situation would be permanently excluded from the export register. Although the suspensions did not completely halt their operations, they did result in the loss of key fiscal benefits.

These governmental interventions proved effective in specific moments, helping to secure much needed foreign currency inflows and to recover a portion of the tax debt. However, beginning in 2013, the growing dependence on export liquidations gradually shifted the balance of power in negotiations in favor of the companies. The change in context began around 2011, when global commodity demand and prices entered a downward phase. This shift was compounded by Argentina-specific dynamics: a widening trade deficit in the energy sector, and a growing inability to access international credit markets. At the same time, the government persisted in its efforts to avoid currency devaluation. As a result, by 2010 the Argentine peso had appreciated significantly in real terms compared to the currencies of other countries (see Fig. 6.4), making it increasingly difficult for the economy to accumulate foreign currency.

The impact began to be felt directly on the Central Bank's international reserves. By the end of 2012, reserves had reached US$ 45 billion, a record high during the Kirchners administrations. However, beginning in 2013, they began to fall sharply: from US$ 37 billion in June to US$ 30

Fig. 6.4 Real Effective Exchange Rate, REER (2003–2015) (*Source* Prepared by author based on BCRA data)

billion in December of that year, eventually dropping below US$ 28 billion by December 2014.

In an effort to curb currency speculation by exporters, Resolution 142 was introduced in April 2012. This measure significantly shortened the timeframe allowed for foreign currency liquidation, targeting in particular the grain and oilseed export complex, by reducing the period from 180 to 15 days. The measure was justified on the grounds that, in many cases, "the timeframes set for the entry of foreign currency were not aligned with the operational dynamics required by these sectors" (Carrillo, 2017).[68] In response to complaints from some companies regarding operational difficulties, the government issued a new resolution a month later, extending the period to 30 days.

[68] *Página 12*, 21/01/2017 https://www.pagina12.com.ar/15343-con-mas-tiempo-para-poder-especular.

In June of that same year, export pre-financing plummeted—these operations function in practice as advances on currency liquidation—further weakening the stability of foreign exchange flows.[69] Rather than obtaining external financing to purchase grain—which requires converting dollars into pesos to pay producers—traders turned to local financing, taking advantage of lower domestic interest rates. This shift made sense in a context of accelerating inflation, negative real interest rates, and growing expectations of devaluation. Under stable macroeconomic conditions, external financing would typically be cheaper. However, in a context marked by inflation and anticipated devaluation, it becomes rational to take on debt in pesos and delay dollar liquidation in hopes that the government will be forced to devalue the currency.

In 2013, expectations of devaluation intensified, and with them, the tug-of-war between traders and the government escalated. Central Bank officials from that period recall that this was the year when the practice of stockpiling grain became particularly visible:

> You see these actors throughout all those standoffs—and especially during the final phase of the Kirchner administration—quite clearly sitting on their stocks and refusing to liquidate. [...] In 2013 the standoff was particularly palpable. The expectation of devaluation accompanied us throughout those years. We had the capacity to endure it, but one cannot ignore that such resilience exists only so long as the objective conditions allow it—and those conditions were marked by a shortage of dollars. [...] The objective data show that starting in 2011, we began to experience balance of payments imbalances, and when we ceased to be net exporters of oil to become net importers, the global crisis became more acute in terms of commodity prices, global trade, etc. The trade surplus shrank, we moved into deficit, and capital flight took off.[70]

The fluctuation of structural power in relation to the macroeconomic context is evident in that, as one Central Bank authority explained, one option considered to induce exporters to change their behavior was the

[69] Mercedes Marco del Pont, personal interview, 03/16/2017. See also: "Comercio exterior: reemplazan créditos en dólares por créditos en pesos", *Ámbito Financiero*, June 26, 2012. https://www.ambito.com/edicion-impresa/comercio-exterior-reemplazan-creditos-dolares-pesos-n3742861 and https://www.pagina12.com.ar/diario/economia/2-232777-2013-11-03.html.

[70] Interview with an authority from the Central Bank.

threat of removing specific benefits. In this particular case, exporters could have been denied access to public pre-export financing loans from Banco Nación. However, this course of action was ultimately not pursued due to the high economic costs it would have entailed at such a sensitive time:

> What could be done to ensure the liquidation of foreign currency? You could resort to extreme measures, like having Banco Nación stop lending to those actors, but those are highly disruptive decisions. Such repressive measures have real costs for the economy, which is why the rules of the game should be clarified from the outset—during the good times. It's no use trying to regulate during the bad times. To ensure the governability of the foreign exchange market, we need to rethink the institutions that regulate it.[71]

Between 2013 and 2015, a shift can be observed in the government's stance toward traders: the tax agency (AFIP), the Central Bank, and the Secretariat of Commerce, which had previously adopted a confrontational posture, began to adopt a more conciliatory approach. Representatives of the export sector themselves acknowledge that by 2014 and 2015, administrative controls and restrictions on the allocation of export permits had been significantly relaxed.[72] At the beginning of 2013, the government reached an agreement with Cargill under which the company received 77% of the wheat export permits, on the condition that it would liquidate foreign currency in advance. A few months later, in September, the Secretary of Commerce proposed that traders purchase bonds issued as part of a tax amnesty initiative—the so-called BAADE bonds—aimed at recovering undeclared foreign assets and alleviating the shortage of foreign currency. In exchange for purchasing US$ 500 million in bonds, the

[71] Interview with an authority from the Central Bank.

[72] Interview with representatives of CIARA.

government offered a preferential exchange rate.[73] However, after several weeks of negotiations, exporters rejected the proposal.

Following the failure of this measure—which also faced opposition from the Central Bank—alternative strategies were pursued to guarantee the inflow of foreign currency, including regulatory adjustments to ease the requirements for currency entry.[74] At the same time, the new Secretary of Commerce, who replaced Moreno in December 2013, acknowledged that his first order of business was to sit down with traders and negotiate the early liquidation of export revenues.[75] Regarding outstanding tax liabilities, the government also scaled back its pressure beginning in 2013. More than 50% of the debt remained unpaid or became subject to litigation. AFIP succeeded in collecting around US$ 350 million from a revised total of US$ 700 million. Only three companies paid the full amount owed, while twenty others made partial payments and pursued legal action to avoid paying the rest.

In sum, this third subsection demonstrates that the dynamics and structural power tied to the control of foreign currency are highly dependent on the macroeconomic context. During a crisis in the external sector, the State's need for foreign currency intensifies, thereby increasing the structural power of the traders. The source of this power can be exogenous—such as a negative external shock—or endogenous—for example, an expansive government policy that creates foreign currency shortages. In other words, structural power is always present, but in times of foreign currency scarcity, it becomes a greater constraint on government action.

[73] https://www.cronista.com/economiapolitica/Marco-del-Pont-Y-Lorenzino-vs.-Moreno-Y-Kicillof-la-pelea-que-ya-nadie-oculta-20131025-0048.html. "For the Central Bank, this operation bordered on scandalous. Had it been approved, it would have benefited grain companies like Cargill and Bunge & Born [...]. The government would, in effect, have created a dual exchange rate system for a handful of companies involving US$ 500 million. *See also* https://www.iprofesional.com/finanzas/172325-banco-central-empresas-baade-A-traves-de-una-circular-Marco-del-Pont-frusto-la-negociacion-que-llevaba-Moreno-con-las-cerealeras.

[74] https://www.cronista.com/finanzasmercados/-El-BCRA-forzo-A-cerealeras-A-liquidar-divisas-Y-compro-us-40-millones-20131108-0052.html. *See also* https://www.infobae.com/2013/11/04/1521151-el-banco-central-flexibilizo-sus-normas-que-los-exportadores-entren-mas-dolares-al-pais/.

[75] Interview with the Secretary of Commerce in the 2014–2015 period.

CHAPTER 7

Environmental Regulations: GMOs and Agrochemicals

7.1 Actors and Power Resources

This chapter analyzes environmental regulations on agricultural production in Argentina, specifically regarding the use of GMOs and agrochemicals. As we will see, environmental regulations in Argentine agriculture tend to be flexible. This leniency is explained by the central role of the technological package—glyphosate-resistant transgenic soy—in the agro-export model, which causes the regulations to follow a commercial logic: in short, the prevailing rationale is not based on assessing the sustainability of production, environmental protection, or public health, but rather on ensuring access to international markets.

This analysis begins from the premise that environmental policy is also a distributive policy (Merlinsky, 2013; Alcañiz and Gutierrez 2022), in the sense that regulation affects how risks are allocated and how the benefits of the production model are distributed among the population and economic sectors.

Since flexible regulations typically imply lower production costs and greater product demand, the actors who benefit from this flexibility are the companies that commercialize and consume agricultural inputs. The actors who are harmed are the populations exposed to agrochemical contamination. Although it falls outside the scope of this study, other disadvantaged groups include small-scale and family farmers, displaced populations, and those affected by riverine flooding associated with

J. O'Farrell, *Business Power in Agriculture Value Chains*, Latin American Political Economy, https://doi.org/10.1007/978-3-032-06589-6_7

Table 7.1 Actors and power resources

Actors	*Export agricultural chain (especially input companies and agricultural producers)*	*Populations exposed to pollution with agrochemicals*
Power resources	Cohesion of the chain Instrumental power of input companies: access to regulation development Structural power of the chain: provision of foreign exchange and fiscal resources	Weak instrumental and structural power: territorial dispersion and organizational weakness Instrumental power increases when negative effects gain visibility and/or are judicialized

the unregulated expansion of the agricultural frontier and deforestation.[1] Another important distributive effect—though more difficult to attribute—is the cost of environmental degradation, sometimes interpreted as a transfer from future generations to present ones. Some estimates place the economic cost of environmental degradation in Argentina at 8.11% of GDP (World Bank, 2016) (Table 7.1).

In countries like Argentina—characterized by their status as food exporters, middle-income economies, and relatively large agricultural sectors—foreign trade interests (particularly the expansion of export markets) typically take precedence in governmental agendas, even over objectives such as mitigating environmental or public health risks. The greater the country's dependence on agricultural exports (as a share of total exports), the more vulnerable its trade balance and fiscal outcome become to environmental regulations that limit arable land or raise production costs. Additionally, middle-income countries face populations with substantial unmet needs and pressing demands for social policy. In this context, imposing strict environmental regulations or precautionary bans on specific technologies entails significant economic costs, while the environmental benefits are often uncertain. Moreover, whereas costs are

[1] The expansion of the agricultural frontier and the displacements of populations are also associated with increases in poverty in indigenous and peasant communities, which are often forced to abandon their lands and migrate to the cities. "The displacement of the agricultural frontier has forced traditional producers to abandon their lands and move to the cities where they commonly fall into poverty and marginalization if they do not find a job" (World Bank, 2016).

typically clearly assigned to a particular sector and indirectly yet certainly impact public finances, the benefits tend to be more diffuse.

Unlike other regulatory domains examined in this book, the interests of the various segments of the agricultural value chain are closely aligned on environmental matters: input suppliers, producers, and exporters all benefit from lax environmental regulations. Conversely, actors opposed to the large-scale export-oriented agricultural model carry less political weight: smallholder farming focused on the domestic market has historically been marginalized in Argentine agricultural policy, as have environmentalist and consumer advocacy organizations.

For these reasons, the state also has a vested interest in promoting the use of the technological package and, more broadly, agricultural technologies at low cost. State interests seek to strike a balance between encouraging exports and mitigating adverse effects on health and the environment. Relaxing environmental regulations improves the short-term profitability of the production model, thereby allowing the government to make greater headway in other regulatory areas, such as those related to export duties, already discussed.

In other words, in contrast with the policy areas analyzed in previous chapters, this case highlights the structural power of the export-oriented agricultural chain (rather than that of any individual link or company). At the same time, instrumental power also plays a key role: input-supplying firms wield overwhelming influence over decision-making on environmental issues that affect them directly, to the extent of conducting the very studies relied upon in assessing and regulating their technologies.

Among the sources of instrumental power identified in the theoretical framework, those that explain the regulatory outcome in this case include close ties with the Ministry of Agriculture, participation in public–private bodies such as the *Comisión Nacional Asesora de Biotecnología Agropecuaria* (National Advisory Commission on Agricultural Biotechnology (CONABIA)), intermediation by the U.S. Embassy, and the availability of resources to illegally finance public officials and election campaigns. In sum, as discussed in the literature reviewed in Chapter 1, business influence is most effective when firms possess both structural and instrumental power (Fairfield, 2015).

Finally, the mobilization of affected populations and grassroots organizations can mitigate negative impacts through judicial rulings and municipal ordinances, particularly when triggered by crises or public scandals that draw attention to the environmental and health consequences of the production model.

Although a comparison between governments of different political orientations lies beyond the scope of this study, it is important to underscore that regulatory flexibility and the institutional weakness of enforcement agencies have been consistent features across all Argentine administrations since at least the 1990s.

7.2 Policies and Distributive Outcomes

Assessments conducted by government oversight bodies (AGN, 2015), international organizations (World Bank, 2016), NGOs (Di Paola, 2016), and academic research (Newell, 2009; Arancibia, 2013; Lapegna, 2017; Paz Belada, 2017) have reached a common conclusion: Argentina's environmental policy during the analyzed period was characterized by regulatory and institutional weakness, with detrimental effects on both the environment and public health. This section focuses on two regulations directly related to the export-oriented agricultural value chain: biosafety (GMO approvals) and agrochemical management.

7.2.1 Biosafety Regulations

Biosafety regulations, which govern the approval and use of genetically modified organisms (GMOs), encapsulate the tension between minimizing environmental and health risks and maximizing the potential benefits of new genetic events. The decisions of regulators reflect their stance on how risky they believe a given technology is and how to mitigate those risks (Pellegrini, 2013).

In Argentina, the regulatory framework for GMO approvals involves several agencies under the Ministry of Agriculture: the National Advisory Commission on Agricultural Biotechnology (CONABIA), *Servicio Nacional de Sanidad y Calidad Agroalimentaria* (the National Service for Agri-Food Health and Quality (SENASA)), and the National Directorate of Agricultural Markets (la Dirección Nacional de Mercados Agrícolas (DNMA)). CONABIA advises the Ministry on biosafety risks; SENASA oversees human health risks and ensures food safety; and DNMA assesses commercial impacts (Pellegrini, 2013b:186–191). As noted earlier, numerous studies highlight Argentina's flexible regulatory framework (Vara, 2005; Newell, 2009; Poth, 2019; Amin Filomeno, 2013; Pellegrini, 2013).

This flexibility stems from adherence to the principle of "substantial equivalence," which aligns with the U.S. regulatory model. Introduced by the OECD in 1993, this principle requires that a genetically modified food must be demonstrated to be as safe as its conventional counterpart. On the other hand, the European Union follows the "precautionary principle," which holds that even in the absence of full scientific certainty, the mere threat of serious or irreversible environmental damage justifies withholding approval of a genetic event or new technology.[2] Unlike substantial equivalence, the precautionary principle prioritizes unknown risks over specific traits of the product (Pellegrini, 2013).

Unlike Brazil, Argentina does not have a biosafety law and has not ratified the Cartagena Protocol (in force since 2003), which would entail moving toward stricter regulatory standards. During the period analyzed, GMO approval procedures in Argentina became more permissive, particularly after 2009.

7.2.2 *Agrochemical Regulations*

One of the most significant environmental controversies centered on the intensified use of agrochemicals, especially glyphosate. As discussed in Chapter 3, glyphosate consumption increased from 28 million liters in 1997–1998 to 200 million liters in, 2012 (Lapegna, 2019). In, 2015, the WHO classified it as a probable carcinogen. Yet despite these warnings and the central role of agrochemicals in the production model, no national legislation provides for comprehensive management of agrochemical use (Di Paola, 2016; Paz Belada, 2017).

Efforts to reduce exposure risks and regulate use largely failed during this period, with a few exceptions in the form of provincial court rulings and municipal ordinances. The lack of clear national standards

[2] For the most studied comparison between the United States and Europe, some authors argue that differences in biosafety regulations (precautionary principle in Europe and substantial equivalence in the United States) reflect the delay in the efforts of the European biotechnology industry to organize and influence legislation (Newell, 2002; Dunlop, 2000). However, some authors also underline that the European biotechnology industry and the European farmers lean toward regulations that discourage the expansion of GMOs since they cannot compete with their American counterparts (Anderson 2003 cited in Pellegrini, 2013).

led to litigation linking agrochemicals to environmental and public health damage. Some rulings set precedents, including precautionary measures and injunctions (in the form of constitutional *amparo* actions) that imposed restrictions on land and aerial applications (Di Paola, 2016).

The national government's response was limited to initiatives from the Ministry of Health aimed at mitigating poisoning risks and health impacts, without direct regulatory action on agrochemical products themselves, no strengthening of SENASA's role, and no critical examination of the place of these substances in the agricultural model (Gobet, 2018).

These two regulatory approaches do not fully account for the environmental effects of agriculture. Deforestation stands out as another major consequence. From 1990 to, 2015, nearly 20% of Argentina's forested area was cleared (World Bank, 2016), especially in the country's northwest, driven by crop production, livestock ranching, and urban expansion. Since 2001, Argentina has lost an average of 0.67 hectares of forest per minute—the approximate size of a soccer field.[3]

Though outside the central scope of this book, forestry legislation reinforces several points discussed here—particularly the approval of Forest Law No. 26,331 in 2007. Although passed in 2007, it was not enacted until February 2009. The law encountered strong resistance from northern provincial governors, agricultural institutions such as INTA, and members of the Agriculture Secretariat.[4] The strongest opposition came from congressmen representing provinces where soybean-driven deforestation was accelerating, such as Formosa and Salta.

Experts agree the law provides a sound regulatory framework, but implementation has been hindered by insufficient funding and lack of transparency (World Bank, 2016), and enforcement has been inconsistent across provinces (Fernández Milmanda & Garay, 2019).[5] The National Forest Fund created by the law is still under development, the budgetary

[3] Deforestation is associated with a higher occurrence of floods and represents "the greatest threat among natural disasters in Argentina, in terms of economic damage and the number of people affected" (World Bank, 2016).

[4] One interpretation of the government's decision to finally enact the law is that a few weeks before there had been a landslide in the town of Tartagal, in the province of Salta, which had given national visibility to the risks of deforestation, such as floods. In fact, in the announcement of the enactment of the law, the president referred several times to the landslide.

[5] This dynamic is similar to other laws of the period on natural resources, such as for example the Glaciers Law approved in, 2011.

Table 7.2 Summary Environment: policies, distributive outcome, and relevant power resources

Policy	*Distributive Outcome*	*Power Resources*
Biosafety Regulations	Flexible regulations favor biotechnology companies	Chain cohesion Instrumental power of input companies: access to regulatory drafting. Structural power of the chain: provision of foreign currency and fiscal resources
Agrochemical Regulations	Flexible regulations benefit input companies and agricultural producers, while harming populations exposed to contamination	Weakness of negatively affected populations

allocations are inadequate, and public information on fund usage remains limited.

In sum, alongside lax regulations governing critical technologies, export-oriented agricultural production has resulted in numerous negative externalities—including deforestation, population displacement, and deteriorating public health—that have not been addressed. The national government's inaction effectively favors actors in the export agriculture chain, mainly producers and input suppliers.

7.3 Episodes

This section offers a reconstruction and analysis of policymaking episodes in this field and the power dynamics between actors that explain the outcomes (Table 7.2).

7.3.1 Biosafety

As previously noted, Argentina does not have a law specifically regulating genetically modified organisms (GMOs). However, there is an institutional mechanism in place for the approval process of GMOs. In fact, the country was a pioneer both in the commercialization of transgenic seeds and in their regulation.

In 1986, the Argentine government found out that a U.S. institute and a French laboratory were conducting experiments in the country with a recombinant vaccine for immunizing animals. The vaccine had entered Argentina through a diplomatic pouch, which, according to some studies, served as evidence that large laboratories were carrying out experiments in Latin America to test high-risk technologies with potential environmental impacts. Although this case did not involve genetically modified plants, it exposed the legal void in Argentina concerning agricultural and livestock biotechnology research (Pellegrini, 2013b:183–184). More significantly, in the early 1990s, INASE began receiving requests to evaluate genetically modified (GM) seeds but lacked established criteria for their assessment.

It was on the basis of these precedents that the *Comisión Nacional Asesora de Biotecnología Agropecuaria* (CONABIA) was created in 1991. This agency is responsible for evaluating biosafety impacts and formally advises the Ministry of Agriculture on biotechnology matters. Like other bodies, once an assessment of a GMO is conducted, it issues a recommendation that may be favorable or not; however, the final decision on approval lies with the Ministry of Agriculture. Although in practice GMOs are the main focus of its work, CONABIA is dedicated to biotechnology as a whole, not just transgenesis.

A distinctive feature of CONABIA is the prominent role played by representatives of interested companies in its decision-making, which has led some to question whether the companies are, in effect, regulating themselves (Pellegrini, 2013b). The institutional model for this body was the National Seed Commission (CONASE), established in 1973 under the Seed Law, which brings together various actors from the agricultural sector. The public–private composition of CONABIA means that certain seats are reserved for experts nominated by sectoral associations and NGOs, but in practice it operates as a sphere for distributing power among multinational corporations in the sector (Pellegrini, 2013„ 2013b). During the period of interest for this book, there were two representatives from ASA, one from Syngenta and one from Dow Agrosciences; two from CASAFE, one from Monsanto and one from Bayer CropScience; and two from the Agricultural Biotechnology Forum, one from Pioneer and one from Biosidus. Thus, although companies do not formally hold seats, the expert positions within the body are distributed among the largest firms, while local biotechnology companies are few and have limited representation. Public sector actors participating in CONABIA include INTA, CONICET, INASE, SENASA, the Secretariat of the Environment, and the Ministry of Health. Despite their formal presence, it has been noted that either due to their numerical minority or because the commission rejected their precautionary stances, the Secretariat of the Environment played an ineffective role in the body (Poth, 2019).

In, 2015, the *Auditoría general de la Nación* (National Audit Office (AGN)) criticized CONABIA's operations for its lack of transparency (its decisions were not published), for relying on information provided directly by companies without criteria to evaluate its veracity, and for failing to provide for the monitoring of GMO impacts once approved—contrary to the environmental policy principles established by the General Environmental Law (Law No. 25.675). No monitoring is conducted on the social, economic, or environmental impacts of GMO use in agroecosystems either.[6]

The first transgenic seed approved in Argentina was RoundUp Ready soybean, resistant to the herbicide marketed by Monsanto, in 1996. Within a few years, it became the single most important product for the country's exports. The evaluation and approval process for RR soy was criticized not only for its lack of transparency but, more importantly, because the main input for the file consisted of a series of reports prepared by Monsanto that were never verified by the relevant government bodies. Approval was granted without conducting any of the biosafety studies proposed by Ministry of Agriculture officials.[7]

Its approval and swift adoption by the majority of producers triggered no immediate significant protests or resistance from social actors. In this regard, numerous studies highlight the striking absence of opposition to the rapid expansion of transgenic soybean in Argentina (Poth, 2019; Trigo, Chudnovsky & López, 2002), particularly when compared to countries such as Brazil,[8] Mexico, and Peru. This can be

[6] The AGN report also noted that "CONABIA does not carry out experimental analyses on the materials to be approved. The environmental risk assessments are of a documentary type, carried out based on the technical-scientific information submitted by the applicant (the company) as a sworn statement. [...] They are not standardized "the criteria for conducting the verifications carried out by CONABIA regarding the falsity or inaccuracy of the information that the applicant presents.."

[7] https://www.pagina12.com.ar/diario/elpais/1-123932-2009-04-26.html https://www.pagina12.com.ar/diario/elpais/1-124649-2009-05-10.html https://www.pagina12.com.ar/diario/elpais/subnotas/124649-39881-2009-05-10.html

[8] In Brazil, regulations governing GMOs were established in 1995 (Law No. 8.974), and RR soybeans were approved in 1998. However, consumer advocacy organizations (IDEC) and Greenpeace immediately filed a legal challenge questioning the legitimacy of

explained, on one hand, by the fact that most GMO production in Argentina is intended for export rather than domestic consumption; and on the other, by the comparatively weaker presence of actors opposed to the transgenic production model—primarily peasants and environmental organizations—than in other countries in the region.

A key milestone in understanding the commercial logic underpinning biotechnology regulation occurred in 1998, when the European Union established a de facto moratorium that lasted four years, during which it banned the commercialization of genetically modified seeds in Europe unless they had already been approved there. In response to this event, which had significant repercussions for Argentina, the National Directorate of Agricultural Markets (DNMA) was created and incorporated into the GMO evaluation process to assess the commercial impacts of their approval. This marked the consolidation of a "mirror policy," whereby the process came to be guided by its potential effect on exports (Poth, 2019).

Between the late 1990s and early 2000s, several bills were introduced in Congress aimed at regulating GMOs and establishing a labeling policy, but none progressed. In 2001, two bills were introduced in the Agriculture Committee of the Chamber of Deputies to legislate on biosafety, but neither received a report. According to CONABIA members, this was due to an intention to avoid politicizing the issue and opening it to social actors who until then had not been involved. For this reason, even more "productivist" biosafety proposals—which, while aimed at increasing the safety of agrarian policy, could also have opened the door to social contestation—were avoided, as they created uncertainty about the outcome such bills might have in Congress. As one CONABIA member explained, this logic is similar to the politicization surrounding the glyphosate conflict

the biosafety policy and disputing the scientific authority of the regulatory body, the National Technical Commission on Biosafety (CTNBio). After 20 months of appeals by Monsanto, the Brazilian federal judiciary imposed an indefinite moratorium on the commercialization of GMOs. It was not until 2003 that President Lula da Silva, under pressure from the European Union—which had reported the arrival of transgenic soybeans from Brazil—issued a decree authorizing commercialization. In 2005, a new biosafety law (Law No. 11.105) was passed, replacing the 1995 legal framework. Some studies suggest that, as a consequence of public controversies, Brazil now has more transparent regulatory agencies (Pellegrini, 2013). Others emphasize the influence of social movements opposed to the RR technology package, particularly the Landless Workers' Movement (MST) and Greenpeace, and their impact on successive governments (Poth, 2019; Scoones, 2008; Paarlberg, 2001).

(analyzed in the next section): "Many politicians prefer the issue not be discussed, rather than having a debate whose consequences could be worse than any benefits that might result from having a law (...) suddenly a law might pass saying 'We ban GMOs'" (Poth, 2019).

Technical objections raised by public research institutions regarding the new production model associated with no-till farming and the technological package of GMOs also failed to translate into initiatives for more rigorous regulation and risk control. INTA authorities pointed out the sustainability problems linked to soybean monoculture, especially in non-Pampas regions, and as early as 2003 reports by INTA warned that the prevailing production model would lead to irreversible depletion of natural resource stocks. However, it also noted that "soybeanization" generated a significant source of fiscal revenue, and that rotation with other crops—although more sustainable in the long term—would in the short term entail considerable fiscal costs and more expensive production methods (INTA, 2003).

In sum, between 1996 and, 2015, a total of 35 transgenic events were approved (Table 7.3). If classified by company, only five firms (Monsanto, Syngenta, Pioneer, Dow, Bayer) submitted 27 of these applications, representing 77% of the total. The company with the most approved applications was Monsanto, with 12, followed by Syngenta with seven. In terms of crop species, maize stood out with 22 approved events, followed by soybean with eight, although in terms of cultivated area, soybean accounted for the majority. Regarding the traits introduced, resistance to glyphosate or glufosinate appeared in 25 of the 35 approved applications, most often in combination with insect resistance.

A central feature that defines GMO approval criteria in Argentina is, as previously mentioned, the prevalence of export-oriented objectives over social, environmental, or health considerations. This is confirmed by various studies on biotechnology regulation in the country (Vara, 2005, Newell, 2009, Pellegrini, 2013). As Vara (2005) notes: "Argentina adopted GM crops within a food for export framework: this is a central aspect that must be considered in order to understand the GM crops it adopted, the policies it implemented, and the state of the public discussion on the subject."

Pellegrini (2013) adds that the predominance of the country's export interests also implies that technologies with high local utility are unlikely to gain approval: "Developments that have a local utility, such as transgenic maize resistant to local disease, have no possibilities to satisfy this

Table 7.3 Transgenic events approved per year, species, characteristic, and firm

Year	*Species*	*Introduced Trait*	*Applicant*
1996	Soybean	Glyphosate tolerance	Nidera S.A
1998	Maize	Lepidoptera resistance	Ciba-Geigy S.A
1998	Maize	Ammonium glufosinate tolerance	AgrEvo S.A
1998	Cotton	Lepidoptera resistance	Monsanto Argentina S.A.I.C
1998	Maize	Lepidoptera resistance	Monsanto Argentina S.A.I.C
2001	Cotton	Glyphosate tolerance	Monsanto Argentina S.A.I.C
2001	Maize	Lepidoptera resistance	Novartis Agrosem S.A
2004	Maize	Glyphosate tolerance	Monsanto Argentina S.A.I.C
2005	Maize	Lepidoptera resistance and Ammonium glufosinate tolerance	Dow AgroSciences and Pioneer Argentina
2005	Maize	Glyphosate tolerance	Syngenta Seeds S.A
2007	Maize	Glyphosate tolerance and Lepidoptera resistance	Monsanto Argentina S.A.I.C
2008	Maize	Lepidoptera resistance and Ammonium glufosinate tolerance	Dow AgroSciences and Pioneer Argentina S.A
2009	Cotton	Lepidoptera resistance and Glyphosate tolerance	Monsanto Argentina S.A.I.C
2009	Maize	Glyphosate tolerance and Lepidoptera resistance	Syngenta Agro S.A
2010	Maize	Glyphosate tolerance and Coleoptera resistance	Monsanto Argentina S.A.I.C
2010	Maize	Lepidoptera resistance	Monsanto Argentina S.A.I.C
2010	Maize	Glyphosate tolerance and resistance to Lepidoptera and Coleoptera	Monsanto Argentina S.A.I.C
2011	Maize	Lepidoptera resistance	Syngenta Agro S.A
2011	Soybean	Ammonium glufosinate tolerance	Bayer S.A
2011	Soybean	Ammonium glufosinate tolerance	Bayer S.A
2012	Maize	Lepidoptera resistance and Ammonium glufosinate and glyphosate tolerance	Syngenta Agro S.A
2012	Maize	Glyphosate tolerance and herbicide tolerance (enzyme inhibition)	Pioneer Argentina S.R.L
2012	Maize	Lepidoptera and Coleoptera resistance and glyphosate tolerance	Syngenta Agro S.A

(continued)

Table 7.3 (continued)

Year	*Species*	*Introduced Trait*	*Applicant*
2012	Maize	Coleoptera resistance	Syngenta Agro S.A
2012	Maize	Lepidoptera resistance and Ammonium glufosinate tolerance	Dow AgroSciences and Monsanto Argentina
2012	Maize	Lepidoptera resistance and Glyphosate tolerance	Monsanto Argentina S.A.I.C
2012	Soybean	Lepidoptera resistance and Glyphosate tolerance	Monsanto Argentina
2013	Soybean	Tolerance to imidazolinone herbicides	BASF Argentina S.A
2013	Maize	Lepidoptera resistance and Ammonium glufosinate tolerance	Pioneer Argentina S.R.L
2014	Maize	Lepidoptera resistance and tolerance to glyphosate and Ammonium glufosinate	Syngenta Agro S.A
2015	Soybean	Tolerance to 2,4-D, Ammonium glufosinate, and glyphosate	Dow AgroSciences Argentina S.A
2015	Soybean	High oleic acid content and glyphosate tolerance	Pioneer Argentina S.R.L
2015	Cotton	Glyphosate and Ammonium glufosinate tolerance	Bayer S.A
2015	Soybean	Drought resistance and glyphosate tolerance	INDEAR S.A
2015	Potato	Virus resistance	Tecnoplant S.A

Source Prepared by the author based on data of the Directorate of Agricultural Biotechnology, Ministry of Agriculture

requirement, as grains and oils derived from that maize may be rejected by other countries. This reveals the weight of commercial interests: as a GM crop producer, Argentina promotes the commerce of transgenic crops with no special barriers, but it may stop the approval of local GMO technology in order to avoid conflicts with international agricultural commerce" (Pellegrini, 2013: 136).

In the same vein, Newell (2009) points out that the dynamics of export markets are decisive in shaping domestic biotechnology policy: "The politics of biotechnology have to be understood in relation to Argentina's trade politics, within Latin America and globally. What happens in

Argentina's key export markets is a significant determinant of the course of events within the country."

All the studies reviewed highlight the influence—particularly the instrumental power—of corporations in biotechnology regulation (Vara, 2005, Newell, 2009, Pellegrini, 2013, Delvenne et al., 2013). Biotechnology firms report holding regular meetings with officials from various ministries, and major exporting companies with significant market share state that they are frequently consulted by the DNMA. Some government officials recount being repeatedly approached by Monsanto with job offers, which almost always involved higher salaries than those in the public sector (Newell, 2009). The presence of corporate representatives on key GMO approval bodies such as CONABIA, SENASA, and the DNMA also reflects the state's reliance on the expertise and resources of these companies to carry out the required evaluations.

Unlike in other areas of policymaking, there were no significant changes in biosafety regulations during the period covered by this book (2003–2015). The most notable turning point occurred in 2009, when the GMO approval process was relaxed in parallel with the improved relationship between the national government and Monsanto, analyzed in Chapter 4. As detailed in Table 7.3, 40% of the transgenic events approved since 1996 were authorized between 2009 and 2011, indicating a clear acceleration. Representatives from the sector interpret this as a sign of a good relationship with the government: "This government was very pro-biotechnology, pro-GMO: one indicator of that is the number of transgenic events approved during the period; many were approved during Domínguez's administration, and the relationship was very positive."[9] The shortening of approval times and the Ministry of Agriculture's good relationship with ASA did not go unnoticed by the U.S. Department of Agriculture, which has a clear interest in this agenda through its national biotechnology firms:

> This new framework was a result of a two year long coordinated effort by many sectors in Argentina. In December, 2010 Argentine Secretary of Agriculture Lorenzo Basso signed an agreement with ASA to develop a working plan to identify the problems in the Argentine regulatory system. To comply with this goal they created five working groups where each

[9] Personal interview with a representative of CASAFE.

group analyzed a different phase of the approval process, and developed proposals to improve its efficiency.[10]

As analyzed in the chapter on intellectual property, beginning in 2009 biotechnology companies also attempted to promote a new Seed Law, but failed to get it introduced in Congress. The contrast with the regulatory flexibilization achieved in GMO approval reflects the greater instrumental power of multinational corporations in Executive Branch bodies such as CONABIA and the Ministry of Agriculture, compared to Congress, where the visibility of the issue and electoral incentives work against an industry with a very poor public image, as expressed by the government officials quoted in Chapter 4.

7.3.2 *Agrochemicals*

Glyphosate was approved in Argentina in 1977 and revalidated by SENASA in 1992 as a "low-toxicity" product, which implied no risk to public health. This revalidation, in which the Ministry of Health curiously did not participate (Arancibia, 2013: 83), was based on WHO's toxicological classification, which placed glyphosate in Toxicity Category III (IV being the least hazardous).

During the period covered by this book, concerns over glyphosate's health impacts grew, both internationally and domestically. Starting in the early 2000s, several scientists challenged the WHO's position, arguing that glyphosate use in agriculture was associated with health problems in rural populations, such as reproductive issues, congenital malformations, neurocognitive deficits in embryos, and cancer. In 2009, the WHO re-examined its toxicological classification and confirmed the previous categorization. Based on this decision, SENASA upheld the same classification in 2011 (Arancibia, 2013). In 2015, glyphosate was classified as a "probable carcinogen" by the International Agency for Research on Cancer (IARC), a branch of the WHO. This report was used by thousands of cancer patients in the United States who had been exposed to Roundup to file lawsuits—often successfully—against Monsanto. More recently,

[10] USDA Annual Report Argentina (2014) https://apps.fas.usda.gov/newgainapi/api/report/downloadreportbyfilename?filename=Agricultural%20Biotechnology%20Annual_Buenos%20Aires_Argentina_8-15-2014.pdf

some EU countries have begun restricting its use or even banning it altogether.[11] Other studies indicate that while glyphosate itself may not be carcinogenic, certain ingredients in the herbicide Roundup are, which aligns with leaked internal emails from Monsanto staff, in which they admit that carcinogenicity cannot be ruled out due to the absence of the necessary tests.[12]

In Argentina, although protests and complaints from populations exposed to glyphosate spraying had been multiplying since the early 2000s, it was only in 2009 that the issue gained visibility and entered the national government's agenda. In April of that year, a group of researchers presented preliminary results from studies concluding that glyphosate caused malformations in embryos. The work was led by Andrés Carrasco, a physician specializing in molecular biology with an established track record and reputation in the scientific community: he had been president of CONICET (2000–2001), head of the Embryology Laboratory at the University of Buenos Aires (UBA), and Undersecretary of Scientific Innovation at the Ministry of Defense's Planning Secretariat (2007–2009).

The study's findings were published on the front page of *Página/12*,[13] a newspaper aligned with the government at the time. In this regard, it is worth noting that the 2008 conflict over agricultural export taxes, previously described, created a political window of opportunity for actors seeking to question agrochemical regulation.[14]

[11] https://www.dw.com/es/ee-uu-no-permitir%C3%A1-etiquetar-el-glifosato-como-cancer%C3%ADgeno/a-49972851

[12] A Monsanto scientist stated in 2003: "You cannot say that Roundup is not a carcinogen … we have not done the necessary testing on the formulation to make that statement. The testing on the formulations are not anywhere near the level of the active ingredient" Another scientist, in, 2010 "With regards to the carcinogenicity of our formulations we don't have such testing on them directly." And an internal Monsanto email from 2002 stated: "Glyphosate is OK but the formulated product … does the damage." https://www.theguardian.com/business/2020/jan/23/formulations-glyphosate-based-weedkillers-toxic-tests

[13] https://www.pagina12.com.ar/diario/elpais/1-123111-2009-04-13.html

[14] Given that the newspaper had an editorial line sympathetic to the government, it is likely that the chances of publishing the findings as a front-page story increased at that particular political moment—something that could be interpreted as a warning that public opinion might turn against agricultural producers due to the negative impact of agrochemicals (Arancibia, 2013:89).

The response from the agribusiness sector to Carrasco's study was swift. On April 16, 2009, the agrochemical chambers CIAFA and CASAFE issued a joint statement asserting that SENASA considered glyphosate among the group of lowest toxicological risk substances, that it was successfully used worldwide, and that it had no harmful effects on fauna, microfauna, or human health, nor any unacceptable environmental impacts.[15] Additionally, producer-linked associations highlighted the benefits of conservation agriculture enabled by glyphosate and other herbicides, along with Argentina's comparative advantage in soybean production and its role in the modern global economy. Sectoral technical associations like AACREA added that replacing glyphosate with other products would increase costs and "lead to greater reliance on active ingredients with higher toxicological risk."[16]

The government responded through the Minister of Science and Technology, who stated in an interview with *Clarín* that Carrasco's work did not reflect CONICET's institutional position and had not been evaluated by a panel of experts.[17] From a methodological standpoint, the ministry argued that the study was conducted on amphibian embryos and that no direct extrapolation to humans could be made. The minister added that Argentina had regulations for agrochemical application, and that spraying directly on humans was "a crime that should be punished."[18]

Carrasco's study, ultimately published in, 2010 in an international toxicology journal, concluded that precautionary measures should be taken to ban or heavily restrict glyphosate use in populated areas near soybean fields and became one of the main sources of evidence used by scientists and environmental and human rights groups advocating for stricter regulation of the herbicide.

Following the initial response by the Minister of Science and Technology, over 600 scientists and social, human rights, and environmental organizations signed a declaration warning of corporate influence on the scientific system. The statement, signed by intellectuals and journalists close to the government, denounced the "mercantilist and pragmatic

[15] https://www.pagina12.com.ar/diario/elpais/1-123932-2009-04-26.html

[16] https://www.crea.org.ar/producir-sin-glifosato/

[17] https://www.youtube.com/watch?v=h5m8fqJ7hUQ

[18] https://www.youtube.com/watch?v=FjmoOhZNlFA

intrusion of economic power over the autonomy of the scientific-university system" and concluded with a direct reference to "the public release of the findings from a widely discussed study on agrochemicals in Argentine agriculture," affirming their "commitment to maintaining a scientific-university system autonomous from large corporate economic interests."[19]

In May 2009, the National Committee on Ethics in Science and Technology recommended that the Ministry of Science and Technology create an interdisciplinary commission to assess the risks of glyphosate. Consequently, an interdisciplinary council was established within CONICET, which included the *Comisión Nacional de Investigación sobre Agroquímicos* (National Commission for Research on Agrochemicals ((CNIA) from the Ministry of Health, with the aim of compiling national and international evidence on glyphosate's health and environmental impacts. The report, published in July 2009, cited numerous studies by the very companies that market agrochemicals and did not include Carrasco's work or those of other CONICET scientists (Arancibia, 2013, Gobet, 2018). It acknowledged that some pesticides, including glyphosate, were associated with miscarriages and reduced fertility in both women and men, but stated that there was no scientific evidence for Argentina and that further research should be encouraged. Despite these conclusions, the report failed to mention the Environmental Law, whose Article 4 establishes that the absence of scientific certainty must not be used to postpone effective measures to prevent environmental degradation (Arancibia, 2013:88). In July 2009, due to the political controversy surrounding his research, Carrasco resigned from his position as Undersecretary of Scientific Innovation at the Planning Secretariat of the Ministry of Defense (Blois, 2016). In 2014, he was denied a promotion from Principal Researcher to Senior Researcher at CONICET, which some interpreted as a response to his activism against glyphosate (Sández, 2016).

The commission established to investigate the impacts of glyphosate (CNIA) was quickly dismantled. As noted in the Environmental Management report by the AGN, despite "the relevance of the information produced, the CNIA has remained inactive since 2010, was defunded and stripped of its institutional standing; since then, it has left its projects unfinished. In short, it has not fulfilled its objectives, and in every aspect

[19] http://voces-de-alerta.blogspot.com/2009/05/voces-de-alerta-pagina-principal.html

or dimension of the agrochemical issue, weaknesses and problems can be observed" (AGN, 2015).

The increasing visibility and politicization of the issue prompted the introduction of several bills in Congress aimed at reducing the risks associated with agrochemical use, none of which were approved. In August 2010, congresswoman Cecilia Merchán of the *Libres del Sur* party introduced a bill to ban all aerial spraying and restrict ground spraying, co-signed by deputies from *Libres del Sur*, *Proyecto Sur*, *GEN*, and *Nuevo Encuentro* (5857-D-2010). The bill proposed a nationwide ban on aerial spraying of "pesticides, agrotoxins or biocides, whether chemical or biological" intended for agricultural use, regardless of the active ingredient, formulation, or dosage. It also banned ground applications within a 1000-meter radius from the limits of urban and peri-urban areas across the country. The bill provided for imprisonment from three to ten years in the event of violations.[20] The bill was discussed in legislative committees and included a public hearing in which Carrasco participated, although without the involvement of representatives from agricultural producers or the input sector.[21] Ultimately, the bill did not receive a committee ruling to be debated on the floor. Similarly, in 2011, GEN and the Socialist Party deputies introduced a bill proposing exclusion zones for both aerial and ground agrochemical applications. However, that bill was not even taken up in committee.

In 2013, the Ministry of Agriculture issued the "Guidelines on the Application of Phytosanitary Products in Peri-urban Areas" based on recommendations compiled by a working group composed of institutions representing agrarian interests, without any participation of public health or environmental experts (Gobet, 2018).

In September, 2014, national congressman Luis Basterra of the ruling FPV party introduced a bill to regulate the registration, commercialization, and control of agrochemicals. The bill was sent to the Agriculture and Commerce committees and received a favorable ruling for floor discussion. Various health and environmental organizations opposed the bill, especially because it included an article that would allow SENASA

[20] https://www.pagina12.com.ar/diario/sociedad/3-153587-2010-09-22.html

[21] https://www.lanacion.com.ar/economia/fuertes-criticas-al-glifosato-en-el-congreso-nid1307076

to approve the commercialization and use of products banned by international organizations, including the WHO. The bill also restricted the possibility of granting authorization based on independent research.

The bill was later revised and reintroduced the following year after public hearings on the issue. While the new version improved upon the previous draft, environmental and health organizations remained dissatisfied, primarily because it left the approval process unchanged and continued to exclude health and environmental agencies from the decision-making process (Gobet, 2018). The government ultimately submitted the bill, which passed the lower house on November 26, 2015 in a special session, just weeks before the change of administration. The bill, titled "Production, Registration, Commercialization, and Control of Phytosanitary Products," was signed by both ruling and opposition legislators, including those aligned with agricultural producers (3880-D-2015). Several environmental organizations noted that the bill did not significantly improve the registration or categorization of agrochemicals and only provided oversight up to the point of retail commercialization (Di Paola, 2016). The approval by the Chamber of Deputies went largely unnoticed by the media. Ultimately, the Senate did not take up the bill, and it lost parliamentary status in 2018.[22]

Evidence collected in interviews for this study suggests that this regulatory outcome reflects both the structural and instrumental power of agribusiness firms—an example of how corporate power is most effective when both forms are combined. As discussed in the chapter on intellectual property, representatives from input companies and officials from the Ministries of Science and Agriculture noted that relations had become very close and fluid since 2008; some officials from the Ministry of Science even described Monsanto as "the government's favorite child."[23]

These accounts are consistent with those of representatives from agrochemical companies organized under CASAFE and with previous studies

[22] Other projects that did not directly impact production—such as the regulation of used phytosanitary containers—were able to generate broader consensus. The Container Law was introduced by the National Executive Branch in, 2014, with the aim of establishing "minimum environmental protection standards for the management of empty phytosanitary containers." The stated goal was to "ensure that the management of empty phytosanitary containers and the recovered material does not pose risks to human or animal health or to the environment, while clarifying that agrochemicals themselves are not subject to regulation under this law" (Di Paola, 2016).

[23] Interview with an official from the Ministry of Science and Technology.

(Newell, 2009). CASAFE representatives stated that they had "a very fluid and friendly relationship" with SENASA, the agency responsible for regulation. They noted that they had "a direct line," were regularly consulted by the agency, and held monthly meetings where the chamber expressed its concerns.[24]

The lack of clear national regulations led many conflicts to be resolved in the courts, resulting in precautionary measures and legal injunctions that imposed restrictions on both aerial and ground spraying (Di Paola, 2016). In December 2009, for the first time, a provincial court in Córdoba banned glyphosate spraying in populated areas of Ituzaingó, setting a 500-meter buffer zone for ground spraying and 1500 meters for aerial spraying.[25] Similar rulings followed in 2010 in the towns of San Jorge (Santa Fe) and La Leonesa and Las Palmas (Chaco), in 2011 in Antillas (Salta), and in 2012 in Firmat (Santa Fe) (Arancibia, 2013). That same year, a court issued the first suspended sentence against a producer and an applicator, finding them guilty of intentional environmental contamination in the Ituzaingó Anexo neighborhood of Córdoba (Di Paola, 2016). These outcomes were heavily influenced by the mobilization of affected communities, particularly the "Mothers of Ituzaingó," a group formed in 2001 that coordinated with scientists and lawyers to pursue legal action. Among the organizations that joined their protest was the *Grupo de Reflexión Rural* (Rural Reflection Group) (GRR), composed of intellectuals and technicians. From the meetings held by these groups emerged the "Stop the Spraying" campaign. These organizations played a key role in raising awareness and shaping public opinion (Arancibia, 2013), although they faced challenges in coordinating a unified national strategy due to the heterogeneity of actors involved (Lapegna, 2019).

Another episode in which social and environmental movements prevailed over input companies was the failed attempt by Monsanto to build a genetically modified corn plant in Malvinas Argentinas, Córdoba. The project—"Latin America's largest GM corn plant"—was announced by President Cristina Fernández de Kirchner in 2012 at a press conference with company representatives, where the launch of Intacta RR2 soybean in Argentina was also announced. As previously mentioned,

[24] Interview with a director of a sectoral chamber.

[25] http://www.pagina12.com.ar/diario/elpais/1-118075-2009-01-12.html

several sources and media reports indicated that the plant's construction and the launch of Intacta in Argentina were part of a broader agreement between the company and the government, which included the introduction of a bill to reform the Seed Law in Congress.

A few months later, a group of local residents, supported by the organization Club del Derecho, filed an injunction to halt the construction of the Monsanto plant until an environmental impact assessment was conducted and a public consultation was held.[26] In September 2013, the "*Asamblea de Vecinos Malvinas Lucha por la Vida*" ("Malvinas Assembly for Life") began a protest that included an encampment and blockade at the construction site, with the support of activists and social organizations from across the country. Several academic institutions—including the Catholic University of Córdoba, the National University of Córdoba, and the National University of Río Cuarto—highlighted irregularities in the plant's approval process. In January 2014, the judiciary ordered a halt to construction in response to the injunction filed by the Assembly. The ruling required the municipality to suspend the project until an environmental impact assessment and a public hearing were completed. In February 2014, Córdoba's Environment Secretary, Néstor Pratto, announced that the government would not authorize the environmental impact study submitted by Monsanto. "As presented, the company failed to clarify how it plans to mitigate the environmental impacts of its operations," he said,[27] specifically noting that Monsanto had not explained how it would handle waste and water contaminated with agrochemicals.[28]

The conflict gained such relevance that CASAFE developed a specific strategy to contain it, fearing it would spread to other provinces. The "*Plan de contención Córdoba*" ("Córdoba Containment Plan") included a communication strategy, increased advertising budgets, efforts to strengthen ties with local government, outreach to reluctant agricultural producers, and infiltration of the organizations blocking the Monsanto plant.[29] Other CASAFE member companies pressured Monsanto to

[26] https://www.lavoz.com.ar/noticias/politica/presentaron-amparo-contra-radicacion-monsanto

[27] http://www.lavoz.com.ar/politica/rechazaron-el-estudio-de-impacto-ambiental-de-monsanto-en-malvinas-argentinas

[28] https://www.bbc.com/mundo/noticias/2014/12/141128_argentina_transgenicos_monsanto_vs

[29] Interview with a representative from the input sector.

abandon the project. Although doing so would be seen as a defeat for the industry and might embolden social movements, they believed the conflict was taking too great a toll. Other sources within the input sector pointed to Monsanto's reputational problems as a key factor, describing it as a matter of corporate culture marked by arrogance and a belief that it could impose its will, which provoked backlash from governments. One industry consultant even remarked that Monsanto's reputation was so tarnished that "they would have to change their name" because "they lost their social license."[30] This, in fact, happened a few years later when Bayer acquired Monsanto and dropped the brand name.

In sum, the laxity of environmental regulations can be explained by the central role of the technological package (glyphosate-resistant transgenic soy) in the agro-export model, which results in regulations following a commercial logic—in other words, their design is not primarily driven by assessments of production sustainability or environmental protection, but rather by the goal of opening international markets. Power over environmental regulation is particularly strong because, unlike in other regulatory areas, the interests of the entire agribusiness chain—input suppliers, producers, and exporters—are aligned in favor of weak oversight. The less dependent the Argentine economy is on agricultural exports (as a share of total exports), the less sensitive its trade balance and fiscal performance will be to environmental regulations that restrict arable land or increase production costs.

[30] Interview with a consultant from the agricultural input sector.

Final Comments

The question of the political power of Argentina's agricultural sector runs through much of the recent work in the social sciences. However, far from being settled, the literature offers polarized representations—ranging from depictions of a politically weak agricultural sector unable to stop a hostile government, to portrayals of a dominant or hegemonic force dictating government policy. One of the motivations behind this work has been to nuance this polarization and analyze in greater depth the power of agrarian elites in the policymaking process.

In this book, I have argued that the structural power wielded by multinational corporations (MNCs) in export agriculture constrains the government's policy options and skews profitability in favor of foreign over domestic actors. As business power is unevenly distributed along the value chain—which is composed of heterogeneous actors with sometimes diverging interests—the government can impose greater costs on the weakest link: agricultural producers. The input and commercialization segments, controlled by MNCs, have more influence over government decisions and greater capacity to capture rents, as they hold privileged access to international markets and technology. This privileged position emerges then as the main source of the structural power of MNCs, allowing them to tilt distributional conflicts in their favor and limit government autonomy.

Contrary to much recent comparative politics literature, I have argued that this structural power is more relevant than instrumental power

J. O'Farrell, *Business Power in Agriculture Value Chains*, Latin American Political Economy, https://doi.org/10.1007/978-3-032-06589-6

in explaining distributive outcomes. Moreover, it is crucial to understanding the limits on the government's ability to pursue certain regulatory goals, thus serving as a constraint on development. Structural power, however, is variable: it depends on economic conditions—since the government's bargaining power *vis-à-vis* MNCs increases when the economy has access to alternative sources of foreign currency and technology—and institutional conditions—since local actors' power *vis-à-vis* MNCs is strengthened in the legislative arena and in high-visibility issues.

The first contribution of this work is to identify and discuss the analytical limitations of existing conceptualizations of power in the literature and to propose a way to reconcile the apparent contradiction between a weak and a dominant agricultural sector. I argue that doing so requires avoiding sweeping conclusions about the power of agribusiness based on one policy domain or one actor in the chain. Instead, it requires a clearer definition of three dimensions of analysis: (i) the business actors in agriculture, (ii) their sources of power, and (iii) the policy areas in which they hold interests.

Reaching this conclusion involved three key moves. First, I sought to more precisely and thoroughly describe recent transformations in agriculture, thereby connecting political analysis with sectoral economic studies. This allowed me to broaden the focus beyond producers and bring attention to previously overlooked actors in political science. In Chapter 4, I argued that economic transformations over recent decades challenge the characterization of producers (or landowners) as the "agrarian elite" and call into question the primacy of their conflict with urban sectors. Since the 1980s, technological innovation, economic liberalization, and privatization have fundamentally reshaped agricultural politics in Latin America. New actors have emerged, turning what was once a bilateral distributive conflict between producers and consumers into a broader conflict that also includes input suppliers and traders.

The second move was to adopt a value chain perspective instead of the more conventional sectoral approach. This represents an analytical innovation for comparative political economy, not only in agriculture but more broadly, with significant advantages. First, it makes visible the heterogeneity of interests and conflicts among private actors—not only between firms and the state. By focusing on the chain, I show how the resolution of distributive conflicts and sectoral development depends not only on the state-business relationship but also on inter-firm dynamics. Understanding intra-chain conflict is important because it limits the sector's ability to coordinate political actions and creates room for the government to disrupt collective action. Additionally, this perspective offers a more holistic view of both government policy objectives and the preferences of private actors. This is relevant because conflicts over taxes, trade, intellectual property, and the environment do not unfold in isolation: outcomes in one area can influence the intensity of preferences in others. For instance, it helps explain why the government delayed reforming the Seed Law or implemented weak environmental regulations—it was already taxing the sector through export duties.

The third move was to problematize, through the lens of structural and instrumental power, the types of resources available to each actor in the chain and the mechanisms through which they influence public policy. This helps position my contribution within the existing literature. For example, a key insight from research on the commodity boom is that, since producers lack structural power, under democratic conditions only investments in electoral politics through political parties can sustainably guarantee their influence—even when governments pursue policy goals at odds with agricultural interests (Freytes, 2015). This book shows that while this may be true for producers, MNCs possess sufficient structural power to influence public policy sustainably, without the need for investing in political parties.

Together, these three analytical moves allow for a more accurate and thorough account of what constitutes power in the agricultural export value chain, and the mechanisms through which it is exercised.

The second contribution of this study is to explain policy outcomes in three regulatory areas—intellectual property, trade, and environmental regulation—that, unlike export duties, have received little attention in comparative political economy. The research shows that outcomes in these areas can be explained by the power of economic actors. This finding complements the literature on export duties but also reveals a more general argument: the government's capacity to pursue fiscal or regulatory goals is negatively correlated with business power. This, in turn, explains variation in regulatory outcomes (greater or lesser regulatory capacity), apparent deficits in certain areas (e.g., the environment), and broader structural challenges to advancing developmental goals. In this sense, the study seeks to revisit and deepen the classical but still relevant question of whether agrarian elites constrain development. Addressing this question requires moving beyond both "fiscalist" approaches—which argue that elites in Argentina pose no constraint—and "environmentalist" approaches—which suggest a highly dependent government with little nuance.

To advance the argument that business power explains the outcomes of policy conflicts, I have provided concrete examples of the mechanisms through which their power resources translate into influence in specific policy episodes. Using the case studies from Chapters 5 to 7, I analyzed how the structural power of MNCs enables them to shape policymaking and prevail in distributional conflicts. I also identified the conditions under which local actors can assert their interests.

A key finding is that the structural power of MNCs in export agriculture flows from their control over access to international markets and technology—resources upon which producers depend for productivity and governments rely on to support the broader economy. This privileged position also enhances their instrumental power, as governments grant them greater access to formal and informal decision-making arenas out of concern for the economic consequences of their choices. However, this power can be moderated—or even strongly conditioned—when local actors gain alternative access to markets, technology, or finance.

In the case of traders, structural power flows from their dominant role in international grain trade, through which they can influence Argentine exports at destination ports. This has consistently shaped the sector's relationship with the government and ultimately explains why no initiative to expand state control over trade advanced during the period analyzed. Their power grew following the deregulation and privatization of grain trade since the 1980s, as state-to-state commerce gave way to firm-to-firm transactions. Domestically, traders can block the flow of foreign currency by delaying settlement or even temporarily suspending exports. This structural power—derived from their control over foreign exchange—is sensitive to macroeconomic conditions, diminishing when the economy has a trade surplus, high reserves, or access to debt. An economy in a better position to create foreign currency flows strengthens the government's bargaining position *vis-a-vis* those usually securing such flows.

Through the empirical reconstruction of policy episodes, I showed that traders emerged as the main beneficiaries of the commodity boom in terms of value capture along the chain. They also showed the greatest capacity to resist or reject government initiatives. While policies such as export duties and export permits adopted in that period successfully transferred resources to the state and consumers, this occurred at the expense of producers. Achieving greater taxation of traders and greater government autonomy would have required deeper reforms to expand state control over foreign trade. But as Chapter 6 shows, such reforms did not advance because public officials and legislators feared traders could punish the country by ceasing to purchase at destination ports.

In the case of agricultural biotechnology firms, structural power flows from control over proprietary technology. However, this power reaches its peak—and allows firms to reverse conflicts with producers—when complemented by legal and political capacities to restrict access to that technology. This power is sufficient to block policies that go against their interests, but insufficient to secure legislative changes aligned with their preferences. Its effectiveness is expressed in public regulation—by disciplining other actors in the chain and aligning them during negotiations with the government—and in private law—through commercial contracts. At its strongest, and thanks to their weight in global input markets, these firms can even block local actors' access to export markets. Still, biotech companies' power is not sufficient to achieve maximal goals in Congress (offensive power) when their interests conflict with the governing party's electoral base, with mobilized constituencies, or on issues resonating with public opinion. In such conflicts, social legitimacy and electoral incentives outweigh the structural or instrumental power of MNCs.

I illustrated these arguments about the power of biotechnology companies through an in-depth study of the most important conflict in the agricultural input segment during the period analyzed. This conflict revolved around Monsanto's pressure to collect higher royalties, either by modifying the Seed Law or through private agreements. As analyzed in Chapter 5, Monsanto's disinvestment threats were ineffective for most of the period, and the government was able to resist its pressure for a more restrictive intellectual property regime. In doing so, it achieved the redistributive goal of compensating agricultural producers and preventing the company from increasing control over seeds. However, multinational biotechnology companies also blocked government initiatives aimed at charging royalties to large agricultural producers to create a biotechnology development fund promoting national companies. This harmed the domestic seed sector and is a clear example of the limits developmentalist strategies face in sectors controlled by MNCs. I also showed that the conflict over royalties took a turn in Monsanto's favor when it managed to implement a private collection system for its Intacta technology, whereby from 2014 onward producers began paying royalties upon selling their harvest to grain handlers or exporters. This arrangement favored Monsanto over traditional seed companies, which continued to appropriate a low share of sector profitability.

The laxity of environmental regulations can be explained by the central role of the technological package (glyphosate-resistant transgenic soybeans) in the agro-export model. This centrality explains why regulations follow a commercial logic: sustainability and environmental or health impact assessments are subordinated to the goal of opening international markets. The actors who benefit from flexible environmental regulations are input-selling companies and export-oriented agricultural producers. Those harmed are populations exposed to agrochemical contamination, smallholder and family farmers, and communities displaced or affected by riverside flooding, associated with the deregulated expansion of the agricultural frontier and deforestation.

My argument complements the existing consensus among economists regarding the asymmetric economic relationships within the value chain—unfavorable to producers—by showing that the asymmetry is also political. In this sense, the findings resolve the apparent contradiction with Rogowski's (1989) argument that a favorable external shock should politically benefit owners of the abundant resource, namely, landowners or agricultural producers. What I show in this book is that such an outcome is decisively mediated by the organization of the value chain. At the same time, I clarify the mechanisms through which this outcome unfolds.

Theoretical Implications

The argument developed in these pages has implications for theoretical debates on business power, and specifically, the power of multinational corporations. First, the arguments in this work contribute to recent theoretical discussions that revisit the classic distinction between structural and instrumental power (Hacker & Pierson, 2002; Fairfield, 2010; Culpepper and Reinke 2014; Fairfield, 2015a, 2015b; Bril Mascarenhas and Madariaga 2019) and to studies of Argentine business politics from a structuralist perspective (Etchemendy, 2014; Shadlen, 2017). In this book, I applied recent conceptual innovations—particularly the variable, relational, and strategic nature of structural power—through a detailed case study with cross-policy and temporal comparisons, and by disaggregating actors based on their type of activity.

Through the reconstruction of specific episodes, I showed how the structural power exercised by companies was decisive in shaping policy outcomes. In contrast to classical approaches that understand structural power statically and fail to explain its variation, I demonstrated how it shifts according to economic conditions (e.g., availability of alternative sources of foreign currency and technology for local actors) and institutional factors (e.g., issue visibility and electoral incentives). To do so, building on recent contributions, I placed policymakers' and officials' perceptions at the center of the analysis and shed light on the mechanisms through which sources of structural power are translated into influence.

A second contribution lies in analyzing how companies use these resources in relation to other private actors in the chain. In this regard, the work represents an innovation in the comparative politics literature, which usually focuses on the power of companies relative to governments. An example of this, as I analyzed in Chapter 5, is how biotechnology companies used technological licenses politically to align seed companies' interests with theirs during negotiations with the government, or how Monsanto used its capacity to block Argentine exports to China to force other actors in the chain (traders, grain handlers, and producers) to accept its private royalty system. I thus emphasize that the use of structural and instrumental power in inter-company negotiations is an underexplored and promising research agenda.[1]

A third contribution relates to the recent debate among scholars in this field on whether structural power is expressed indirectly or can also be strategic. Some authors argue that it only manifests indirectly through market decisions, while others claim it can also be expressed strategically, through deliberate political actions.[2] This work contributes to the latter position and provides concrete instances in which structural power is expressed strategically. For example, Monsanto's explicit threats not to release new technology in the market or to suspend its R&D program in the country. In the case of traders, structural power derived from their provision of foreign currency sometimes manifests through market behavior—such as delaying exports in anticipation of a devaluation—but also politically, through coordination and deliberate action to extract concessions from the government. One of the challenges in analyzing this type of power is how to empirically identify traders' motivations when

[1] Farrell y Newman (2015) make a similar suggestion.

[2] As I analyzed in Chapter 1, Hacker and Pierson (2002) and Fairfield (2015a, 2015b, 2019) argue that it is expressed indirectly; Culpepper and Reinke (2014) contend that it can also be strategic.

delaying currency liquidation, and to distinguish market-based speculative decisions from political moves aimed at pressuring or weakening the government. Relatedly, I also show that structural power can play a role in the agenda-setting stage (Hacker & Pierson, 2002)—e.g., when government officials anticipate that traders could punish them in destination markets and therefore abandon intervention proposals—as well as in doing "the causal hard work in specific parts of legislation" (Culpepper and Reinke 2014), such as when traders negotiate concessions from the government in exchange for accelerating or delaying foreign currency settlement.

A fourth contribution to the literature on business power, and to globalization studies more broadly, is the finding that the main source of structural power does not lie in disinvestment (or exit), but rather in the ability to block local actors' access to markets and technology. This finding is directly related to—and updates, in light of current global conditions—classical literature on dependent development and MNCs. I show that MNCs in the input and trading sectors have limited capacity to exit because of high sunk costs (in seed conditioning plants, ports, elevators, and processing plants) and a high opportunity cost of disinvestment, given Argentina's status as a leading global producer of agricultural commodities. Instead of flowing from their ability to disinvest, the structural power they wield to appropriate higher returns and protect their market position comes from their ability to affect exports at destination ports or block access to technologies.

This also has implications for the globalization literature and differs from the conventional view that liberalization and market integration have increased corporate power by making it easier to exit. I argue that globalization enhanced MNCs' power by giving them greater capacity to influence domestic actors' participation in international markets. It is this kind of power that has sidelined initiatives to increase state control over grain trade. I also showed that Monsanto, during this period, twice tried to leverage its legal and market power in other jurisdictions to pressure the Argentine government by putting national exports at risk. The first attempt, in the European Union, failed; the second, in China, succeeded. To clarify the scope of the argument, this type of power operates in specific situations—such as when MNCs see their property rights threatened, or after other, less extreme forms of power have failed to achieve their goals.

Fifth, I show that structural power depends on the context in which companies operate and offer a notion of structural power tailored to the Argentine context. One particular feature of Argentina's political economy is the recurrence of balance-of-payment crises. In this context, corporate actions that jeopardize foreign currency inflows carry special weight, greater than in countries with less exposure to this type of crisis. A second characteristic is the country's heavy reliance on commodity exports, and a third is the concentration of these exports in a few companies. These traits give greater relative weight to firms operating in this sector. A counterweight to MNC power lies in the fact that, as Argentina is a global leader in agricultural production, exiting this market carries high opportunity costs. This reinforces the government's bargaining position and creates a situation of mutual indispensability—not absolute control or hegemony, as other works have concluded.

This research also contributes to the literature on the role of MNCs in shaping the economies of developing countries by proposing a deeper study of their influence on policymaking processes. One of the assumptions derived from this literature—from global value chain theories to varieties of capitalism—is that MNCs play an indispensable role as channels for access to markets, technology, and financing (Gereffi et al. 2005; Schneider, 2013). I argue that both literatures, due to their functionalist bias and focus on coordination over conflict, have tended to overlook questions of power asymmetry in state–MNC negotiations. The varieties of capitalism approach has made major strides in understanding the roles MNCs play in regional economies and their political strategies and preferences, focusing on some sources of instrumental power. But it tells us little about their level of influence. With this work, I aimed to contribute to this approach by showing how MNCs use the privileged economic position described in the literature—as gateways to technology, finance, and markets—as a source of power. Regarding the global value chains literature (Gereffi et al. 2005), which argues that income distribution across the chain is a function of chain structure and governance, I offer a more political view by showing that companies are actively involved in shaping and protecting their market positions, as well as in designing the institutional arrangements that regulate their activities.

Finally, this work engages with the discussion on development and dependency. One definition of dependent development characterizes it as a growth process in which the control exercised by MNCs results in an unequal distribution of benefits—favoring the MNCs more than the countries in which they operate—and, at the level of domestic policy-making, a clear restriction on the options available to governments, as these may conflict with the global priorities of the corporations (Gereffi, 1978). In this book, I show how the literature on business power can productively engage with dependency theories and how the structural power of MNCs can obstruct the developmental prospects of a semi-peripheral economy. This, in part, addresses one of the criticisms leveled against dependency theories—that they lost relevance because they failed to specify the political and economic mechanisms through which dependency operates, and did not generate causal arguments that could be empirically tested (Stallings, 2020; Wibbels, 2009a, 2009b). In these pages, I present a framework and a causal argument that identifies the actors (multinational corporations, officials, politicians, voters), their preferences, and the constraints under which they operate, resulting in greater or lesser dependency.

To conclude, this work offers an analytical and theoretical approach with three types of implications for future research. This approach can contribute to studies on (i) other value chains, (ii) export agriculture in other countries, and (iii) public policy design. First, the usefulness of adopting a framework that simultaneously considers different types of power and the complexity of the chain could be replicated in other sectors where both local and international actors operate, or where their positions depend on control over different types of economic resources. Second, a future research agenda lies in the need to explore how this framework functions in cross-national comparisons. To that end, the precise description of how economic structure characteristics intersect with different forms of power and their conditioning factors provides a relevant analytical map. Third, and most importantly, the detailed and in-depth analysis of the political economy of policymaking processes is a necessary input for improving diagnostics and policy design in each of the areas analyzed.

Annex

List of interviews (55).

Public sector (21), Private sector input link (9), Private sector agricultural producers link (13), Private sector traders link (11).

Public Sector

1. Miguel Campos, Secretary of Agriculture, Livestock and Fisheries of the Nation (2003–2006), interview 1, 11/15/2016
2. Miguel Campos, Secretary of Agriculture, Livestock and Fisheries of the Nation (2003–2006), interview 2, 07/11/2017
3. Julián Domínguez, Minister of Agriculture, Livestock and Fisheries of the Nation (2009–2012), 11/8/2016;
4. Lorenzo Basso, Secretary of Agriculture, Livestock and Fisheries of the Nation of MAGyP. 2009–2013, 11/4/2016
5. Oscar Solis, Undersecretary of Agriculture, of MAGyP, 2009–2013, 2/11/2016
6. Gabriel Delgado, Secretary of Agriculture, Livestock and Fisheries of the Nation of MAGyP. 2013–2015, 11/11/2016
7. Javier Rodríguez, Secretary of Political Institutional Coordination and Agricultural Emergency (2014–2015)
8. Roxana Blasetti, Director of International Agri-food Relations of MAGyP (2004 and 2012), 07/05/2019
9. Raymundo Lavignolle, National Institute of Seeds (INASE), 06/12/2019
10. Anonymous interview at Biotechnology Directorate of the Ministry of Agriculture
11. Augusto Costa, Secretary of Commerce, Ministry of Economy (2013–2015), 4/3/2016
12. Guillermo Moreno, Secretary of Commerce, Ministry of Economy (2007–2013), 3/23/2017
13. Anonymous interview with official at Ministry of Science, Technology and Productive Innovation, 7/7/2014
14. Mercedes Marco del Pont, president of the Central Bank of the Argentine Republic (BCRA), 3/16/2017
15. Andrea García, Deputy Frente para la Victoria (FPV)
16. Luis Basterra, Deputy Frente para la Victoria (FPV)
17. Alberto Cantero, Deputy Frente para la Victoria (FPV), president of the agriculture commission 2007–2009
18. Anonymous interview with advisor in the chamber of deputies, AACREA member, Secretary of Agriculture (2017–2019), 05/21/2019
19. Isidoro Felcman, Director Strategic Agri-Food Plan (PEA), 2010–2011
20. Lara Goyburu, consultant Strategic Agri-Food Plan (PEA), 2010–2011

21. Javier García Espil, lawyer specializing in environmental policy and former Director in the National Environment Secretariat (2016–2019)

Private Sector

Agricultural Inputs Link

22. Miguel Rapela, Executive Director of the Asociación de Semilleros Argentinos (ASA), 07/2014
23. Alfredo Paseyro, President of the Asociación de Semilleros Argentinos (ASA), 07/2014
24. Anonymous interview with representative at Cámara de Sanidad Agropecuaria y Fertilizantes (CASAFE), 06/18/2014
25. Federico Trucco, CEO of Bioceres
26. Anonymous interview with Director of Institutional Relations and Sustainability of an exporting company (trader), Interview 1, 03/15/2016
27. Anonymous interview with Director of Institutional Relations and Sustainability of an exporting company (trader), Interview 2, 03/17/2017
28. Juan Iglesias Perez, founder and former owner of Ipesa (agrochemical company) 05/20/2019
29. Manuel Mihura, Manager at GDM (Don Mario), 07/10/2019
30. Anonymous interview with institutional representative of the input link, 06/25/2016

Agricultural Producers Link

31. Ricardo Buryaille, national deputy for ACyS Formosa and former second vice president of Confederaciones Rurales Argentinas (CRA)
32. Ernesto Ambrosetti, chief economist of the Sociedad Rural Argentina (SRA), 07/04/2019
33. Pilar Giraudo, President of the Asociación Argentina de Productores en Siembra Directa (AAPRESID), 07/31/2014
34. Ulises Forte, Deputy (UCR) 2009–2013, Second Vice President of Federación Agraria (FAA), 03/29/2016

35. Guillermo Martini, member of Corriente Agraria Nacional y Popular (CANPO), 06/03/2019
36. Ricardo Negri, Responsible for research at Asociación Argentina de Consorcios Regionales de Experimentación Agrícola (AACREA), president from the National Service of Agrifood Health and Quality (Senasa) (2018) 06/10/2019
37. Enrique Duhau, agricultural businessman, manager of Administration Enrique Duhau SA Agricultural and Livestock (AED), advisor at MAIZAR, 06/13/2019
38. Luis Zubizarreta, President of Asoc. de la Cadena de la Soja Argentina (ACSOJA), 3/3/2017
39. Jorge Solmi, Vice-president FAA, 06/10/2019
40. Roberto Campi, Confederaciones Rurales Argentinas (CRA) 06/21/2019
41. Gustavo Grobocopatel, Los Grobo Group, AACREA, 07/24/2019
42. Carlos Vicente (GRAIN), June 27, 2014
43. Lucas Villamil, agricultural journalist, Clarín Rural

Traders Link

44. Adrián Vera, executive director of the Bolsa de Cereales de Buenos Aires; interview 1, 03/10/2016
45. Adrián Vera, executive director of the Bolsa de Cereales de Buenos Aires, interview 2, 2016
46. Raúl Dente, Manager of the Federación de Centros de Acopiadores de Cereales, interview 1, 2016
47. Raul Dente, Manager of the Federación de Centros de Acopiadores de Cereales, interview 2 05/30/2019
48. Alejandro Terre, export manager of Agricultores Federados Argentinos (AFA), 03/23/2016
49. Alberto Rodriguez, President of Cámara de la Industria Aceitera de la República Argentina (CIARA), 03/07/2017
50. Louis Dreyfus Company (LDC), anonymous interview, 03/2017
51. Gustavo Lopez – Consultant at Agritrend, 03/06/2017
52. Trader at Nidera, 03/15/2016
53. Trader at COFCO 1, anonymous interview, 06/2019
54. Trader at COFCO 2, anonymous interview, 02/2020

55. Anonymous interview at Confederación Intercooperativa Agropecuaria Limitada (CONINAGRO), 07/2019

Bibliography

Acemoglu y Robinson. (2006). *Economic Origins of Dictatorship and Democracy.* Cambridge University Press

Acuña, C. (1990) Intereses empresarios, dictadura y democracia en la Argentina actual (o sobre por qué la burguesía abandona estrategias autoritarias y opta por la estabilidad democrática), documento CEDES/39, CEDES, Buenos Aires.

Acuña, C. (1995). *La Burguesía Industrial como actor político.* Department of Political Science University of Chicago.

AGN. (2015). Informe sectorial sobre Gestión Ambiental de la Auditoría General de la Nación.

Ahmed, G., Hamrick, D. Y., & Gereffi, G. (2014). *Shifting Governance Structures in the Wheat Value Chain: Implications for Food Security in the Middle East and North Africa*, Duke University Center on Globalization, Governance and Competitiveness.

Albertus, M. (2015). *Autocracy and Redistribution: The Politics of Land Reform (Cambridge Studies in Comparative Politics).* Cambridge University Press. https://doi.org/10.1017/CBO9781316227107

Alcañiz, I., & Gutierrez, R. A. (2022). *The Distributive Politics of Environmental Protection in Latin America and the Caribbean.* Elements in Politics and Society in Latin America.

Amin Filomeno, F. (2013a). State capacity and intellectual property regimes: Lessons from South American soybean agriculture. *Technology in Society, 35*, 139–152.

J. O'Farrell, *Business Power in Agriculture Value Chains*, Latin American Political Economy, https://doi.org/10.1007/978-3-032-06589-6

Amin Filomeno, F. (2013b). How Argentine farmers overpowered Monsanto: The mobilization of knowledge users and intellectual property regimes. *Journal of Politics in Latin America, 3*, 35–71.

Amsden, A. (1991). Diffusion of development: The late-industrializing model and Greater East Asia. *The American Economic Review, 81*(2), 282–286.

Amsden, A. (1989). *Asia's Next Giant: South Korea and Late Industrialization*. Oxford University Press.

Anchorena, B. (2017). La autonomía en disputa: capacidades estatales y poder empresario en el conflicto agropecuario argentino de 2008, A Thesis submitted to the Faculty of the Graduate School of Arts and Sciences of Georgetown University in partial fulfillment of the requirements for the degree of Master of Arts in Development Management & Policy.

Anlló, Guillermo, Roberto Bisang y Mercedes Campi. 2013. *Claves para repensar el agro argentino*. Buenos Aires: Eudeba.

Arancibia, F. (2013). Challenging the bioeconomy: The dynamics of collective action in Argentina. *Technology in Society, 35*(2013), 79–92.

Arza y Van Zwanenberg, (2014). The politics of technological upgrading: international transfer to and adaptation of GM cotton in Argentina. *World Development, 59*, 521–534.

Arza, Valeria (2014) "Modernización tecnológica en transgénicos como estrategia de negociación política de multinacionales" Realidad Económica N 288,12/2014.

ASA-UBATEC. (2017). Estudio del Sistema de Agronegocios de Semillas Argentino: Una visión sistémica desde la investigación y el conocimiento, Asociación de Semilleros Argentinos (ASA), UBATEC SA, Buenos Aires, 3 de abril de 2017, http://www.asa.org.ar/wp-content/uploads/2020/01/Impacto-del-sistema-de-semillas-en-Argentina-20170403.pdf

Azcuy Ameghino, E. (2016). La cuestión agraria en Argentina. Caracterización, problemas y propuestas Revista Interdisciplinaria de Estudios Agrarios No 45 | 2do. Semestre de 2016.

Azpiazu, Basualdo y Khavise. (1986). El nuevo poder económico en Argentina de los años 80, Siglo XXI, Buenos Aires.

Bair, J. (2005). Global capitalism and commodity Chains: Looking back, going forward. *Competition & Change, 9*(2), 153–180.

Banco Mundial. (2016). Argentina: Análisis Ambiental del país. Serie de informes técnicos del Banco Mundial en Argentina, Paraguay y Uruguay No 9, 2016. Oficina Regional de América Latina y el Caribe.

Barsky, O. Y., & Gelman, J. (2009) Historia del Agro Argentino: desde la conquista hasta comienzos del siglo XXI, tercera edición actualizada, Editorial Sudamericana.

Basualdo, E. (2008). El agro pampeano: sustento económico y social del actual conflicto en la Argentina. Cuadernos del CENDES, vol. 25, núm. 68, mayo-agosto, 2008, pp. 29–54.

Basualdo, E., & Arceo, N. (2009). Características estructurales y alianzas sociales en el conflicto por las retenciones móviles, en La crisis Mundial y el conflicto del agro, Arceo, E., Basualdo E. y Arceo, N. Universidad Nacional de Quilmes, Centro Cultural de la Cooperación y Página12.

Bates, R. (2014, 1981). Markets and States in Tropical Africa: The Political Basis of Agricultural Policies. 1st ed., University of California Press, 2014. JSTOR.

Beach, D. & Pedersen, R. B. (2011). What is process tracing actually tracing? The three variants of process tracing meth- ods and their uses and limitations. Paper prepared for presentation at The American Political Science Association annual meeting, Seattle, Washington, USA, September 1–4, 2011.

Bell, S. (2012). The power of ideas: The ideational shaping of the structural power of business. *International Studies Quarterly, 56*, 661–673.

Bisang, R. (2003). Apertura económica, innovación y estructura productiva: La aplicación de la biotecnología en la producción agrícola pampeana argentina. Desarrollo Económico, 43(171).

Bisang, R., Anllo, G., & Campi, M. (2008). Una revolución (no tan) silenciosa. Claves para repensar el agro en Argentina. Desarrollo Económico 48(190–1), 165–207.

Bisang, S., & Anlló. (2011). Las empresas de biotecnología en Argentina, Documentos de proyectos, Cepal.

Block, F. (1977). The Ruling Class Does not Rule: notes on the marxist theory of the state, Socialist Revolution, number 33, may-june 1977.

Blois, M. P. (2016). Ciencia y glifosato: interpelando órdenes. Una investigación en la prensa en el contexto argentino. Cuadernos de Antropología Social /43 (2016).

Blyth, M. (2003). Structures Do Not Come with an Instruction Sheet: Interests, Ideas and Progress in Political Science. *Perspectives in Politics, 1*, 695–706.

Bril-Mascarenhas, T., & Madariaga, A. (2019). Business power and the minimal state: The defeat of industrial policy in Chile.*The Journal of Development Studies, 55*(6), 1047–1066. https://doi.org/10.1080/00220388.2017.1417587

Bril-Mascarenhas, T., Millet, A., & Mayaux, P-L. (2017). Process tracing: inducción, deducción e inferencia causal. Revista de Ciencia Política, 2017, Vol. 37 / N° 3 / 2017 / 659–684.

Bril-Mascarenhas, T., & Maillet, A. (2019). How to Build and Wield Business Power: The Political Economy of Pension Regulation in Chile, 1990–2018. *Latin American Politics and Society, 61*(1), 101–125. https://doi.org/10.1017/lap.2018.61

Caligaris y Pérez Trento. (2018). Propiedad de la tierra y acción política de la clase terrateniente argentina. Una crítica a la tesis del poder terrateniente, **temas y debates 35 / año 22 /** enero-junio 2018 / pp. 71–92.

Campello, D. (2015). *The Politics of Market Discipline in Latin America*. Nueva York, Cambridge University Pres.

Cardoso, F. H., & Faletto, E. (1979). Dependency and Development in Latin America, University of California Press.

Castellani, A. (2006). Estado, Empresas y Empresarios. La relación entre intervención económica estatal, difusión de ámbitos privilegiados de acumulación y desempeño de las grandes firmas privadas. Argentina 1966–1989, Tesis de Doctorado en Ciencias Sociales, Universidad de Buenos Aires.

Cepal. (2012). Cambio estructural para la igualdad: una visión integrada del desarrollo, Trigésimo cuarto período de sesiones de la cepal, Julio 2012.

Chang, H. (2002). *Kicking Away the Ladder Development Strategy in Historical Perspective*. Anthem Press.

Clapp, J. (2015). ABCD and beyond: From grain merchants to agricultural value chain managers, Canadian Food Studies, Section IV
Corporate Role in Food and Agriculture
Special Issue: Mapping the Global Food Landscape.

Clapp, J. (2009). Corporate interests in US food aid policy: global implications of resistance to reform. In J. Clapp & D. Fuchs (Eds.),*Corporate Power in Global Agrifood Governance*. MIT Press.

Clapp, J. (2018). Mega-mergers on the menu: Corporate concentration and the politics of sustainability in the global food system. *Global Environmental Politics, 18*, Number 2, 12–33.

Collier, D., Brady, H. E., & Seawright, J. (2004). Sources of leverage in causal inference: toward an alternative view of methodology. In H. E. Brady & D. Collier (Eds.), *Rethinking Social Inquiry: Diverse Tools, Shared Standards*. Lanham: Rowman and Littlefield.

Collier, R. B., & Collier, D. (1991). *Shaping the Political Arena: Critical Junctures, the Labor Movement, and Regime Dynamics in Latin America*. Princeton.

Correa, C. (2006). Monsanto vs. Argentina, LeMondeDiplomatique, abril de 2006.

Culpepper, P. (2010). *Quiet Politics and Business Power: Corporate Control in Europe and Japan (Cambridge Studies in Comparative Politics)*. Cambridge University Press. https://doi.org/10.1017/CBO9780511760716

Culpepper, P. (2015). Structural Power and political science in the post-crisis era. *Business Politics, 17*(3), 391–409.

Culpepper, P., & Reinke. (2014). Structural power and Bank Bailouts in the United Kingdom and the United States. *Politics & Society, 42*, 427–454.

Dallas, P., & Sturgeon. (2019). Power in global value chains. *Review of International Political Economy, 26*(4), 666–694. https://doi.org/10.1080/09692290.2019.1608284

De La, Torre, A., Nash, J., & Sinnott, E., (Eds.) (2010). *Natural Resources in Latin America and the Caribbean. Beyond Booms and Busts?* Washington D.C.: The World Bank.

Delvenne, P., Vasen, F., & Vara, A. M. (2013). The "soy-ization" of Argentina: The dynamics of the "globalized" privatization regime in a peripheral context. *Technology in Society, 35*, 153–162.

Di Paola, M. (2016). Divide y reinarás: dispersión en el tratamiento legislativo de los agroquímicos. *Informe Ambiental Anual 2016 Farn.*

Doner, R., & Schneider, B. (2016). The Middle-Income Trap: More Politics than Economics. *World Politics, 68*(4), 608–644. https://doi.org/10.1017/S0043887116000095

Dunning, J. (1992). *Multinational Enterprises and the Global Economy.* Addison-Wesley.

Etchemendy, S., & Garay, C. (2011). Argentina: Left Populism in Comparative Perspective (2003–2009). en Steven Levitsky and Kenneth Roberts eds. Latin America's Turn to the Left: Causes and Implications, Johns Hopkins University Press.

Etchemendy, S. (2014). *Models of Economic Liberalization: Business, Workers, and Compensation in Latin America, Spain, and Portugal.* Cambridge University Press. Paperback Edition.

Evans, P. (1979). *Dependent Development: The Alliance of Multinational, State, and Local Capital in Brazil.* Princeton University Press.

Evans, P. (1985). Transnational linkages and the economic role of the state: An analysis of developing and industrialized nations in the Post–World War II period. In P. Evans, D. Rueschemeyer, & T. Skocpol (Eds.), *Bringing the State Back In* (pp. 192–226). Cambridge University Press. https://doi.org/10.1017/CBO9780511628283.009

Evans, P. (1995). *Embedded Autonomy: States and Industrial Transformation.* Princeton University Press.

Evans, P. (2009). From situations of dependency to globalized social democracy. *Studies in Comparative International Development, 44*, 318–336.

FADA. (2019). El campo argentino en números, Fundación Agropecuaria para el Desarrollo de Argentina.

Fairfield, T. (2010). Business Power and Tax Reform: Taxing Income and Profits in Chile and Argentina. *Latin American Politics and Society, 52*, 2.

Fairfield, T. (2011). Business power and protest: Argentina's agricultural producers protest in comparative context. *Studies in International Comparative Development, 46*(4), 424–453.

Fairfield, T. (2015a). *Private Wealth and Public Revenue in Latin America: Business Power and Tax Politics*. Cambridge University Press.

Fairfield, Tasha. (2015b). Structural power in comparative political economy: perspectives from policy formulation in Latin America. *Business and Politics, 17*(3), 411–441. ISSN 1469–3569.

Fairfield, T. (2019). Taxing Latin America's economic elites. In G. Flores-Macías (Ed.), *The Political Economy of Taxation in Latin America* (pp. 172–192). Cambridge University Press. https://doi.org/10.1017/9781108655934.007

Falkner, R. (2009). 'The troubled birth of the "Biotech Century": Global corporate power and its limits. In J. Clapp & D. Fuchs (Eds.), *Corporate Power in Global Agrifood Governance* (pp. 225–252). MIT Press.

Farrell & Newman. (2015). Structuring power: business and authority beyond the nation state. *Business Politics, 17*(3), 527–552.

Fernández Milmanda, B. (2019). *Agrarian Elites and Democracy in Latin America after the Third Wave*. Oxford University Press. Publisher's Version.

Fernández Milmanda, B. (2024). *Agrarian Elites and Democracy in Latin America*. Cambridge University Press.

Fernández Milmanda, B., & Garay, C. (2019). The Multilevel Politics of Enforcement: Environmental Institutions in Argentina. *Politics and Society, 48*(1), 3–26.

Fernandez, V. (2015). Global value chains in global political networks: Tool for development or neoliberal device? *Review of Radical Political Economics, 47*(2), 209–230.

Figueroa, V., & Leiras, M. (2014). Tierra, clubes y poder: la influencia política de los terratenientes en las repúblicas oligárquicas. Evidencia de Argentina (1880–1912). Trabajo presentado en el Encuentro Anual 2014 de la Red para el Estudio de la Economía Política de América Latina, Santiago de Chile, 9 y 10 de Junio de 2014.

Freytes, C. (2015). *The Cerrado Is Not the Pampas*: Explaining Tax and Regulatory Policies on Agricultural Exports in Argentina and Brazil (2003–2013). Ph.D. Dissertation, Northwestern University.

Freytes, C., & O'Farrell, J. (2017). Conflictos distributivos en la Agricultura de exportación en la Argentina reciente (2003–2015), Desarrollo Económico, vol. 57, N 221 (mayo-agosto 2017).

Frieden, J. (1991). *Debt, Development, and Democracy: Modern Political Economy and Latin America, 1965–1985*. Princeton University Press.

George, Alexander, L., & Bennett. (2005). *Case Studies and Theory Development in the Social Science*. MIT Press.

Gerchunoff, P., & Llach, L. (2003). El ciclo de la ilusión y el desencanto: un siglo de políticas económicas argentinas, Ariel Sociedad Económica.

Gereffi, G. (1978). Drug firms and dependency in Mexico: The case of the steroid hormone industry. *International Organization, 32*(1), 237–286. https://doi.org/10.1017/S002081830000391X

Gereffi, G., & Korzeniewicz, M. (Eds.). (1994). *Commodity Chains and Global Capitalism*. Praeger.

Gereffi, G., & Evans, P. (1981). Transnational corporations, dependent development, and state policy. *Latin American Research Review, 16*(3).

Gereffi, G. H., & Sturgeon. (2005). The governance of global value chains. *Review of International Political Economy, 12*(1), 78–104. https://doi.org/10.1080/09692290500049805

Gerring, J. (2001). *Social Science Methodology: A Critical Framework*. Cambridge University Press.

Giarracca, N. (2011) Del paro agrario a las elecciones de 2009: tramas, reflexiones y debates, Antropofagia, Buenos Aires.

Gibson, E. (1996). *Class and Conservative Parties*. The Johns Hopkins University Press.

Gill & Law. (1989). Global Hegemony and the structural power of capital. *International Studies Quarterly, 33*(4), 475–499.

Goertz, G., & Mahoney, J. (2012). *A Tale of Two Cultures: Qualitative and Quantitative Research in the Social Sciences*. Princeton University Press.

Gras, C., & Hernandez, V. (2016). Radiografía del nuevo campo argentino: del terrateniente al empresario transnacional. Buenos Aires: Siglo XXI Editores.

Gras, C., & Hernandez, V. (2009). La Argentina rural: de la agricultura familiar a los agronegocios, Editorial Biblos, Buenos Aires.

Guillén, M. F. (2001). *The Limits of Convergence: Globalization and Organizational Change in Argentina, South Korea, and Spain*. Princeton University Press. JSTOR,

Hacker J., & Pierson P. (2002). Business power and social policy: Employers and the formation of the American welfare state. *Politics and Society, 2*, 277–305.

Haggard, S. (1989) The political economy of foreign direct investment in Latin America. *Latin American Research Review, 24*, 1.

Haggard, S. (1990). Pathways from the periphery: In *The Politics of Growth in the Newly Industrializing Countries*. Cornell University Press.

Hall, P (2003). Aligning ontology and methodology in comparative research. In J. Mahoney, & D. Rueschemeyer (Eds.), *Comparative Historical Analysis in the Social Sciences*. Cambridge University Press, Ch. 11.

Haunss, S., & Shadlen, K. (2009). *Politics of Intellectual Property: Contestation Over the Ownership, Use, and Control of Knowledge and Information*, Edward Elgan.

Heller, R., & Snyder. (2009). Dependency and development in a globalized world: looking back and forward. *Studies in Comparative International Development, 44*, 287–295

Henrich Boll. (2017). AgriFood Atlas. Facts and figures about tcorporations that control what we eat. Heinrich Böll Foundation, Berlin, Germany, Rosa Luxemburg Foundation, Berlin, Germany Friends of the Earth Europe, Brussels, Belgium

Heredia, M. (2003). Reformas estructurales y renovación de las élites económicas en Argentina: estudio de los portavoces de la tierra y del capital. *Rev. Mex. Sociol 65*(1). México ene./mar. 2003.

Hernandez, V. (2007), El fenomeno economico y cultural del boom de la soja y el empresariado innovador. *Desarrollo Económico, 47*(187), 331–365.

Hertel-Fernandez, A. (2014). Who Passes Business's "Model Bills"? Policy Capacity and Corporate Influence in U.S. *State Politics. Perspectives on Politics, 12*(3), 582–602. https://doi.org/10.1017/S1537592714001601

Hopkins, T., & Wallerstein, I. (1977). Patterns of development of the modern world-system. *Review, 1*(2), 11–145.

Hora, R (2010). La crisis del campo del otoño de 2008. Desarrollo Económico, Vol. 50, No. 197 (ABRIL-JUNIO 2010), pp. 81–111.

Hora, R. (2002). La evolución del sector agroexportador argentino en el largo plazo, 1880–2010, Historia Agraria, 58, Diciembre 2012, pp. 145–181, ISSN: 1139–1472.

Hora, R. (2002). Los terratenientes de la Pampa Argentina: una historia social y política, 1860–1945. Buenos Aires. Siglo XXI. pp 201–248.

Hora, R. (2009). Los estancieros contra el Estado: la liga agraria y la formación del ruralismo político en la argentina. Siglo XXI.

Hora, R. (2015). Los terratenientes de la pampa argentina. Una historia social y política. Siglo XXI editores. Buenos Aires.

Hora, R. (2018). ¿Cómo pensaron el campo los argentinos? y cómo deberían pensarlo hoy, cuando ese campo ya no existe. Siglo XXI editores, Buenos Aires.

INTA. (2003). INTA on the Concern on Long-Run Sustainability of the Argentine Agricultural Production, December 4, p. 1. Available at: http://www1.inta.gov.ar/ies

Johnson, C. (1982). *MITI and the Japanese Miracle*. Stanford University Press.

Kholi, A. (2009). Nationalist versus dependent capitalist development: alternate pathways of Asia and Latin America. *A Globalized World, St Comp Int Dev 44*, 386–410. https://doi.org/10.1007/s12116-009-9048-x

Kulfas, M. (2019) Los tres kirchnerismos: una historia de la economía argentina, siglo XXI editores, segunda edición

Lapegna, P. (2017). The political economy of the agro-export boom under the Kirchners: Hegemony and passive revolution in Argentina. *Journal of Agrarian Change, 17*(2).

Lapegna, P. (2019). La argentina transgénica: de la resistencia a la adaptación, una etnografía de las poblaciones campesinas. Siglo XXI.

Lattuada, M. (2006). *Acción colectiva y corporaciones agrarias en la Argentina*. Universidad Nacional de Quilmes Editorial.

Levitsky, S., & Roberts, K. M. (2011). "Introduction: Latin America's "Left Turn": A framework for analysis" and "conclusion: Democracy, development and the left in Latin America." In S. Levitsky & K. Roberts (Eds.), *The Resurgence of the Latin American Left. Baltimore*. Johns Hopkins University Press.

Levy, D. (2008). Political contestation in global production networks. *The Academy of Management Review, 33*(4).

Levy, D., & Prakash, A. (2003). Bargains old and new: Multinational corporations in global governance. *Business and Politics, 5*(2), 1051–1051.

Lindblom, C.E. (1982), The market as prison. *Journal of Politics. 44*(2): 324–336.

Lopez, G. (2010). ¿Vamos al grano? El rol del Estado en el comercio granario argentino, SEMA.

Losada, L. (2009). Historia de las Elites en la Argentina (Sudamericana).

Lupu, N., & Stokes, S. (2009). Las bases sociales de los partidos políticos en Argentina, 1912–2003, Desarrollo Económico, vol.48 Nro 142, ene-mar 2009.

Mahon, J. (1996). Mobile Capital and Latin American Development, Pennsylvania State University Press.

Mahoney, J. (1999). Nominal, ordinal, and narrative appraisal in macrocausal analysis. *American Journal of Sociology, 104*(4), 1154–96.

Mahoney, J., & Goertz, G. (2006). A Tale of Two Cultures: Contrasting Quantitative and Qualitative Research. *Political Analysis, 14*(3), 227–249.

Mangonnet, J. y Murillo, V. (2017) El boom sojero y la protesta fiscal de los productores rurales, Desarrollo Económico, vol. 57, N 221 (mayo-agosto 2017).

Mangonnet, J., Murillo, M., & Rubio, J. (2018). Local Economic Voting and the Agricultural Boom in Argentina, 2007–2015. *Latin American Politics and Society, 60*(3), 27–53. https://doi.org/10.1017/lap.2018.23

Manzetti, L. (1992). The Evolution of Agricultural Interest Groups in Argentina. *Journal of Latin American Studies, 24*(03), 585–616.

Marín, A. y Stulbrin, L. (2017) Oportunidades y desafíos para convertirse en un innovador mundial en Recursos Naturales (RN). Argentina Desarrollo Económico; Lugar: Buenos Aires; Año: 2017 vol. 56 p. 471–497.

Mazzuca, S. (2013). Lessons from Latin America: The rise of rentier populism. *Journal of Democracy, 24*(2), 108–122. Project MUSE, https://doi.org/10.1353/jod.2013.0034

Merlinsky, G. (2013). Cartografías del conflicto ambiental en Argentina, compilado por Gabriela Merlinsky. - 1a ed. - Ciudad Autónoma de Buenos Aires: Fundación CICCUS, 2013.

Monsanto Annual Report. (2016). A limitless perspective.

Moore, B. (1996). Orígenes Sociales de la Dictadura y la Democracia, Prologo y Caps. 7, 8 y 9, Ed. Península.

Moran, T. (1975). *Multinational Corporations and the Politics of Dependence: Copper in Chile*. Princeton University Press.

Moran, T. (1978). Multinational corporations and dependency: A dialogue for dependentistas and non-dependentistas. *International Organization, 32*(1), 79–100.

Morgan, D. (1979). Los Traficantes de Granos. La historia secreta del pulpo mundial delos cereales, Editorial abril, segunda edición 1984.

Mullner, J. y Puck, J. (2018). Towards a holistic framework of MNE–state bargaining: A formal model and case-based analysis. *Journal of World Business, 53*, 15–26.

Murillo, O., Vaishnav. (2011). Economic constraints and presidential agency. In S. Levitsky and K. Roberts (Eds.) *The Resurgence of the Latin American Left*. Johns Hopkins University Press.

Murillo, V. (2009). *Political Competition, Partisanship, and Policy Making in Latin American Public Utilities*. Cambridge University Press.

Murphy, S. (2006). Concentrated Market Power and Agricultural Trade. Ecofair Trade Dialogue, Discussion Papers, No. 1 / August 2006, Heinrich Boell Stiftung.

Murphy, S. (2008). Globalization and corporate concentration in the food and agriculture sector. *Development, 51*(4), 527–533.

Murphy, S., Burch, D., & Clapp, J. (2012). *Cereal Secrets: The World's Largest Grain Traders and Global Agriculture*. Oxfam International.

Nellen-Stucky & Meienberg (2006). Harvesting Royalties for Sowing Dissent? Monsanto's Campaign against Argentina's Patent Policy, Berne Declaration.

Newell, P. (2009). Bio-Hegemony: The Political Economy of Agricultural Biotechnology in Argentina. *Journal of Latin American Studies, 41*, 27–57.

Nolke, A. y Vliegenthart, A. (2009) Enlarging the Varities of Capitlism: the Emergence of Dependent market Economies in East Central Europe, World Politics 61, ño. 4 (october 2009), 670–702.

O'Donnell, G. (1972) Modernización y Autoritarismo, Editorial Paidós.

O'Donnell, Guillermo. (1977). "Estado y alianzas en la Argentina, 1956–1976." Desarrollo Econo´mico 16(64):523–554.

O'Donnell, S. (2011). Argenleaks: Los cables de Wikileaks sobre la Argentina, de la A a la Z.

O'Keefe, P. (2018). Supply chain management strategies of agricultural corporations: A resource dependency approach, Competition & Change 2016, Vol. 20(4) 255–274

Paarlberg, R. (2001). The politics of precaution: genetically modified crops in developing countries, IFPRI, Food policy statement, number 35, October 2001.

Paz Belada, A. (2017). *Regulación de los agroquímicos en la Argentina: Hacia una ley general de presupuestos mínimos regulatorios*. Universidad de San Andrés Departamento de Derecho.

Pellegrini, P. (2013). Transgénicos: Ciencia, agricultura y controversias en la Argentina, Universidad Nacional de Quilmes.

Pellegrini, P. (2013b). *What risks and for whom? Argentina's regulatory policies and global commercial interests in GMOs, Technology in Society 35, 02/2013*. Elsevier.

Perelmuter, T. (2018). Propiedad intelectual en semillas: los dispositivos del cercamiento jurídico en Argentina, Mundo Agrario, diciembre 2018, vol. 19, n° 42, e099. ISSN 1515-5994.

Pierri, J. (Ed.) (2014) Producción y comercio de granos (1980–2012); Políticas Públicas, Grandes Empresas y Dependencia, Editorial Biblos, Buenos Aires

Post, A. (2014). *Foreign and Domestic Investment in Argentina: The politics of privatized infrastructure*. Cambridge University Press.

Poth, C. (2019). Biotecnología, Ciencia y Poder. Un análisis crítico sobre la regulación en torno a las semillas genéticamente modificadas, Universidad Nacional de General Sarmiento.

Pucciarelli, A. (1986). El capitalismo agrario pampeano, 1880–1930: la formación de una nueva estructura de clases en la Argentina moderna, Buenos Aires, Hyspamérica.

Regúnaga, M. (2009). Implications of the organization of the commodity production and processing industry: Case Studies in Latin America and the Caribbean Region, The Soybean Chain in Argentina.

Richardson, N. (2009). Export Oriented Populism: Commodities and Coalitions in Argentina. *Studies in International Comparative Development, 44*(3), 228–255.

Richardson, N. (2012). *The Politics of Abundance: Export Agriculture and Redistributive Conflict in South America*. Ph. D. Dissertation, University of California at Berkeley.

Sábato, J. (1988). La clase dominante en la Argentinamoderna: formación y características, Colección CISEA, Imago Mundi, Segunda edición 1991, Buenos Aires.

Sández, F. (2016). La Argentina Fumigada: Agroquímicos, enfermedad y alimentos en un país envenenado. Espejo de la Argentina, Planeta

Santarcángelo, Schteingart y Porta (2017). Cadenas Globales de Valor: una mirada crítica a una nueva forma de pensar el desarrollo, CEC Año 4, No 7 (2017) pp. 99–129.

Sbatella y Barrera, (2011). Regulación del comercio exterior y apropiación de rentas. Pasado y presente de la medida, en Ensayos en honor a Marcelo Diamand: Las raíces del nuevo modelo de desarrollo argentino y del pensamiento económico nacional, Buenos Aires: Miño y Dávila, 2011.

Schneider, B. R. (2004). *Business Politics and the State in Twentieth-Century Latin America*. Cambridge University Press.

Schneider, Ben R. (2010). Business Politics in Latin America: Patterns of fragmentation and centralization. In D. Coen (Eds.), *The Oxford Handbook of Business and Government*. Oxford University Press.

Schneider, B. R. (2013). *Hierarchical Capitalism in Latin America: Business, Labor, and the challenges of equitable development*.

Scoones, I. (2008) Mobilizing against GM crops in India, South Africa and Brazil. *Journal of Agrarian Change, 8*(2) and (3), 315–344.

Sell, S. (2003). *Private Power, Public Law: The Globalization of Intellectual Property Rights (Cambridge Studies in International Relations)*. Cambridge University Press. https://doi.org/10.1017/CBO9780511491665

Sell, S. (2009). Corporations, seeds, and intellectual property rights governance. In J. Clapp & D. Fuchs (Eds.), *Corporate Power in Global Agrifood Governance*. MIT Press.

Sexton, R. (2013). Market power, misconceptions, and modern agricultural markets. *American Journal of Agricultural Economics, 95*(2), 209–219.

Shadlen, K. (2017). *Coalitions and Compliance The Political Economy of Pharmaceutical Patents in Latin America*. Oxford University Press.

Shadlen, K. (2011). The politics of patents and drugs in Brazil and Mexico: the industrial bases of health policies. In K. C. Shadlen, S. Guennif, A. Guzmán, & N. Lalitha, (Eds.), *Intellectual Property, Pharmaceuticals and Public Health: Access to Drugs in Developing Countries*. (pp. 178–201). Edward Elgar Publishing. ISBN 9781849800143

Smith, P. (1968). Carne y política en la Argentina. Biblioteca Argentina de Historia y Política. Hyspamerica.

Smythe, E. (2009). In whose interests? Transparency and accountability in the global governance of food. In J. Clapp & D. Fuchs (Eds.), *Corporate Power in Global Agrifood Governance*. MIT Press.

Stallings, B. (2020). *Dependency in the twenty first century?* Cambridge Elements, Politics and Society in Latin America, Cambridge University Press.

Strange, S. (1989). *States and Markets*. Continuum.

Sturgeon, (2009). From commodity chains to value chains: interdisciplinary theory building in an age of globalization. In J. Bair (Ed.), *Frontiers of Commodity Chain Research* (pp. 110–135). Stanford University Press.

Svampa, M. (2013). «Consenso de los Commodities» y lenguajes de valoración en América Latina, revista Nueva Sociedad No 244, marzo-abril de 2013, ISSN: 0251-3552.

Sztulwark, S. (2012). *Renta de innovación en cadenas globales de producción. El caso de las semillas transgénicas en Argentina*. Editorial de la Universidad Nacional de General Sarmiento.

Trigo, E. (2011). Fifteen years of genetically modified crops in Argentine agriculture. Buenos Aires: Argentine Council for Information and Development of Biotechnology

Turzi, M. (2010). The política economy of soybean production in Brazil, Argentina and Paraguay, dissertation submitted to the John Hopkins University, Baltimore, Maryland.

UNCTAD. (2006). Tracking the trend towards market concentration: the case of the agricultural input industry AUTHOR: Irene Musselli Moretti PUBLICATION: UNCTAD report DATE: 20 April 2006

UNCTAD (2019) UNCTAD Commodity Dependence Report 2019, United Nations.

UNCTAD/FAO. (2017). Commodities and Development Report 2017, Commodity Markets, Economic Growth and Development, United Nations and Food and Agriculture Organization of the United Nations.

Vaitsos, C. (1974). *Intercountry income distribution and transnational enterprises*. Clarendon Press.

Van Zwanenberg, P., Eli, A., & Smith, A. (2011). *Regulating Technology: International Harmonization and Local Realities*. Routledge.

Vara, A. M. (2005). Argentina, GM nation, chances and choices in uncertain times. Project on international GMO regulatory conflicts. NYU; 2005.

Vernon, R. (1971). Sovereignty at bay: The multinational spread of U. S. enterprises, The International Executive, Autumn (Fall) 1971.

Vogel, D. (1987). Political science and the study of corporate power: a dissent from the new conventional wisdom. *British Journal of Political Science (October 1987)*, 385–408.

Vommaro, G. (2019). Estado y alianzas…, cuarenta años después. Elementos para pensar el giro a la derecha en Argentina, Revista de Ciencias Sociales vol.32 no.44 Montevideo jun. 2019.

Wade, R. (1990). *Governing the market: Economic theory and the role of government in east Asian industrialization*. Princeton.

Wallerstein, I. (1974). The rise and future demise of the world capitalist system: Concepts for comparative analysis. *Comparative Studies in Society and History, 16*(4), 387–415.

Wibbels, E. (2009). Cores, peripheries, and contemporary political economy. *St Comp Int Dev 44*, 441–449. https://doi.org/10.1007/s12116-009-9044-1

Wibbels, E. (2009). Cores, peripheries, and contemporary political economy. *St Comp Int Dev*, *44*, 441–449

Williams, M. (2009). Feeding the World? Transnational corporations and the promotion of genetically modified food. In J. Clapp & D. Fuchs (Eds.), *Corporate Power in Global Agrifood Governance*. MIT Press.

Zeolla. (2014). Elementos sobre la historia de la regulación estatal de la comercialización de granos en la Argentina, Centro Cultural de la Cooperación Floreal Gorini, Buenos Aires, agosto de 2014.

Kolibri 360 GmbH
Ferdinand-Jühlke-Straße 7
99095 Erfurt, Deutschland
produktsicherheit@kolibri360.de